Making Sense of SCIENCE™

ENERGY

for teachers of GRADES 6–8

TEACHER BOOK

Kirsten R. Daehler

Jennifer Folsom

Mayumi Shinohara

Published in partnership with

National Science Teachers Association

Printed in the United States of America.

ISBN: 978-0-914409-86-1

Library of Congress Control Number: 2011929664

The book cover is printed on 30% recycled paper. The text paper is certified by the Sustainable Forest Initiative.

WestEd, a national nonpartisan, nonprofit research, development, and service agency, works with education and other communities to promote excellence, achieve equity, and improve learning for children, youth, and adults. WestEd has 17 offices nationwide, from Washington and Boston to Arizona and California. Its corporate headquarters are in San Francisco.

WestEd books and products are available through bookstores and online booksellers. WestEd also publishes its books in a variety of electronic formats. To order books from WestEd directly, call our Publications Center at 888-293-7833 or visit us online at www.WestEd.org/bookstore.

For more information about WestEd:

Visit www.WestEd.org

Call 415-565-3000 or toll free 877-4-WestEd

Write WestEd, 730 Harrison Street, San Francisco, CA 94107-1242

This material is based upon work supported in part by the National Science Foundation under Grant ESI-0455856; the Institute of Education Sciences, U.S. Department of Education, through Grant R305B070233; the Stuart Foundation; and the W. Clement & Jessie V. Stone Foundation. Any opinions, findings, and conclusions or recommendations expressed in this material are those of the authors and do not necessarily reflect the views of these agencies.

MAKING SENSE OF SCIENCE PRODUCTION

Production Director: Kirsten R. Daehler

Production Leads: Jennifer Folsom & Jennifer Mendenhall

Illustrator & Graphic Designer: Jennifer Mendenhall

Editor: Noel White

Publications Manager: Danny S. Torres

Proofreader: Joan D. Saunders

Production Assistant: Mikiya Alexander Matsuda

Publications Assistant: Tanicia Bell

WESTED

Chief Executive Officer: Glen Harvey

Chief Program Officer: Gary Estes

Chief Policy & Communications Officer: Max McConkey

Director of STEM: Steve A. Schneider

Editorial Director: Joy Zimmerman

Design Director: Christian Holden

Table of Contents

CORE COURSE

LOOKING AT STUDENT WORK™

CD Contents

Looking at Student Work™ Guide masters

All the makings of a Looking at Student Work™ Guide are provided on the CD for you to reproduce (according to the End User License Agreement), including:

- Binder covers and spine inserts
- Looking at Student Work™ Guide (including Sessions A–E, Learning Objectives & Misconceptions, Task Bank, sample sets of student work, and completion certificate)

Information sheets

One-page summaries about the project and about the research results related to benefits for teachers and students are provided for you to share as needed, for example, with district or school leaders.

End User License Agreement

We have chosen to make the materials easily available for the benefit of teachers and their students. In exchange, we ask you to honor the hard work that goes into developing these materials. Before reproducing any part of the Looking at Student Work™ Guide, please sign and return a copy of the End User Registration to WestEd.

To order additional Making Sense of SCIENCE™ course materials, please visit our product website: **www.WestEd.org/mss**

Acknowledgments

Hundreds of people — classroom teachers, scientists, literacy specialists, science educators, and researchers — contributed to the development, evaluation, and refinement of this **Making Sense of SCIENCE**™ course. A core development team did much of the heavy lifting over several long years. They researched misconceptions, helped conceptualize the course's scope and sequence, wrote teaching cases, and participated in fun give-and-take discussions to shape the ideas and activities found on the pages of this book. At key junctures, our advisors from the fields of science, literacy, adult learning, cognitive science, and education infused their expertise into the work to make sure we got the science "right," stayed true to the principles of best practices, and pushed the envelope of what is possible.

Thanks to the committed partnership of our deep-thinking external evaluator, Joan I. Heller, and her staff at Heller Research Associates, these materials benefited from a true R&D process in which both research and development balanced and conversed with one another along the way. Some of the best insights, helpful hints, and essential details came from dozens of teachers and staff developers from across the country who piloted this course. We counted on such critical friends to share their honest advice and recommendations, even when it meant revamping an entire activity or dumping many pages of hard-written text.

Some of the more invisible contributions came from the intellectual community who planted the seeds for this **Making Sense of SCIENCE** approach to teacher learning and over the past decade helped the vision mature. In particular, the case-based elements evolved from the generously shared work and stimulating conversations with colleagues including Judy Shulman, Lee Shulman, Carne Barnett-Clarke, Alma Ramírez, and Tania Madfes. Other contributions to our thinking came from Judith Warren Little, Mary Budd Rowe, Hilda Borko, Susan Mundry, Page Keeley, Jennifer Knudsen, and many others. The marriage between the science and literacy elements was forged through the truly collaborative and selfless contributions of Elyse Eidman-Aadahl, Gina Hale, Cyndy Greenleaf, and Ruth Schoenbach.

WestEd has provided institutional support for this work at untold turns. Steve Schneider and Art Sussman made it possible for this journey to begin and have been unwavering sources of encouragement, opportunity, and trust over the years. WestEd staff in institutional development, communications, marketing, and publications have opened many doors and added polish to our work. Noel White's attention to detail kept us honest, Danny Torres made publication a reality, and our project handyman, Mikiya Matsuda, provided the glue to hold things together and the wheels to keep things moving. These materials wouldn't be nearly as fun to read, beautiful to hold, or comprehensible and clear without Jennifer Mendenhall's gifted illustrations and graphical design. She's a rare Renaissance gal who insists on making sense of the science for herself before drafting images to help others do the same.

Some famous person once wrote, "The best way to learn to write a book is to…write a book." For us this process of learning and writing has been a marathon, one that has been simultaneously exhilarating, arduous, rewarding, and at times comical. Perhaps we haven't said "thank you" enough to our unbelievable family and friends who have hung in there. You made us dinner, weighed in with advice and "quick reads" at a moment's notice, nurtured the kids, and were understanding and supportive of our passion for this work. Thank you one and all.

~Kirsten, Jen, and Mayumi

Development Team

Project Staff

Kirsten R. Daehler, Director of Understanding Science for Teaching, WestEd

Jennifer Folsom, Curriculum Writer and Staff Developer, WestEd

Jennifer Mendenhall, Illustrator and Graphic Designer, WestEd

Mayumi Shinohara, former Co-Director of Understanding Science for Teaching, WestEd

Teachers

Liz Abrahams, Teacher, San Francisco USD

Vicki Baker, Teacher, New Haven USD

Rebecca Carino, Science Resource Teacher, Cupertino Union SD

Bill Dolyniuk, Teacher, Woodside SD

Brian Donovan, Teacher, The San Francisco School

Khadija Iyer, Teacher, Cupertino Union SD

Keith A. Karraker, Teacher, Windrush School

Science Educators

Matt Ellinger, Teacher Educator and Researcher, Carnegie Foundation for the Advancement of Teaching

Lawrence Lowery, Professor, University of California at Berkeley

Richard J. Merrill, Past-president NSTA, Curriculum Specialist, Mt. Diablo USD

Shannon Merrill, Lecturer, Supervisor of Student Teachers and Interns, California State University East Bay

Literacy Specialists

George Bunch, Assistant Professor of Education, University of California at Santa Cruz

Elyse Eidman-Aadahl, Director, National Programs and Site Development, National Writing Project

Cynthia Greenleaf, Co-Director of the Strategic Literacy Initiative, WestEd

Gina Hale, Professional Development Associate, WestEd

Ruth Schoenbach, Co-Director of the Strategic Literacy Initiative, WestEd

Jerome M. Shaw, Assistant Professor of Science Education, University of California at Santa Cruz

Scientists

Michael B. Heaney, Staff Physicist, Xerox Palo Alto Research Center

James Hetrick, Professor, University of the Pacific

Barry Kluger-Bell, Physicist, Science Educator, former Assistant Director of the Exploratorium Institute for Inquiry

Evaluation & Research Team

Joan I. Heller, Director, Heller Research Associates

Cara Peterman, Research Assistant, Heller Research Associates

National Field Test Contributors

Stephanie Anderson, Science & Special Projects Coordinator, San Joaquin Office of Education

Theron Blakeslee, Science Specialist and District Staff Developer, Ingham Intermediate SD

Ella Boyd, Teacher, Charlotte-Mecklenburg Schools

David Boyles, Teacher, Puyallup SD

Martha Couretas, Science Specialist and District Staff Developer, Ingham Intermediate SD

Paul Gardner, Director of Science and Special Projects, San Joaquin County Office of Education

Stephanie Hathaway, Director of Education, Discovery Place, Inc.

Deena Hoch, Teacher Leader, Science Specialist, and District Staff Developer, Puyallup SD

Kathy Huncosky, Science Instructional Resource Teacher, Madison Metropolitan SD

Michelle Hurst, Teacher, Hampton Township SD

Kathryn Kelsey, Science Coach, Seattle PS

Barbara Lease, Science Coordinator, Allegheny Intermediate Unit Math & Science Collaborative

Gabriela Rose, Science Coordinator, Allegheny Intermediate Unit Math & Science Collaborative

Andrew Schwebke, Director of Student Learning, Puyallup SD

Lesli Taschwer, Science Instructional Resource Teacher, Madison Metropolitan SD

Teresa Vail, Assistant Project Coordinator, San Joaquin Office of Education

Elaine Woo, Project Director of Seattle's K–5 Inquiry-Based Science Program, Seattle PS

Pilot Test Contributors

Jeanette Amador, Teacher, Newman-Crows Landing USD

Karen Arnold, Teacher, Stockton USD

Joel Austin, Teacher, San Francisco USD

Mia Ball, Teacher, Newman-Crows Landing USD

Megan Barrington, Teacher, Fremont USD

Cathy Boicelli, Teacher, Redwood City SD

Dana Brown, Teacher, Santa Clara USD

Laura Del Barba Dominguez, Teacher, Stockton USD

Audrey Diaz, Teacher, Alum Rock SD

Ann Duesterberg, Teacher, Palo Alto USD

Jennifer Duren, Teacher, Stockton USD

Elaine Fong, Teacher, New Haven USD

Abigail Garrison, Teacher, Palo Alto USD

Charlotte Hall-Austin, Teacher, Stockton USD

Irene Hirota, Teacher, San Francisco USD

Kim Hutson, Teacher, Lodi USD

Jenny Jaeger, Teacher, Georgiana Bruce Kirby Prep School

Terri Jones, Teacher, Stockton USD

Tom Kang, Teacher, Palo Alto USD

Chip Knox, Teacher, Stockton USD

Jessica Kulik, Teacher, Stockton USD

Nicole Lewis, Teacher, Ceres USD

Emily Mellentine, Teacher, Cupertino Union SD

Shelli Murphy, Teacher, San Carlos SD

Nancy Parker, Teacher, Moreland SD

Sarah Pierce, Teacher, Palo Alto USD

Jon Poggi, Teacher, Newman-Crows Landing USD

Shauna Poong, Teacher, San Francisco USD

Nancy Rankin, Teacher, Menlo Park City SD

Cheryl Remkus, Teacher, San Mateo–Foster City SD

Jim Rohan, Teacher, Pajaro USD

Angela Rugani, Teacher, Commodore Stockton Skills School

Leslie Schoenberg, Teacher, San Francisco USD

Susan Sherman, Teacher, Chinese American International School

Michele Stockburger, Teacher, Newman-Crows Landing USD

Julie Willard, Teacher, Menlo Park City SD

Dana Wright, Teacher, Menlo Park City SD

Course Introduction

> **"** The world looks so different after learning science.
> For example, trees are made of air, primarily. When they are
> burned, they go back to air, and in the flaming heat is released
> the flaming heat of the Sun which was bound in to convert
> the air into tree... These are beautiful things and
> the content of science is wonderfully full of them. **"**

~Richard Feynman
The Physics Teacher, 1968

We hope this course will challenge you to see the world and science in different, beautiful ways. The best challenges are invigorating. They awaken new ideas and insights. And we believe the most fun and rewarding way to take on such challenges is in the company of others — that's what this course is all about.

The activities, readings, and discussions in this course are preparation for the challenges and pleasures of your own classroom. Teaching science is complex and often messy. It requires you to navigate tricky science, work with students' preconceptions and misconceptions, and make difficult decisions on the fly. To prepare you for the hard work of teaching, this course helps deepen your understanding of the science, reveals students' ways of thinking, and adds to your knowledge of how students learn and what works in your classroom — all key things that support your very best teaching.

Making Sense of SCIENCE™ courses use a case-based approach. Cases play an important role in the education of many kinds of professionals, such as doctors and lawyers, who work with specialized knowledge and engage in complex decision making. Through discussions and active reflection, as well as hands-on science learning and an extensive focus on literacy issues related to science, this professional development course strengthens multiple areas of professional expertise. Most activities target the "sweet spot" — often called pedagogical content knowledge — where science content knowledge, specialized knowledge of students, and teaching expertise converge.

The course builds on more than a decade of research and development by the Understanding Science for Teaching project at WestEd. The project's fundamental goal is to improve the science achievement and college/career preparation of students by strengthening teachers' content knowledge, pedagogical reasoning, and instructional skills. In pursuit of this goal, the project created **Making Sense of SCIENCE** professional development courses. In multiple, rigorous studies of teachers and their students across the country, these courses have been shown to benefit all students, especially English learners and students with poor literacy skills.

What should you expect from this course?

True to its name, the course is about making sense of the science of energy. It focuses on science, inquiry, and literacy — all in the service of building a scientific way of thinking and instilling that way of thinking in students.

Through the course activities, you'll learn practical, relevant things for science teaching — for example, how to guide hands-on science learning, support evidence-based discussions, and help your students develop the academic language, habits of mind, and communication skills necessary for sense making and scientific reasoning.

As a way to investigate teaching, you'll read and discuss cases written by teachers for teachers. The cases, which include rich examples of student work, allow you to grapple with science content, navigate typical teaching challenges, and experience authentic dilemmas that occur when teaching energy to students.

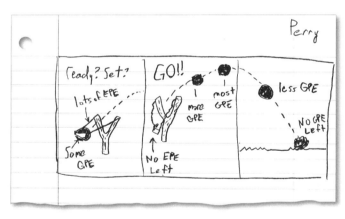

You will also try on the science yourself, working through hands-on investigations with colleagues. And you'll read, talk, and think a lot about the language of science because literacy is key to accessing underlying science concepts and expressing complete, accurate, and precise scientific understanding.

While you're likely to learn or brush up on a lot of science content, the course is not just about getting "right answers." Rather, it focuses on the aspects of energy that often raise the most misunderstandings — things such as the difference between energy and matter, the notion of energy as a measurable quantity, and the role of systems in calculating energy and tracking energy transfers. In other words, the course focuses on the tricky issues, the misconceptions, the places where accurate understanding may require departing from everyday intuition and language.

Although energy is a familiar part of our everyday experience, this topic can be surprisingly difficult to teach, filled with stumbling points for both teachers and students. It is full of nuance and precision. It involves diagrams, symbols, and equations. Plus, energy is defined in many ways, for example, as different types and as a measure. And the language used to describe energy in a complete, accurate, and precise way can be unfamiliar and complex. It can also be confusing to people who are accustomed to speaking more casually about energy and what it means to conserve energy. In this course, you'll work through the stumbling points, the misconceptions, the math, and the language on your way to becoming confident and effective in helping students handle the challenges of energy.

We do not recommend trying this course alone. It's not particularly dangerous, but the course is meant to be experienced in collaboration with other teachers and guided by a facilitator. If you're an energy veteran, it's a place to talk about the things that have puzzled or bothered you for years and a place to engage in in-depth study of the logic (or illogic!) of students' incorrect and correct ideas. If you're newer to the concept of energy, it's a place to get started, ask questions, try on new ideas, and take advantage of the experience of peers. Regardless of the perspective you bring, this course has immediate relevance to the work you do in your own classroom, and each of us has something to add to the mix.

IDEAS ABOUT *Insulators*

INCORRECT

Wool hats are warmer than their surroundings.

39°C   21°C

CORRECT

Wool hats are the same temperature as their surroundings. They keep you warm by reducing the transfer of heat energy to the surroundings.

21°C   21°C

How does this course differ from other professional development?

While parts of this course may feel familiar, there are also unique elements. The *combination* of traits, rather than any single trait, is really what makes the course work. As you experience the course, you're likely to notice characteristics such as the following.

Teacher-centered

This course assumes you're an adult, a working professional, not a blank slate. The activities and discussions should surface and build on your own existing knowledge, skills, and dispositions and leverage the resources of a group of professionals to benefit everyone's learning. So although you'll focus a lot on science content and on students' conceptions of science, you'll be doing so in order to build toward a solid analysis of pedagogy, helping you consider the impact of specific teaching moves on specific students at specific moments.

Rather than pushing groups to arrive at absolute judgment that a particular teaching decision is correct (or incorrect), the sessions typically have you discuss the pros and cons of what the teachers in the cases do. The biggest learning opportunities come from such analysis and evaluative discussion, not necessarily from evaluative decision making. In this manner, the course is meant to support your own professional judgment and strengthen your

reflective habit of mind, rather than offer absolutes and right answers or recommend teaching moves and activities for you to replicate.

Collaborative

Science by nature is a social endeavor. In this course, you are encouraged to take advantage of the colleagues around you. Your role is to actively explore the science with them, ask questions and learn from each other, and serve as a resource to other participants by sharing your own experiences and insights. The facilitator's role is to help the group learn together as you collectively make sense of the science and how to teach the science.

Rigorous and standards-based

You'll be learning serious science. Nothing is watered down. The course was built by people with science backgrounds and reviewed by scientists. It delves deeply into science connected to real classrooms, real students, real teaching dilemmas, in typical school settings. And the content is aligned with national and state standards, leading student curricula, the *Benchmarks for Scientific Literacy,* and the *2009 National Assessment of Educational Progress (NAEP) Science Framework*.

We know you have real work to do in your classroom that requires a deep understanding of science, deep enough to guide student learning and enable you to field tough questions. This course is all about preparing you for the challenges of classroom work.

Focused on the intersection of science content, student learning, and teaching

Most other professional development experiences deal only with science content or only with teaching strategies or approaches. **Making Sense of SCIENCE** is different because it weaves together science content, student thinking, *and* instruction.

Despite the rigorous content, you may notice that you're asked to spend as much time thinking about *wrong* answers as *right* answers. The focus on common-yet-incorrect ideas is one of the ways this course weaves together content and pedagogy, building your pedagogical content knowledge, not just your knowledge of the straight science. Understanding the specifics of and rationale behind common misconceptions is part of understanding students and the ways they make sense of science. To this end, the course encourages you to reflect on your own process of learning, in terms of both what and how you are learning.

Supported by metacognition

Thinking about your thinking (a.k.a. metacognition) is an especially powerful tool for adult learning (White, Frederiksen, & Collins, 2009). Throughout this course you will take time to pause and step outside yourself to notice how you think and what your brain is doing as you learn, write, read, and solve complex problems. Reflecting on your own processes for learning science, writing, reading, and teaching as well as sharing your actions and thoughts with others are key to this course. Such metacognitive conversations demystify the mostly invisible and highly complex ways we think. In turn, being metacognitive allows you to swap useful strategies, identify sticking points, monitor and regulate your learning, and get to know yourself better as a teacher, as a reader and writer of science, and as a knowledgeable science person.

For similar reasons, metacognition contributes to students' success in learning, both in science and in literacy. In fact, helping students be metacognitive about their literacy process allows them to hone their skills, increase their use of problem-solving strategies, and self-regulate, which can result in significant progress with literacy as well as greater achievement in science (Greenleaf et al., 2009). At this age, the importance of peers and students' natural interest in understanding themselves contributes to the value of metacognitive conversations as a tool for learning (Greenleaf, Schoenbach, Cziko, & Mueller, 2001). This course models how to introduce students to and engage them in thinking about their thinking. It also provides routines and activities to use with students and time for teachers to plan how to incorporate metacognition into their instruction.

Effective — especially for students who need it most

This course has been shown to work — consistently well and repeatedly, with many people, in multiple settings. It works because it was refined over many years and built on solid research. (See the references at the end of this introduction for a list of related resources.) The approach is guided by research on science thinking and reasoning (students' and teachers'), conceptual change, adult learning, and teacher professional development. In extensive national field-testing, the **Making Sense of SCIENCE** approach has been shown to strengthen teachers' content knowledge, transform classroom practices, and boost student achievement (Heller, Shinohara, Miratrix, Rabe-Hesketh, & Daehler, 2010; Heller, 2011).

While research has demonstrated benefits for all types of students, those who make the largest gains are English learners and low-performing students. This is likely the result of the course's unique focus

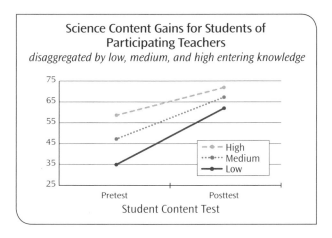

Science Content Gains for Students of Participating Teachers
disaggregated by low, medium, and high entering knowledge

on literacy. Because the course builds important skills for helping students with writing and making sense of science texts, it can be especially beneficial for English learners and students with poor literacy skills, offering the potential to significantly reduce achievement gaps.

Satisfying, worthwhile, and fun

Let's face it, not all professional development is worth your time nor is all of it fun. But we believe learning science should be satisfying and fun. You know that feeling of excitement you can get when you have a great conversation with someone about a topic you are passionate about, or when someone shows you a new way of looking at the world, or when your mind performs some impressive mental gymnastics and you have an "ah-ha" moment? Many teachers who have taken this course tell us it offers just such experiences for them. They find it mentally stimulating, worthwhile, and even life changing. As you experience this course, we hope you have fun learning science — science that is both rigorous and relevant — along with the satisfaction of refining your own art of teaching.

If this is a course on teaching science, why spend so much time on literacy?

A great deal of research has shown that students' capacity to benefit from instruction rests largely on their ability to understand academic content and express themselves through reading, writing, talking, and listening (Krajcik & Sutherland, 2010; Lee & Fradd, 1998; Torres & Zeidler, 2002). For English learners, science language development is yet another challenge (Buxton, 1998; Lee & Fradd, 2001). Science classrooms in particular require students to communicate in specialized ways, such as evidence-based discussions, argumentation, and reasoning (Osbourne, 2010). Communicating in science requires interpretation of many forms of visual and mathematical expression, such as maps, diagrams, pictures, graphs, equations, and tables. Students must also navigate unfamiliar science terms, such as *system,* along with the specialized

meanings of common words, such as *energy.* In addition, students' learning outcomes are often measured through tests that require knowledge of subject-specific language. For all these reasons, this course focuses extensively on literacy to help you support students' talking, reading, and writing in science. The goal is for students to have the means to make sense of the content as well as to develop their academic language proficiency.

Our focus on literacy is not limited to word-based literacy. Images and symbols are inherent in the language of science. Scan the science section of the newspaper, flip through a science magazine, open a science textbook, or look at a scientist's notebook and you'll likely see a plethora of graphs, diagrams, photographs, schematics, tables, and flowcharts, along with arrows, numbers, and equations.

In fact, in an analysis of how scientists communicate (e.g., in scientific journals, textbooks, presentations at professional meetings), Dr. Jay Lemke identified four distinct languages of science: *words, actions, images,* and *symbols* (Lemke, 2002; Lemke, 1998). While each of these four languages can be used independently to convey a particular idea, this course proceeds from the assumption that our deepest conceptual understanding comes from a layered communication involving multiple forms of expression.

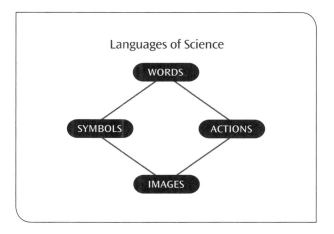

The more readily you can move among words, images, mathematical expressions, physical gestures, and other forms of expression, the more complete and robust your understanding is and the more able you are to convey that understanding to others.

Where does Making Sense of SCIENCE™ come from?

With support from the National Science Foundation, the W. Clement & Jessie V. Stone Foundation, the Institute of Education Sciences, and the Stuart Foundation, the Understanding Science for Teaching project that developed this course has worked with thousands of teachers and staff developers across the country, providing many hours of professional development and impacting hundreds of thousands of diverse students. Rigorous research and national field-testing have gone hand-in-hand with the development of the Understanding Science for Teaching model and the resulting **Making Sense of SCIENCE** materials. More information and related research is available online from WestEd.org/us4t.

The literacy strand of this course is based on the work of the Strategic Literacy Initiative (another WestEd project, which designed the Reading Apprenticeship® framework) and the work of the National Writing Project. Both projects are built on solid research, have developed and extensively evaluated their work in many settings throughout the country over many years, and have proven it effective. More information is available about these projects online from WestEd.org/ra and from NWP.org.

This **Making Sense of SCIENCE** course on energy is part of a professional development series of more than a dozen courses developed by the Understanding Science for Teaching project. Other courses in the series cover topics ranging from living things (for teachers of grades K–2) to electric circuits (for teachers of grades 3–5) and force and motion (for teachers of grades 6–8).

How is the course structured?

This **Making Sense of SCIENCE** course has two main components — the core course with 30 hours of learning and a school-year follow-up with 10 hours of guided analysis of students' work.

Core course

Within the core course, there are five sessions (each offers 6 hours of learning) on different topics related to the concept of energy:

1. What Is Energy?
2. Potential Energy
3. Heat Energy
4. Conservation of Energy
5. Energy in Ecosystems

The first five chapters of this book correspond to these core sessions and contain the print materials you'll need to participate. The activities in these core sessions involve small-group and whole-group work with some solo reading and reflecting mixed in. The exact order of things will vary, depending on what is most strategic for each topic and session.

The next couple of pages provide a visual tour of the components that relate to each session of the core course — teaching, science, and literacy.

Looking at Student Work™

Also integral to the course are five follow-up sessions (each 2 hours in length) on topics related to examining student work and analyzing assessment practices:

A. Mental Models
B. Learning Gaps
C. Next Steps
D. Analyzing Tasks
E. Modifying Tasks

The last five chapters in this book constitute the **Looking at Student Work** guide. These follow-up sessions usually take place during the regular school year so you can utilize student work from your own classroom. This guide provides materials designed to flexibly support self-directed teacher groups (a.k.a. professional learning communities).

The last few pages of this introduction provide a visual tour of the components related to this follow-up. A more detailed introduction is included at the beginning of the **Looking at Student Work** section of this book.

CORE COURSE: TEACHING COMPONENT

The core course offers explicit opportunities for you and colleagues to think about the art of teaching and to reflect on your own teaching. This page shows a sample of what you'll find, including *Teaching Cases* and *Teaching Investigations,* along with *Classroom Connections.*

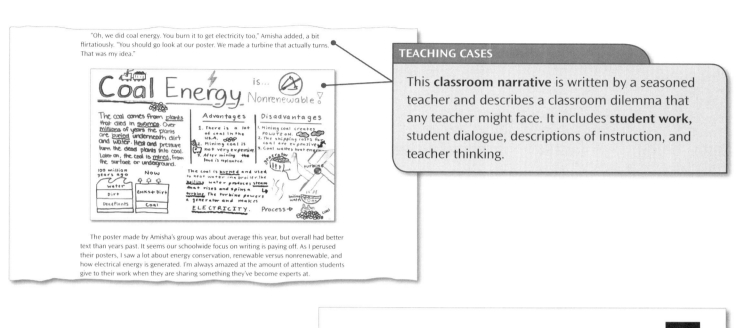

"Oh, we did coal energy. You burn it to get electricity too," Amisha added, a bit flirtatiously. "You should go look at our poster. We made a turbine that actually turns. That was my idea."

The poster made by Amisha's group was about average this year, but overall had better text than years past. It seems our schoolwide focus on writing is paying off. As I perused their posters, I saw a lot about energy conservation, renewable versus nonrenewable, and how electrical energy is generated. I'm always amazed at the amount of attention students give to their work when they are sharing something they've become experts at.

TEACHING CASES

This **classroom narrative** is written by a seasoned teacher and describes a classroom dilemma that any teacher might face. It includes **student work**, student dialogue, descriptions of instruction, and teacher thinking.

Teaching Investigation

SESSION 4

30 MINUTES

20 MINUTES ❶ **Analyzing student thinking**

    a. Look at Raj's work for the *real-world* rocket launch (p. 12) and the *theoretical* rocket launch (p. 13)

- What is correct and not yet correct about his responses?
- What do you think Raj understands and does not yet understand about the conservation of energy?

TEACHING INVESTIGATIONS

The **guiding questions** in Teaching Investigations direct you to analyze student work, grapple with teaching dilemmas, and weigh the tradeoffs of instructional choices.

Classroom Connection

SESSION 4

40 MINUTES

20 MINUTES ❶ **Reviewing key concepts**

    a. Individually, read the Science Review and Literacy Review on the following pages. Feel free to pick and choose the sections that are most valuable to you.

As you read, take notes and think about these questions:

- What is interesting or new to you?
- Which examples and images do you find especially helpful?
- What are you still wrestling with?

CLASSROOM CONNECTIONS

The **guiding questions** in Classroom Connections prompt you to consider the implications for your own students and reflect on your learning from hands-on activities, discussions, and readings.

Science is at the core of this course. These next pages show a sample of how the science is presented for adult learners, sometimes as explanations, other times as guided hands-on activities, including *Content Notes, Science Investigations,* and *Science Reviews.*

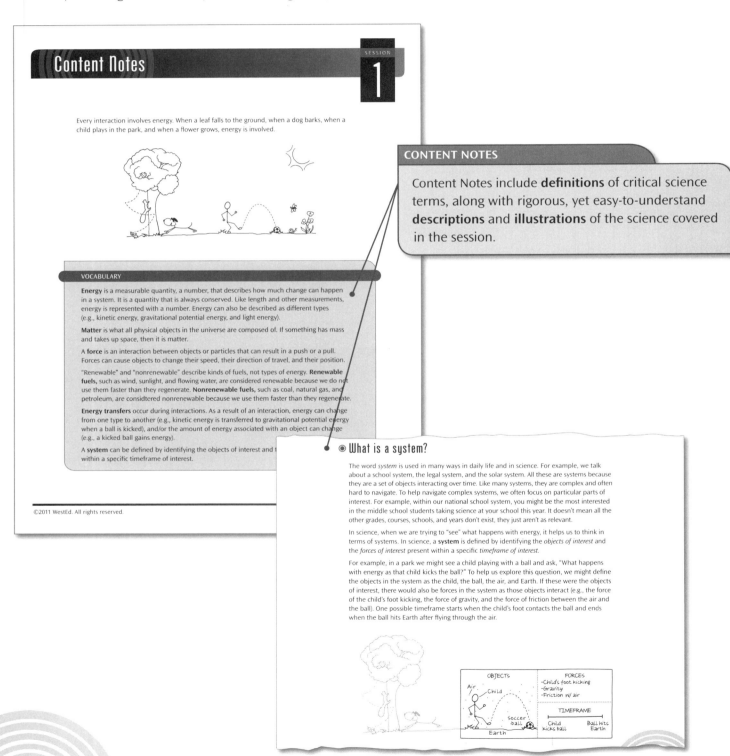

CONTENT NOTES

Content Notes include **definitions** of critical science terms, along with rigorous, yet easy-to-understand **descriptions** and **illustrations** of the science covered in the session.

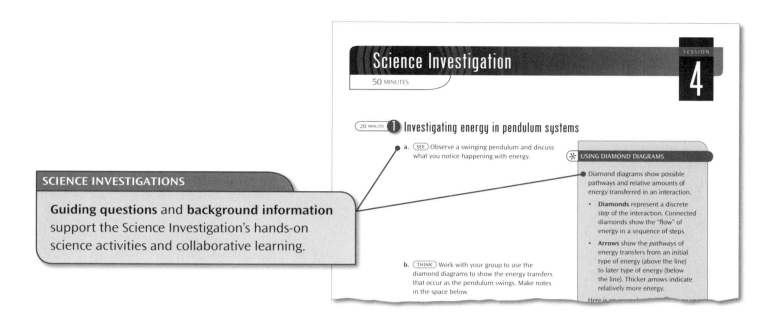

SCIENCE INVESTIGATIONS

Guiding questions and **background information** support the Science Investigation's hands-on science activities and collaborative learning.

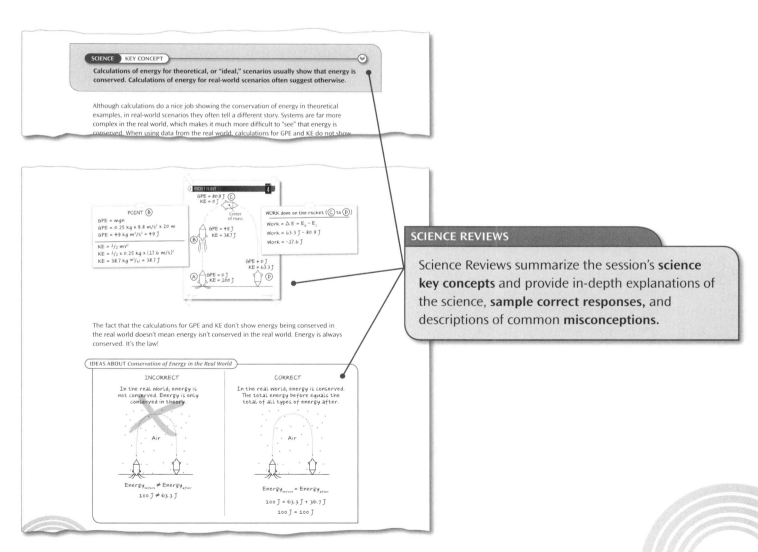

SCIENCE REVIEWS

Science Reviews summarize the session's **science key concepts** and provide in-depth explanations of the science, **sample correct responses,** and descriptions of common **misconceptions.**

While the literacy component is fully integrated into most aspects of the core course, each session also offers dedicated opportunities for literacy learning. This page shows a sample of what you'll find, including *Literacy Investigations* and *Literacy Reviews*.

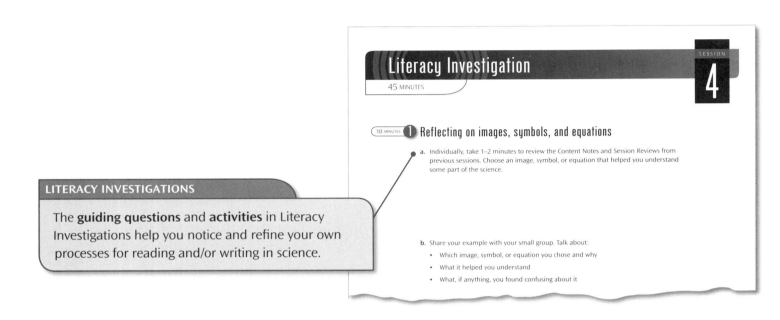

Literacy Investigation

45 MINUTES

SESSION 4

10 MINUTES **1** **Reflecting on images, symbols, and equations**

a. Individually, take 1–2 minutes to review the Content Notes and Session Reviews from previous sessions. Choose an image, symbol, or equation that helped you understand some part of the science.

b. Share your example with your small group. Talk about:
- Which image, symbol, or equation you chose and why
- What it helped you understand
- What, if anything, you found confusing about it

LITERACY INVESTIGATIONS

The **guiding questions** and **activities** in Literacy Investigations help you notice and refine your own processes for reading and/or writing in science.

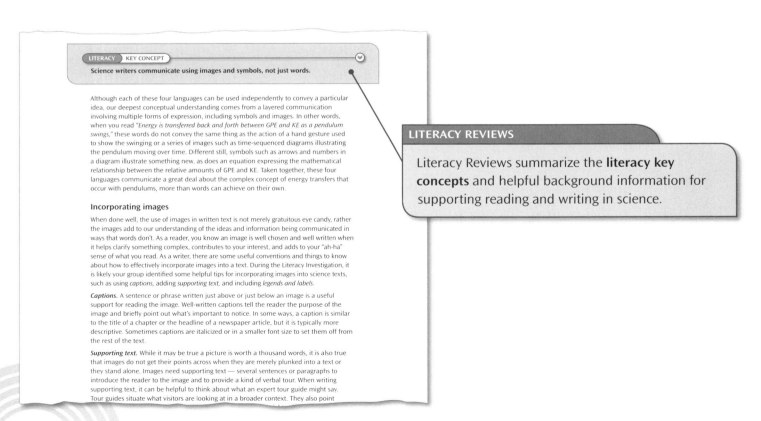

LITERACY) KEY CONCEPT

Science writers communicate using images and symbols, not just words.

Although each of these four languages can be used independently to convey a particular idea, our deepest conceptual understanding comes from a layered communication involving multiple forms of expression, including symbols and images. In other words, when you read *"Energy is transferred back and forth between GPE and KE as a pendulum swings,"* these words do not convey the same thing as the action of a hand gesture used to show the swinging or a series of images such as time-sequenced diagrams illustrating the pendulum moving over time. Different still, symbols such as arrows and numbers in a diagram illustrate something new, as does an equation expressing the mathematical relationship between the relative amounts of GPE and KE. Taken together, these four languages communicate a great deal about the complex concept of energy transfers that occur with pendulums, more than words can achieve on their own.

Incorporating images

When done well, the use of images in written text is not merely gratuitous eye candy, rather the images add to our understanding of the ideas and information being communicated in ways that words don't. As a reader, you know an image is well chosen and well written when it helps clarify something complex, contributes to your interest, and adds to your "ah-ha" sense of what you read. As a writer, there are some useful conventions and things to know about how to effectively incorporate images into a text. During the Literacy Investigation, it is likely your group identified some helpful tips for incorporating images into science texts, such as using *captions*, adding *supporting text*, and including *legends and labels*.

Captions. A sentence or phrase written just above or just below an image is a useful support for reading the image. Well-written captions tell the reader the purpose of the image and briefly point out what's important to notice. In some ways, a caption is similar to the title of a chapter or the headline of a newspaper article, but it is typically more descriptive. Sometimes captions are italicized or in a smaller font size to set them off from the rest of the text.

Supporting text. While it may be true a picture is worth a thousand words, it is also true that images do not get their points across when they are merely plunked into a text or they stand alone. Images need supporting text — several sentences or paragraphs to introduce the reader to the image and to provide a kind of verbal tour. When writing supporting text, it can be helpful to think about what an expert tour guide might say. Tour guides situate what visitors are looking at in a broader context. They also point

LITERACY REVIEWS

Literacy Reviews summarize the **literacy key concepts** and helpful background information for supporting reading and writing in science.

LOOKING AT STUDENT WORK™

This follow-up component is presented in the second part of this book. These next pages show a sample of the *Discussion Protocols* used by colleagues to analyze student work, along with a *Task Bank* of items for you to use with students, and a summary of the *Learning Objectives & Misconceptions* from the core course.

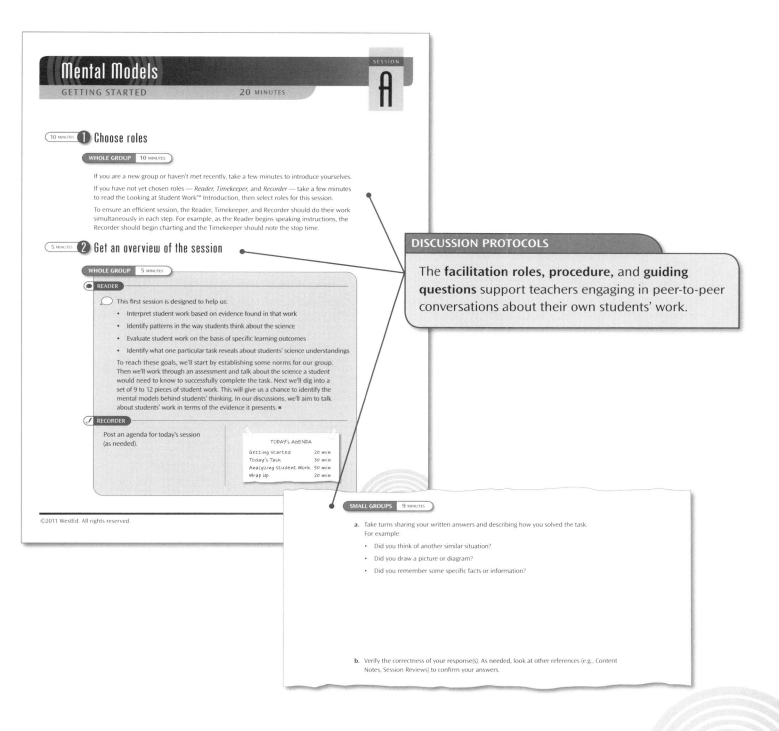

Mental Models
GETTING STARTED   20 MINUTES

SESSION A

10 MINUTES 1 Choose roles

WHOLE GROUP   10 MINUTES

If you are a new group or haven't met recently, take a few minutes to introduce yourselves.

If you have not yet chosen roles — *Reader, Timekeeper,* and *Recorder* — take a few minutes to read the Looking at Student Work™ Introduction, then select roles for this session.

To ensure an efficient session, the Reader, Timekeeper, and Recorder should do their work simultaneously in each step. For example, as the Reader begins speaking instructions, the Recorder should begin charting and the Timekeeper should note the stop time.

5 MINUTES 2 Get an overview of the session

WHOLE GROUP   5 MINUTES

READER

This first session is designed to help us:

- Interpret student work based on evidence found in that work
- Identify patterns in the way students think about the science
- Evaluate student work on the basis of specific learning outcomes
- Identify what one particular task reveals about students' science understandings

To reach these goals, we'll start by establishing some norms for our group. Then we'll work through an assessment and talk about the science a student would need to know to successfully complete the task. Next we'll dig into a set of 9 to 12 pieces of student work. This will give us a chance to identify the mental models behind students' thinking. In our discussions, we'll aim to talk about students' work in terms of the evidence it presents. ∎

RECORDER

Post an agenda for today's session (as needed).

TODAY's AGENDA

Getting Started	20 min
Today's Task	30 min
Analyzing Student Work	50 min
Wrap Up	20 min

DISCUSSION PROTOCOLS

The **facilitation roles, procedure,** and **guiding questions** support teachers engaging in peer-to-peer conversations about their own students' work.

SMALL GROUPS   9 MINUTES

a. Take turns sharing your written answers and describing how you solved the task. For example:

- Did you think of another similar situation?
- Did you draw a picture or diagram?
- Did you remember some specific facts or information?

b. Verify the correctness of your response(s). As needed, look at other references (e.g., Content Notes, Session Reviews) to confirm your answers.

Course Introduction **xv**

LEARNING OBJECTIVES & MISCONCEPTIONS

These lists are detailed compendiums of **learning objectives** for students and common **misconceptions** about the science.

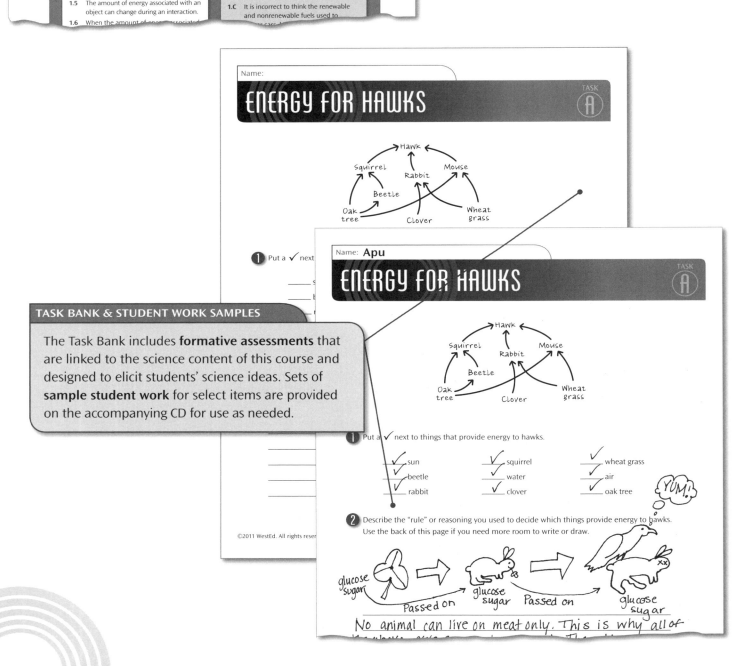

SESSION 1   SCIENCE SUMMARY

LEARNING OBJECTIVES

Energy and Energy Transfers

1.1 Energy is a measure of how much change can happen in a system (e.g., change in motion or change in conditions such as shape, temperature, or composition).

1.2 Energy is not a substance or an object, nor is it a force or power.

1.3 Energy is involved in every interaction.

1.4 Energy is a quantity that is conserved despite the many changes that occur in the world. It is often measured in joules, calories, and kilocalories.

1.5 The amount of energy associated with an object can change during an interaction.

1.6 When the amount of energy associated...

MISCONCEPTIONS

1.A It is incorrect to think of energy as something physical, made of matter or as some yet-to-be-discovered type of magical essence that is pulled out of one object and moved to another object during energy transfers. In fact, only the name and location of the energy really changes, and no physical substance moves object to object.

1.B It is incorrect to think energy is a force, similar to gravity or magnetic force, or to think of it as a nonscientific force (e.g., a magical force).

1.C It is incorrect to think the renewable and nonrenewable fuels used to...

TASK BANK & STUDENT WORK SAMPLES

The Task Bank includes **formative assessments** that are linked to the science content of this course and designed to elicit students' science ideas. Sets of **sample student work** for select items are provided on the accompanying CD for use as needed.

Name:

ENERGY FOR HAWKS

TASK **A**

① Put a ✓ next

Name: **Apu**

ENERGY FOR HAWKS

TASK **A**

① Put a ✓ next to things that provide energy to hawks.

✓ sun	✓ squirrel	✓ wheat grass
✓ beetle	✓ water	✓ air
✓ rabbit	✓ clover	✓ oak tree

YUM!

② Describe the "rule" or reasoning you used to decide which things provide energy to hawks. Use the back of this page if you need more room to write or draw.

glucose sugar → Passed on → glucose sugar → Passed on → glucose sugar

No animal can live on meat only. This is why all of

References

American Association for the Advancement of Science. (1993). *Benchmarks for science literacy.* New York: Oxford University Press.

Bransford, J. D., Brown, A. L., & Cocking, R. R. (Eds.). (2004). *How people learn: Brain, mind, experience, and school,* expanded edition. Washington, DC: National Academies Press.

Buxton, C. (1998). Improving the science education of English language learners: Capitalizing on educational reform. *Journal of Women and Minorities in Science and Engineering, 4*(4), 341–363.

Duschl, R. A., Schweingruber, H. A., & Shouse, A. W. (Eds.). (2007). *Taking science to school: Learning and teaching science in grades K–8.* Washington, DC: National Academies Press.

Greenleaf, C., Hanson, T., Herman, J., Litman, C., Madden, S., Rosen, R., Kim-Boscardin, C., Schneider, S., & Silver, D. (2009). Integrating literacy and science instruction in high school biology: Impact on teacher practice, student engagement, and student achievement. Final report to the National Science Foundation. Grant #0440379.

Greenleaf, C., Schoenbach, R., Cziko, C., & Mueller, F. (2001). Apprenticing adolescents to academic literacy. *Harvard Educational Review, 71*(1), 79–129.

Guskey, T. R., & Yoon, K. S. (2009). What works in professional development? *Phi Delta Kappan, 90*(7), 495–500.

Heller, J. I. (2011). Understanding Science professional development and the science achievement of English language learners: Confirmatory report. Final report submitted to Regional Educational Laboratory West, WestEd, and Institute of Education Sciences, U.S. Department of Education.

Heller, J. I., Shinohara, M., Miratrix, L., Rabe-Hesketh, S., & Daehler, K. R. (2010). *Learning science for teaching: Effects of professional development on elementary teachers, classrooms, and students.* Paper presented at the 2010 Conference of the Society for Research on Educational Effectiveness, Washington, DC.

Krajcik, J., & Sutherland, L. M. (2010). Supporting students in developing literacy in science. S*cience, 328,* 456–459.

Lee, O., & Fradd, S. H. (1998). Science for all, including students from non-English-language backgrounds. *Educational Researcher, 27*(4), 12–21.

Lee, O., & Fradd, S. H. (2001). Instructional congruence to promote science learning and literacy development for linguistically diverse students. In D. R. Lavoie & W-M. Roth (Eds.), *Models for science teacher preparation: Bridging the gap between research and practice* (pp. 109–126). Dordrecht, the Netherlands: Kluwer Academic Publishers.

Lemke, J. (1998). Multiplying meaning: Visual and verbal semiotics in scientific text. In J. R. Martin & R. Veel (Eds.), *Reading science* (pp. 87–113). London: Routledge.

Lemke, J. (2002). Mathematics in the middle: Measure, picture, gesture, sign, and word. In M. Anderson, A. Saenz-Ludlow, S. Zellweger, & V. Cifarelli (Eds.), *Educational perspectives on mathematics as semiosis: From thinking to interpreting to knowing* (pp. 215–234). Ottawa: Legas Publishing.

Little, J. W. (2006). Professional community and professional development in the learning-centered school. In *NEA research reports on best practices.* Washington, DC: National Education Association. Retrieved June 15, 2009, from www.nea.org/tools/30380.htm

Loucks-Horsley, S., Stiles, K. E., Mundry, S., Love, N. B., & Hewson, P. W. (2009). *Designing professional development for teachers of science and mathematics,* 3rd edition. Thousand Oaks, CA: Corwin Press, Inc.

National Assessment Governing Board. (2008). *Science framework for the 2009 National Assessment of Educational Progress.* Washington, DC: Author.

Osbourne, J. (2010). Arguing to learn in science: The role of collaborative, critical discourse. *Science, 328,* 463–466.

Schoenbach, R., & Greenleaf, C. (2009). Fostering adolescents' engaged academic literacy. In L. Christenbury, R. Bomer, & P. Smagorinsky (Eds.), *Handbook of adolescent literacy research* (pp. 98–112). New York: Guilford Press.

Schoenbach, R., Greenleaf, C., Cziko, C., & Hurwitz, L. (1999). *Reading for understanding: A guide to improving reading in middle and high school classrooms.* San Francisco: Jossey-Bass.

Torres, H. N., & Zeidler, D. L. (2002). The effects of English language proficiency and scientific reasoning skills on the acquisition of science content knowledge by Hispanic English language learners and native English language speaking students. *Electronic Journal of Science Education, 6*(3).

Van Driel, J. H., Verloop, N., & De Vos, W. (1998). Developing science teachers' pedagogical content knowledge. *Journal of Research in Science Teaching, 35*(6), 673–695.

White, B., Frederiksen, J., & Collins, A. (2009). The interplay of scientific inquiry and metacognition: More than a marriage of convenience. In D. Hacker, J. Dunlosky, & A. Graesser (Eds.), *Handbook of metacognition in education* (pp. 175–205). Mahwah, NJ: Lawrence Erlbaum Associates.

WHAT IS ENERGY?

Ask students what they think energy is and it's likely you'll hear, "Energy is everything," "Gasoline is energy," or "Energy makes things go, like me." Chances are your textbook offers definitions such as *energy is the ability to do work* or *energy makes things happen*. But what exactly do these definitions mean? What might they help students understand about energy? Where do they mislead students? Do they incorrectly suggest energy is a force or some kind of matter?

Defining a complex concept, such as energy, is tricky business. The definition you choose has to both make sense to students and be scientifically accurate. The following Teaching Case explores this dilemma. It provides a window into a classroom where the teacher initially gives students a simple textbook definition of energy, then provides other opportunities for them to actively make meaning of the concept. For example, students use energy tree diagrams to track energy transfers that occur with wind-up toys and car crashes. In the end, students come full circle to their geoscience studies and track the energy transfers that occur when fuels are burned to produce electrical current and therefore electrical energy. They finish by using a literacy tool called a Frayer Model to write their own expanded definitions of energy.

This Teaching Case is intended to help you start the process of inquiry — inquiry into the science, into the thinking of the students, into words and language, and into the instructional decisions made by the teacher.

As you read this Teaching Case, think about the following questions:

- How do these students initially think about energy?

- What definitions and support does their teacher provide?

- What do students' written definitions show that they understand about energy after this series of instruction?

There is a hubbub of energy in my classroom today, the kid kind. As a wrap-up to our geoscience unit, students taped their Earth Resources posters on the walls and were doing a Gallery Walk to read what others had written.

"Biomass, I never heard of that," Amisha commented to Gino, who had made his poster with a couple of buddies. "How does electricity come from that stuff?"

"Burn it," Gino offered in his typical, matter-of-fact way.

"Oh, we did coal energy. You burn it to get electricity too," Amisha added, a bit flirtatiously. "You should go look at our poster. We made a turbine that actually turns. That was my idea."

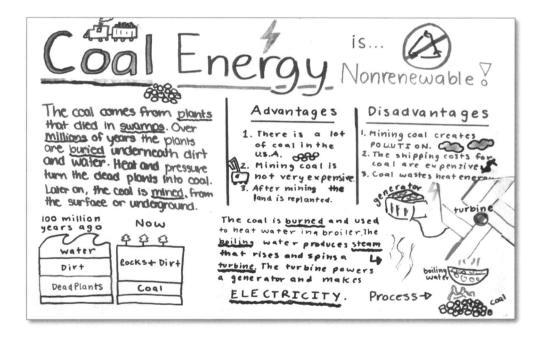

The poster made by Amisha's group was about average this year, but overall had better text than years past. It seems our schoolwide focus on writing is paying off. As I perused their posters, I saw a lot about energy conservation, renewable versus nonrenewable, and how electrical energy is generated. I'm always amazed at the amount of attention students give to their work when they are sharing something they've become experts at.

I was pleased to see students thinking deeply about the science of how natural resources are converted into electrical energy. However, the titles of some posters, for example, Gasoline Energy and Geothermal Energy, jumped out at me. It reminded me of something I noticed last year. My students have a tendency to mix up resources with energy. For example, they described the Sun, water, wind, and oil as energy. But they are not actually energy, rather they are natural resources we use to generate electrical energy.

When I teach about energy, I want my students to learn that energy has to be present for things to happen and it can't be produced or destroyed but it can change in amount. I also want them to understand the role of energy in everything they see, do, and feel. After all, energy is a big, new, and important idea that is introduced in middle school. It is the foundation for deeply understanding most of middle school science — plate tectonics, weather, cell biology, chemical reactions, and motion.

In relation to natural resources, I want my students to understand that coal is made of molecules bonded together and, as a result, has chemical potential energy. When coal is burned, its chemical potential energy is released and in the process warms water and the air above it. Then the heated air and steam rise, which turns a turbine, which turns the shaft of an electromagnet, which generates electrical current. This electrical current is what has electrical energy.

Introducing energy

Following the end-of-unit geoscience test, we launched into our physics unit. I started class today by reading a riddle and asking my students to talk in pairs to figure out the answer.

What is this stuff?

Whatever happens is caused by it. It is everything. Everything needs it. Everything is it. You need it to eat, to run, to walk, to sit, to think, to sleep, "perchance to dream." You use it constantly, every moment, awake or asleep. You can't get mad without it. You can't get glad without it. It makes the wind blow, rain flow, and lightning zap and thunder. It "feeds" volcanoes and earthquakes. It drives tidal waves, typhoons, and tornadoes. It "powers" the universe. It "powers" bacteria. It is the mysterious everything. What is it?

Interestingly, nearly every pair guessed energy. Only a few students wondered if the mystery stuff might be matter instead. Wanting to move the class toward a more scientific understanding of energy, I began, "It sounds like most people have the same answer to this riddle. Even so, it's not so easy to say what energy is. Our textbook says, 'Energy is the ability to do work.' In science, energy is a very important concept because it's part of every interaction. Every time two objects of any size touch one another or get near each other — from cement trucks to those tiny, tiny particles we talked about in chemistry — energy is involved. Every time things change temperature, every time you think or breathe, and every time a light is flipped on, energy is involved."

I saw a good number of heads nodding, so I continued. "Knowing about energy helps scientists predict what will happen in interactions. Yet energy is a very abstract idea. It is not an object, not a fluid, and not smoke. In fact, it is not *anything* made of matter. You can't feel it or hold it, rather the idea of energy helps us think about things interacting or changing. In a way, energy is sort of like the idea of color. Objects have colors, but objects are not the colors themselves. The same is true for energy. Moving cars have energy, but cars are not energy. Maybe a good way to make sense of energy is to think about energy as *a measure of how much can happen*. Like other measures, for example, meters or degrees Celsius, we use numbers to say how much energy exists in a certain situation."

"Can you think of other examples where objects have a certain property, but they aren't the property?" I asked to see if students were following.

Eventually Paris said, "A meter isn't an object but a meter stick is?"

I nodded, and Warner volunteered, "My sister is bossy, but she isn't the boss." The class erupted in laughter.

The sibling attack wasn't what I hoped for, but they seemed to get the difference between a property of an object and the object itself. I hoped students would come to see energy that way too. To help them think more concretely about energy, I introduced the idea that there are different types of energy. I made a list on the board and shared an example or two of each type.

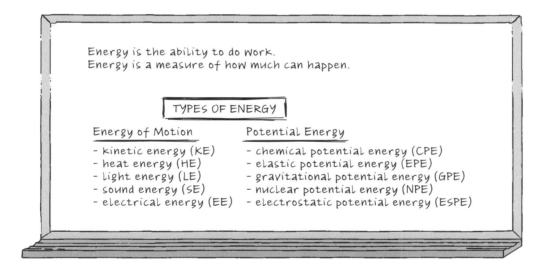

Energy is the ability to do work.
Energy is a measure of how much can happen.

TYPES OF ENERGY

Energy of Motion

- kinetic energy (KE)
- heat energy (HE)
- light energy (LE)
- sound energy (SE)
- electrical energy (EE)

Potential Energy

- chemical potential energy (CPE)
- elastic potential energy (EPE)
- gravitational potential energy (GPE)
- nuclear potential energy (NPE)
- electrostatic potential energy (ESPE)

Then I explained, "There is lots to know about each type of energy. In the next couple of days we'll become more familiar with them. In fact, every table group is going to research one type of energy and make a poster to help your classmates understand it."

The next day, groups got to work. They read various resources I'd gathered for the task: books from the library, printouts from the Internet, and a few video clips. I heard them deciding what to include on their posters and arguing about how best to describe and illustrate things for other students.

When they finished, I had students do another Gallery Walk. This time I taped a blank piece of paper next to each poster and asked students to record one thing they liked about the poster and one question they had for the authors.

As a final step, groups revised their own posters, attaching a second, smaller piece of paper with an answer to one of their classmate's questions. For example, while Tony's group took a somewhat minimalist approach in their initial description of chemical potential energy, they tried hard to answer a question one of their classmates had about their poster: "When does chemical potential energy occur, and how much energy is in chemical bonds?"

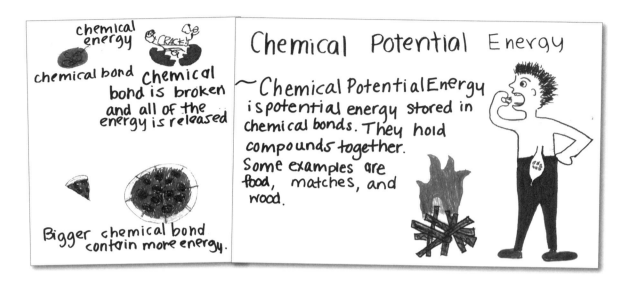

Overall I felt my class was developing a pretty good understanding of the different types of energy. I was fascinated by their various approaches, especially in light of our conversation about what energy is not and what it is. This assignment made me realize how hard it is to explain the types of energy without somehow suggesting energy is some kind of object made of matter.

Transferring energy

I'd planned to start today's classes showing a short movie clip of a dramatic car crash and then work together to figure out the various kinds of energies involved. But the DVD player was on the fritz, of course, so I scrambled for an Internet video and ran into a host of difficulties. Realizing that technology just wasn't on my side, I pulled two Matchbox® cars from my desk drawer and made the best of it.

"Okay, so the red car is zooming along, fast and kind of crazy. What type of energy do you think it has?"

"Gasoline?" offered Paris. Many heads nodded.

"Other ideas?" I pressed. Silence.

Taken aback slightly, I refocused the class. "I was thinking about the different *types of energy* — heat energy, kinetic energy, elastic potential energy, and so on — not about the natural resources or fuels these energies come from. Gasoline is a fuel. When we ignite gasoline, we release heat energy. As a reminder, look at the fabulous posters around the room. What type of energy does this moving car have?"

This time hands shot up, and Amisha confidently answered, "Kinetic energy. That's ours, and it's the energy inside things that are moving."

"Indeed! Kinetic energy is the one related to objects that are moving. Remember, energy is a measure of how much something can do. It's a measure of what can happen in an interaction or a system. So what might happen when this fast-moving red car crashes into the slow-moving blue car?"

Even with my sorry old toy cars, that was all it took to get the conversation rolling. As we talked through the various ways the objects interact, I modeled how to draw an energy tree diagram: "*Ovals* show the types of energy and *arrows* let you know what direction the energy transfers, say from kinetic energy to sound energy when you hear the crashing."

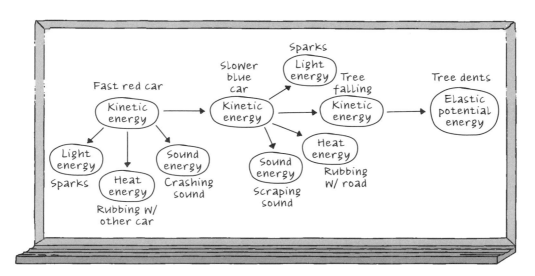

Using the energy tree diagram went surprisingly smoothly. My students excitedly described all the possible energy transfers in gory detail. In the midst of this excitement, I heard things like "the car's energy went into the tree and made it break apart" and "the red car's energy goes into air and makes sparks." Initially, I thought those phrases made it sound like energy was a literal thing, moving around, but I decided the phrases weren't exactly wrong, and honestly I didn't have a better way to describe it.

For the rest of the period, students practiced diagramming the energy transfers in four other interactions — rubbing their hands together, eating food, using a flint lighter, and making a wind-up toy dance.

As I walked around looking at their work, I noticed several things. First, many students had a pretty clear idea of which energies transferred into what. Yet they sometimes weren't clear on the nuances of the different energy types. For example, Warner said sound energy comes from elastic potential energy, which isn't possible because sound energy results from the motion of another object and therefore should come from kinetic energy, but overall his work shows he's making good progress.

Warner

Wind up toy

Elastic Potential Energy — Kinetic Energy — Heat Energy — Sound Energy

Sound Energy

After winding up the toy and releasing all the elastic potential energy, the toy will then move. Also during the wind up, it may create a sound. Also from the kinetic energy, it can give off sound and heat energy.

Revisiting natural resources

Just a few days ago, my students couldn't differentiate between natural resources (e.g., wind, water, and oil) and the scientific types of energy (e.g., kinetic energy, heat energy, and chemical potential energy). Now they'd gotten more precise in their use of the word *energy,* and I wanted them to loop back to where we started with their Earth Resources posters and their descriptions of the mechanical process that converts their resource into electrical current.

When students arrived, I invited them to marvel at the lights in our classroom and think about how the electrical energy used to make this light energy might have come from the natural resource they studied earlier. After a brief warm-up conversation, I instructed students to draw an energy tree diagram showing the transfers of energy involved in going from their natural resource to electrical current with electrical energy.

With minimal clarification, students got right to work. It was thrilling to see the lessons on energy coming full circle. Most diagrams, like Tony's, were quite elaborate, although not many students did as good a job with the specifics. Tony really knows a lot about what happens in a geothermal utility plant!

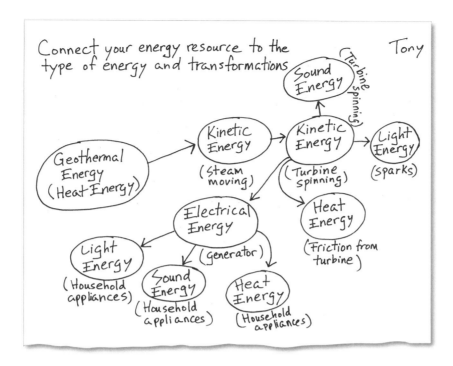

Writing about energy

On Friday, I wanted students to pull together their thoughts about energy. As a warm-up, I pointed students to a seemingly off-topic question I'd written on the board: "*Love* is a word that is hard to define. Which other words are hard to define?"

Judging by their answers, most students had already given plenty of thought to life's abstractions. I heard many hard-to-define words, such as *God, dreams, afterlife, color, lust, big, emotion, number, luck,* and *freedom.* We talked briefly about why some words are so hard to define in a complete, precise way. Then we completed a Frayer Model for the term *love.* We worked step-by-step through listing examples and nonexamples of love, describing love's characteristics, and synthesizing a definition. I like how Frayer Models provide students a useful structure for thinking about complex, hard-to-define words.

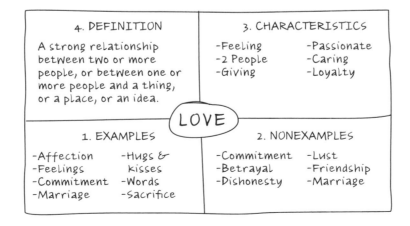

Next I had students complete a Frayer Model for the term *energy*. I was impressed by how the tool helped scaffold students' thinking and writing about energy, but *energy* is a tough word to define, even with a scaffold.

Amisha's work pointed out a really common problem my students had — they tended to describe energy as a "force" or some kind of "power." I think most students were using these descriptions along the lines of magical forces and supernatural powers, not how scientists use the terms *force* and *power,* but neither way is correct.

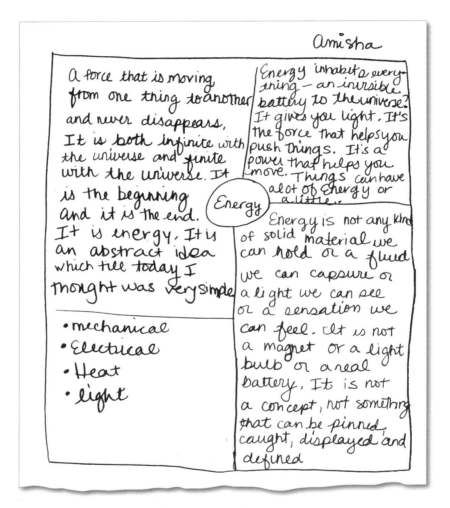

Gino's work highlighted another common problem my students had — energy is closely tied to matter, yet it is not matter, be it moving or stationary!

Looking at their work, I can see my students were thinking hard about this extremely abstract idea. On one hand, I was thrilled with the progress they'd made. On the other hand, it was disappointing that so many of my students seemed to have incorrect mental models about energy.

In hindsight, I'm wondering if it was helpful for students to hear different definitions of energy. We talked about the one in their textbook — *energy is the ability to do work* — but I also used the phrase *energy is a measure of how much can happen,* along with lots of other discussion about what energy is and is not. Maybe I should have picked one and kept coming back to it? If so, which one? Neither really tells the whole story.

Something as foundational to science as energy should have a clear definition, one that we can easily grasp and make use of. But the opposite is true. Energy is such a big, abstract idea that it is not easily defined. Even we adults might know what it is, but we are hard-pressed to explain what it is in a meaningful, accessible way. So where does that leave our kids?

Every interaction involves energy. When a leaf falls to the ground, when a dog barks, when a child plays in the park, and when a flower grows, energy is involved.

VOCABULARY

Energy is a measurable quantity, a number, that describes how much change can happen in a system. It is a quantity that is always conserved. Like length and other measurements, energy is represented with a number. Energy can also be described as different types (e.g., kinetic energy, gravitational potential energy, and light energy).

Matter is what all physical objects in the universe are composed of. If something has mass and takes up space, then it is matter.

A **force** is an interaction between objects or particles that can result in a push or a pull. Forces can cause objects to change their speed, their direction of travel, and their position.

"Renewable" and "nonrenewable" describe kinds of fuels, not types of energy. **Renewable fuels,** such as wind, sunlight, and flowing water, are considered renewable because we do not use them faster than they regenerate. **Nonrenewable fuels,** such as coal, natural gas, and petroleum, are considered nonrenewable because we use them faster than they regenerate.

Energy transfers occur during interactions. As a result of an interaction, energy can change from one type to another (e.g., kinetic energy is transferred to gravitational potential energy when a ball is kicked), and/or the amount of energy associated with an object can change (e.g., a kicked ball gains energy).

A **system** can be defined by identifying the objects of interest and the forces of interest within a specific timeframe of interest.

⊙ What is true about energy?

Energy is a word we use in many different ways. Our students have lots of energy. We are facing a worldwide energy crisis. That car doesn't have enough energy to make it over the hill. Which energy drink will give me the most energy?

The word *energy* first appeared in the work of Aristotle, and the scientific concept of energy came out of early work with objects in motion. In the 1800s, scientists began using the terms *energy, kinetic energy,* and *potential energy,* but at that time the nature of energy was still in question. For years, scientists debated if energy was an undiscovered substance or merely a quantity, like length and temperature. With the development of thermodynamics, energy was determined to be solely a measurable quantity, a number, with no physical substance. Clearly, energy has been and continues to be a confusing concept — a concept that is often incorrectly explained and defined. So what is true about energy?

Energy is a measure of how much change can occur in a system. This includes changes in motion and changes in conditions (e.g., shape, volume, pressure, temperature, chemical composition). Said in another way, the amount of energy — a number — tells you how much change has happened or can happen in a given scenario. For example, if a glass of water has a higher temperature than the surrounding air, it has the ability to warm that air. If the glass of water cools down and ends up at the same temperature as the surrounding air, it no longer has the ability to warm that air (even though it still has the ability to melt ice and react with other substances). Energy is associated with both glasses of water. However, the hotter glass of water has more energy.

The amount of energy is calculated in different ways for different systems. Nobel laureate Richard Feynman once explained energy by saying, "I don't know what energy is but if you have plenty of time, I can teach you how to calculate it." That is perhaps what matters most in understanding energy — realizing that *energy is not something with a physical form, but instead a property, like length, that can be calculated.*

The other big truth about energy is that *energy is a quantity that is always conserved.* If energy is conserved within a system, the total amount of energy in that system doesn't change. Therefore, in a closed system, if the amount of energy in one part of the system increases, there must be an equivalent decrease somewhere else in the system.

Knowing about energy helps us describe and predict what will happen in the world around us. The amount of energy present tells us how much ability there is for something to change in a particular system. For example, the amount of change that can happen in the human digestive system depends on the energy associated with various foods.

⊙ What kinds of energy exist?

Among scientists, there is no standard way to categorize energy, nor is there a single convention for naming the various types of energy. In these materials, we chose to use two generally well-accepted categories of energy — *energy of motion* and *energy of position* — and identify specific types of energy within each category. The following table shows this organizational approach.

ENERGY OF MOTION	ENERGY OF POSITION
Energy due to the motion of matter	Energy due to the relative positions of matter
Kinetic Energy (KE)	Gravitational Potential Energy (GPE)
Heat Energy (HE)	Elastic Potential Energy (EPE)
Light Energy (LE)	Chemical Potential Energy (CPE)
Sound Energy (SE)	Nuclear Potential Energy (NPE)
Electrical Energy (EE)	Electrostatic Potential Energy (ESPE)

Note: You may be familiar with types of energy other than the ones we chose to use for this course (e.g., mechanical energy and thermal energy). Such terms are often synonymous with a type of energy listed in this table or they are the result of several of these types of energy acting in combination with each other within a system.

Energy of motion

Energy of motion is active energy. All the types of energy of motion involve objects moving and changing position.

- Kinetic energy (KE) is a result of an individual object's motion (e.g., a hockey puck sliding on ice, a car speeding along a road, a particle moving through space). When talking about the collective movement of many small objects, such as atoms, molecules, and subatomic particles, we use other terms, such as *heat energy* and *sound energy,* even though technically all energies of motion can be thought of as kinetic energy.

- Heat energy (HE), sometimes called thermal energy, is a result of the atoms and molecules that make up matter vibrating, rotating, and/or moving randomly from one place to another.

- Light energy (LE), sometimes called radiant energy, is a result of photons moving.

- Sound energy (SE) is a result of atoms and molecules moving in concert to form temporary pressure regions of compression and expansion.[1]

- Electrical energy (EE) is a result of charged particles moving through a conductor, (e.g., electrons moving in a wire).

---

[1] You may be familiar with thinking about sound and light in terms of waves, rather than moving particles. While we explain energy in terms of particles, both ways of thinking are valid. Waves are merely particles moving in a coherent manner. Waves transfer energy from one place to another. For example, when an earthquake triggers an ocean wave, water molecules slosh up and down in a coordinated manner. This sloshing motion travels through the water, making it possible to lift boats and knock down trees. The amount of energy associated with a wave can be measured in terms of the frequency of the wave and the square of its amplitude. A wave with twice the frequency transfers twice the amount of energy, while a wave that is twice as high transfers four times as much energy.

Energy of position

Energy of position is passive, or potential, energy. It is present even if objects are not changing position. All types of potential energy are due to the position of one object relative to another.

- Gravitational potential energy (GPE) is a result of the relative spacing of masses, regardless of their size or the distance between them. Most often, GPE refers to the energy associated with Earth and another object, such as a ball.

- Elastic potential energy (EPE) is a result of compressing or expanding an object relative to its natural shape, which causes a change in the relative positions of the object's atoms.

- Chemical potential energy (CPE) is a result of the arrangement of atoms and molecules that make up an object.[2]

- Nuclear potential energy (NPE) is a result of the relative positions and masses of subatomic particles in nuclei, such as protons and neutrons.[2]

- Electrostatic potential energy (ESPE) is a result of the relative spacing of stationary charged particles, such as electrons on a balloon.

◉ What is not true about energy?

Even though the word *energy* is part of our everyday language, energy is a hard concept to define. Even scientists think so. To make matters worse, textbooks often define energy incorrectly, incompletely, and/or imprecisely. It is frequently oversimplified and used interchangeably with other scientific terms that describe different concepts. One good way to better understand energy is to think about all the things that energy is not. Energy is not a force, not matter, and not power. While force, matter, and power are all related to energy, in science, these words have specific definitions that clearly distinguish them from energy.

Energy is not a force

In science, a **force** is a pushing or pulling interaction between objects. Some examples of forces include gravity (the interaction between two objects due to their mass), magnetic force (the attraction or repulsion between two magnetic objects), buoyant force (the force exerted on an object immersed in a fluid), and friction (the force between two solids that resists their sliding across one another).

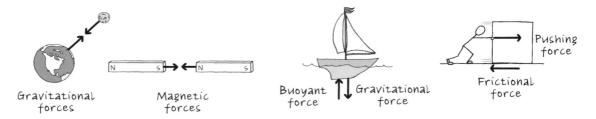

Gravitational forces   Magnetic forces   Buoyant force   Gravitational force   Frictional force   Pushing force

---

[2] CPE and NPE are different from other potential energies due to the interplay between matter and energy. In this course we take a Newtonian physics perspective, as it provides a useful approximation of what happens. A relativistic physics explanation would be quite different. In addition, the term *nuclear energy* is confusing because people refer to radioactive fuels (e.g., uranium) as nuclear energy, to the ability to generate EE from such fuels as nuclear energy, and to the energy released when the nuclei of atoms are either split or fused together as nuclear energy.

Note: In this course we use an arrow with a single tail (➝) to represent force. The length of the arrow tells us the relative magnitude, or strength, of the force. The direction the arrow is pointing shows the direction of the force.

Forces can't be seen, but their effect can be felt. A force between objects can make an object change its motion, change direction, rotate, speed up, slow down, and stop. Forces can also cause objects to deform and change shape. If a force causes a change in either the motion or the position of an object, then there is *also* a change in the energy associated with that object. However, that doesn't mean forces are energy!

For example, imagine you apply a force to a rubber band and stretch it out longer. The force increases the rubber band's *length,* which you can *measure* with a ruler. The force also increases the *energy* associated with the rubber band, which you can *calculate* using a formula. The force is neither the length nor the energy. The force just caused those two quantities to increase.

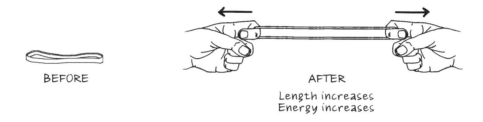

BEFORE

AFTER

Length increases
Energy increases

Another way to think about forces being different from energy is by considering the units used for each. A standard unit for measuring force is a *newton* (N), where $1 \text{ N} = 1 \text{ kg m/s}^2$. A standard unit for measuring energy is a *joule* (J), where $1 \text{ J} = 1 \text{ kg m}^2/\text{s}^2$. The approximate amount of energy needed to lift a small apple 1 meter off the ground is 1 joule. Once that apple is 1 meter off the ground, there is approximately 1 newton of weight (or pulling force) between the apple and Earth.

While the scientific use of the term *force* has a specific meaning, the nonscientific use has many meanings. In everyday language, we use the word *force* to mean authority, influence, and even magical ability, but none of those is a synonym for energy either.

Energy is not matter

According to Newtonian physics, all physical objects in the universe are made up of matter. If something has mass and takes up space, it is **matter.** Energy has no visible or invisible physical form. Energy is not a physical substance, known or unknown. It does not have mass or take up any space. While we say "energy is transferred from one object to another," energy is not a physical thing passed between objects or from place to place.[3]

---

[3] Throughout this course we use Newtonian physics to describe matter and energy. We take this approach because it's a useful way of explaining our everyday experiences. In fact, Newton's ideas are still taught in schools for this same reason, even though our understanding of the universe now includes theories of special relativity, general relativity, and quantum mechanics. Einstein's theory of special relativity, which is famously abbreviated as $E = mc^2$, says the amount of available energy is directly related to the amount of mass. It also says the amount of mass increases as the speed of an object increases, such that near the speed of light mass is infinite. For this reason, some scientists will explain that mass can be converted into energy and vice versa.

Energy is not power

At first blush, it doesn't sound too bad to explain energy as power, but in science, power is the amount of energy expended over a certain period of time. So if you substituted the word *energy* for the word *power* in that definition, you'd have to say, "Energy is the amount of energy expended over a certain period of time." Huh?! Clearly, energy cannot be power, but they are indeed related. In fact, power is the rate at which energy is consumed. As an equation, power (P) is the change in energy (ΔE) over the change in time (Δt) as shown by:

$$P = \frac{\Delta E}{\Delta t}$$

Another way to think about the difference between energy and power is to consider their units. As a reminder, a standard unit for measuring energy is a joule. A standard unit for measuring power is a *watt* (w), where w = J/s or w = kg m²/s³. It requires approximately 1 watt of power to lift a small apple 1 meter off the ground in 1 second.

Even if you think about the nonscientific uses of the term *power,* power doesn't equal energy. For example, we often use the term *power* in phrases such as *the power of the masses, the power of love, the power to rule,* and so on. None of which leads us toward a more scientific definition of energy.

◉ Renewable and nonrenewable

This course does not consider renewable and nonrenewable as types of energy, but rather as kinds of fuels and natural resources. In the scientific community, **renewable fuels** are resources that can be regenerated before we use them up (e.g., wind, sunlight, biomass, and geothermal activity). **Nonrenewable fuels** are resources that are not regenerated before we use them up (e.g., coal, natural gas, and oil). For example, biomass is considered a renewable fuel because it is dead plant matter, typically young trees or other fast-growing crops, that can be regenerated in a relatively short time. Coal, on the other hand, is a nonrenewable fuel because it is compressed, ancient organic matter that takes millions of years to form.

Whether a fuel is *renewable* or *nonrenewable* depends on the timeframe of interest. Often the timeframe of interest is how long it takes humans to use up the fuel. If you shorten the timeframe for the system (e.g., by increasing fuel use), biomass becomes nonrenewable. If you lengthen the timeframe of the system (e.g., by decreasing fuel use), then coal becomes renewable, since it continuously forms at a slow rate. If you dramatically lengthen the timeframe, then no fuel is renewable — eventually, even the Sun will burn out. How you define the timeframe is what determines how fuels are categorized.

Perhaps most importantly, *fuels are matter.* Fuels are important for generating electrical current, which results in electrical energy, but *fuels are not energy.* For example, the following diagram shows that the combustion of biomass heats air and water and that the rising air and steam turns a turbine, which turns a shaft with many coils of wire surrounded by magnets, which generates an electrical current in the wires. The electrical current transmits along these wires to homes. The movement of electrical charges (a.k.a. electrical current) results in the electrical energy in this system.

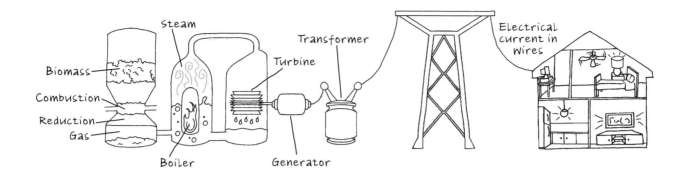

◉ What is a system?

The word *system* is used in many ways in daily life and in science. For example, we talk about a school system, the legal system, and the solar system. All these are systems because they are a set of objects interacting over time. Like many systems, they are complex and often hard to navigate. To help navigate complex systems, we often focus on particular parts of interest. For example, within our national school system, you might be the most interested in the middle school students taking science at your school this year. It doesn't mean all the other grades, courses, schools, and years don't exist, they just aren't as relevant.

In science, when we are trying to "see" what happens with energy, it helps us to think in terms of systems. In science, a **system** is defined by identifying the *objects of interest* and the *forces of interest* present within a specific *timeframe of interest.*

For example, in a park we might see a child playing with a ball and ask, "What happens with energy as that child kicks the ball?" To help us explore this question, we might define the objects in the system as the child, the ball, the air, and Earth. If these were the objects of interest, there would also be forces in the system as those objects interact (e.g., the force of the child's foot kicking, the force of gravity, and the force of friction between the air and the ball). One possible timeframe starts when the child's foot contacts the ball and ends when the ball hits Earth after flying through the air.

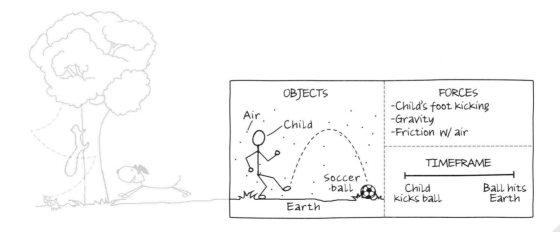

How you define the system depends on what you're interested in. If we asked a different question, for example, "What happens with energy as the leaf falls?" we would need to define the system in a different way. To help us explore that question, we might define the objects in the system as the leaf, the air, and Earth. If these were the objects of interest, there would also be forces in the system as those objects interact (e.g., the force of gravity and the force of friction between the air and the leaf as it falls).

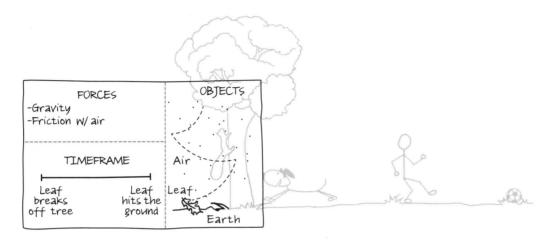

Both of these examples focus on different objects and different aspects of the same park scene. Each system is very different even though both of these interactions take place at the same moment in the same park.

◉ Energy transfers?

Every interaction involves a transfer of energy. Riding your bike is an interaction — an interaction between you and your bike, and between your bike and anything it rolls over. Eating breakfast is an interaction — an interaction between you and the spoon and between the food and your digestive system. Playing with a toy is an interaction — an interaction between you and the toy and between the toy and other objects. Each of these interactions involves a transfer of energy in one way or another.

An **energy transfer** is when the *amount of energy* present in one part of a system changes or when the *type of energy* in the system changes to another type of energy.[4] Because it is not possible to actually see energy being transferred, one helpful way to make these changes more transparent is to draw a representation, or model, such as an energy tree diagram.

---

[4] The term *energy transformation* is sometimes used as a synonym for the way we use the term *energy transfer* in this course. Other times people reserve the term *energy transformation* to refer to a change in the type of energy present and *energy transfer* to mean a change in the amount of energy present. There is no universally accepted way of using these terms, and there are benefits and limitations to each choice.

The following energy tree diagram tracks the energy being transferred in an interaction between a kid and a soccer ball. When the soccer ball is kicked, the kinetic energy from the child's moving foot is transferred to the ball.

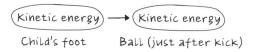

As the soccer ball rises higher above Earth, there is a transfer of energy from one type to another. The following energy tree diagram shows that as the position of the ball changes relative to Earth, the ball's kinetic energy is transferred to gravitational potential energy.

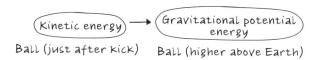

While the energy transfers involved in this soccer ball interaction are relatively easy to track, things can get complex quickly depending on how you define the system. Imagine what the energy tree diagram might look like if you included the food the child ate for breakfast and the Sun!

Science Investigation

50 MINUTES

---

20 MINUTES **1** Identifying energy

a. Play with a wind-up toy for a few minutes. Discuss the energies involved as it moves around, bumps into things, falls off the table, and so on.

b. Draw a picture showing your wind-up toy's adventure and label the types of energy you identify.

c. Ask for "Handout A: Types of Energy" from your facilitator. Individually, read the background information and make notes to yourself, including questions, or rephrase the descriptions in your own words.

d. Discuss how the descriptions on the handout relate to the way you described energy in your picture of the wind-up toy's adventure.

---

2 Tracking energy

a. As a group, make an energy tree diagram to track what happens with energy in your toy's adventure.

Energy tree diagrams show the types of energy involved in an interaction, along with energy transfers that occur. In energy tree diagrams:

- **Ovals** indicate the *types of energy* (e.g., kinetic energy or heat energy) associated with an interaction.

- **Arrows** indicate the *energy transfers*, either from type to type or from one interaction to another.

- **Descriptions** explain the *event* linked to the energy transfer.

Here is an example for a burning log:

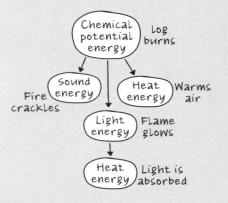

b. Discuss your system and how the energy associated with the wind-up toy changes.

- How did you define your toy system? Which objects are included? When does your energy tree diagram start and end?

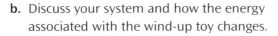

- What *types of energy* are associated with the toy when it's stationary on the table? And when it moves?

- What are some ways to increase the toy's energy? And to decrease its energy?

3 ## Contrasting force and energy

a. Again, play with the wind-up toy. This time discuss the *forces* involved as it moves around, bumps into things, falls off the table, and so on. For more information about forces, refer to your Content Notes.

b. Use a spring scale to measure the strength of the:

- *Pulling force* required to drag an object at a constant speed, counteracting friction

 MEASURING FORCE WITH SPRING SCALES

Spring scales are common tools for measuring pulling forces, such as the force needed to move an object against the frictional force.

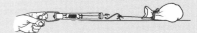

They can also be used to measure the gravitational force between an object and Earth.

- *Gravitational force* between an object and Earth

c. Which requires you to expend more *energy,* dragging an object 1 meter or lifting an object 1 meter off the ground?

Hint: Which requires you to do more *work*?

d. What are you noticing about *energy* and *force*? What does this tell you about what energy is and what energy is not?

 CALCULATING FORCE, WORK, AND ENERGY

Force (F) is the amount of push or pull it takes to make mass (m) accelerate (a).

Force = mass × acceleration

F = ma

Force and energy are related by the concept of work. The **work** (W) done on a system is measured by the amount of force (F) applied over a distance (d).

Work = force × distance

W = Fd

A **change in energy** (ΔE) in a system is measured by the work done.

Change in energy = Work

$\Delta E = W$

A standard unit for measuring force is a *newton* (N), where mass is measured in kilograms (kg) and acceleration is measured in meters per second squared (m/s²).

N = kg m/s²

As a result of the pull of gravity between objects and Earth, things on Earth fall at a constant rate (g).

g = 9.8 m/s²

A standard unit for measuring work and energy is a *joule* (J).

joule = newton × meter

J = (kg m/s²) × m

J = kg m²/s²

20 MINUTES **1** **Exploring students' ideas**

a. Individually, take a few minutes to flip through the Teaching Case and review things students said and wrote about energy. In particular, take a careful look at:

- the Coal Energy poster and students' conversations about resources (p. 3)

- the Chemical Potential Energy poster (p. 6)

- Warner's and Tony's energy tree diagrams (pp. 8–9)

- Amisha's and Gino's Frayer Models (pp. 10–11)

b. Discuss what this case tells us about students' *mental models* for energy. Use specific evidence from students' words and drawings.

- What do these students think energy is?

- What is correct about their ideas?

- What is incorrect or incomplete?

✳ EXPLORING MENTAL MODELS

The way we think about a particular phenomenon is called a **mental model.** Our mental models are how we imagine things work. Our mental models can be accurate, complete, and precise, but often they are not. Sometimes all that's needed is learning that missing piece of information or fine-tuning the idea. Other times incorrect mental models are built on misconceptions.

A **misconception** is an incorrect idea that is often based on sound logic or personal experience. Misconceptions often make good sense, for example, thinking the Sun revolves around Earth matches what we see, yet it's not how things really are — it is a misconception. In other words, many common, yet incorrect mental models are logical and result from something other than mistakes or shortcomings in instruction.

a. As a group, identify the various definitions and descriptions of energy used by the teacher in this Teaching Case.

b. Which descriptions, definitions, and parts of definitions made their way into students' Frayer Models? What didn't seem to stick? Why do you think this is so?

Literacy Investigation

18 MINUTES

---

5 MINUTES **1** ## Reflecting on your writing history

a. Individually, take a few minutes to think about some key moments in your development as a writer.

- Which experiences stand out for you? High points? Low points?

- Were there times when you felt like an insider (or outsider) as a writer?

- What supported your development as a writer? What changed over time? What obstacles did you face?

2 Learning from our writing histories

a. Pair up with another person and take turns sharing the key moments of your writing histories. Make sure each person has 2–3 minutes of uninterrupted time to talk.

b. After you have both shared, discuss what you learned about each other. What do your histories have in common? In what ways are they different?

c. Discuss how your histories inform your understanding of the nature of writing.

- What is writing?

- What supports or hinders people's writing?

- In what ways can writing change for a person over time?

Classroom Connection

35 MINUTES

 15 MINUTES **1** Reviewing key concepts

a. Individually, read the Science Review and Literacy Review on the following pages. Feel free to pick and choose the sections that are most valuable to you.

As you read, take notes and think about these questions:

• What is interesting or new to you?

• Which examples and images do you find especially helpful?

• What are you still wrestling with?

b. Individually, take a few minutes to think and write about your own big takeaways from today.

2 Exploring the ideas of this session

    a. As a group, discuss the Science and Literacy Reviews. Use the questions on the previous page as a guide.

3 Considering classroom implications

    a. Based on your experiences today, discuss implications for *what* and *how* you teach your students.

Session Review

SCIENCE REVIEW

Energy is the kind of word that is everywhere. But it's a slippery word. It represents an abstract scientific concept that is hard to pin down. Energy means different things in different contexts, and it comes in a host of flavors and variations. Frankly, it is quite hard to say exactly what energy is and what energy is not.

> **SCIENCE** **KEY CONCEPT**
>
> **Energy is not a substance. Although force and power are related to energy, they are not energy. Energy is a measurable quantity, a number, that describes how much change can happen in a system.** Energy is a construct, or idea, created by scientists to describe how much change can happen or has happened. Energy is a measure of how much can change, like temperature and length are measures of how warm an object is and how long an object is, respectively. While energy can be represented as a number, sometimes it is also described as having different types (e.g., kinetic energy, potential energy, and heat energy).
>
> **SCIENCE** **KEY CONCEPT**
>
> **Every interaction involves a transfer of energy, and every energy transfer is evidence of an interaction.** An interaction is an event that involves two or more objects acting on or influencing each other to cause an effect or make a change (e.g., a foot moves a soccer ball and the Sun warms Earth). As a result of an interaction, energy can change from one type to another (e.g., from kinetic energy to gravitational potential energy) and/or the amount of energy associated with an object can change (e.g., a kicked ball gains kinetic energy). Both of these types of changes are called energy transfers.
>
> **SCIENCE** **KEY CONCEPT**
>
> **Defining a system means naming the objects of interest and forces of interest that interact during a specific timeframe of interest. Different systems highlight different things.** Given the same set of objects and events, there are many different ways to define a system. Scientists define systems depending on what they are interested in knowing or representing. Systems can be as large as the universe or as small as two subatomic particles. Once you choose your focus, then you define the boundaries of the system by identifying the objects of interest and the forces of interest that are present within a specific timeframe of interest.

The following Science Review elaborates on these science key concepts, including sample "answers" to the Science Investigation and explanations of predictable errors and incorrect ways of thinking about the science.

⊙ Defining energy

Open a dictionary, look in a textbook, or search online and you might be surprised by how many different definitions you find for the word *energy*. Some of these definitions may directly contradict each other or be so complex that your head spins. Others may be overly simplistic or perpetuate misconceptions.

SCIENCE ▸ KEY CONCEPT

Energy is not a substance. Although force and power are related to energy, they are not energy. Energy is a measurable quantity, a number, that describes how much change can happen in a system.

Incorrect definitions

Here are some common definitions of energy that are misleading or flat out incorrect.

- Energy is a force that makes things happen. (INCORRECT)
- Energy is the power to carry out an action. (INCORRECT)
- Energy is the essence of life. (INCORRECT)
- Energy is in everything. (INCORRECT)
- Energy is light, sound, heat, and motion. (INCORRECT)
- Energy does things for us. It takes us to school and runs our computers. (INCORRECT)

Energy is a force that makes things happen. (INCORRECT) A force is a push or a pull. Energy is not a push or a pull. During the Science Investigation, you used a spring scale to measure the pulling force of gravity, as well as the pulling force needed to drag an object. These forces were measured in *newtons,* whereas the energy associated with the interaction was calculated in *joules.*

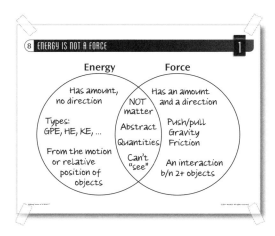

It is important to recognize that both energy and force are constructs, or organizing frames, that have been created by scientists to describe aspects of interactions between objects. Neither force nor energy is made of matter, and neither is visible or tangible. Scientifically speaking, force is not the same thing as energy, but many people who describe energy as a force are not thinking of energy as a force in the scientific sense. Instead they are suggesting energy is something more ethereal, as in "she is a powerful force to be reckoned with" or "may the force be with you," but energy is not this kind of force either.

Even if you take the word *force* out of the definition "Energy is a force that makes things happen," the idea that "energy makes things happen" is still problematic. Just because energy is present doesn't mean anything will happen. For example, a cup of hot coffee has a measurable amount of energy that could make something happen, such as increase the temperature of the air above the cup. However, while the coffee has the potential to do this, it doesn't mean the coffee will make the air hotter — perhaps there is an insulating cover on the cup or perhaps the air is the same temperature as the coffee. Even though the coffee has a lot of energy, it doesn't mean anything will happen. Energy does not make things happen or cause things to change — rather, whenever things happen, there is a change in energy, and because of differences in energy, things can happen.

Energy is the power to carry out an action. (INCORRECT) Scientifically speaking, power is a measure of the rate of change of energy in a given period of time.

$$\text{Power} = \frac{\text{change in energy}}{\text{change in time}} = \frac{\Delta E}{\Delta t}$$

For example, this means a car needs an engine with a greater horsepower to experience a greater change in kinetic energy in a short period of time (i.e., accelerate more quickly). Therefore, it doesn't make sense to equate power and energy. If you did, the definition would read "energy is the amount of energy expended over a certain period of time."

Energy is the essence of life. (INCORRECT) This definition hinges on what is meant by the "essence of life," which is really a philosophical question not meant for science to answer. Scientifically speaking, energy is a quantity that can be measured, calculated, and conserved. It seems unlikely we could do any of those things with the "essence of life."

Energy is in everything. (INCORRECT) The word *in* is problematic in this definition because it implies that energy is a thing or a kind of matter. Atoms and subatomic particles are matter and they are *in* everything. Because energy is in fact a measurement of a property (the ability to change), similar to length being a measurement of a property (size), you could check the definition by interchanging the terms. Does it make sense to say "Length is *in* everything?" Not really.

Energy is light, sound, heat, and motion. (INCORRECT) While energy can be calculated for all types of motion, energy is not motion. Motion is defined as any change in the position of an object. Light is the coordinated change in position of photons. Sound is the coordinated change in position of particles (usually particles in the air or the atoms and molecules in materials). So while energy can be calculated for light, sound, and random molecular movement, energy is not light, sound, or motion.

Energy does things for us. It takes us to school and runs our computers. (INCORRECT)
Energy does not do things. Objects do things. For example, vehicles take us to school and electrical current runs our computers. Energy doesn't physically do things for us, rather energy is a concept that is represented by a number and expresses the potential ability for things to happen.

Generally accepted definitions

With so many possible definitions, it's helpful to figure out a definition to use with your students as they develop their own understanding of energy. Here are some common definitions that are generally accepted as age-appropriate and scientifically accurate.

- Energy allows things to happen.

- Energy is the ability for change to occur.

- Energy is the ability to do work.

These definitions are accessible. They make sense and use simple language. You can imagine that energy is required to get things done. One limitation of definitions like these is they can trigger people to think of energy only in connection with motion, possibly contributing to the following common, yet incorrect idea.

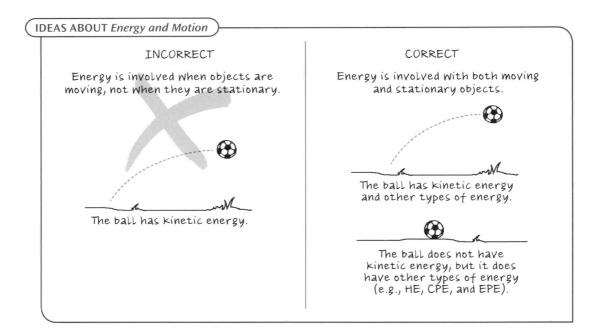

IDEAS ABOUT *Energy and Motion*

INCORRECT

Energy is involved when objects are moving, not when they are stationary.

The ball has kinetic energy.

CORRECT

Energy is involved with both moving and stationary objects.

The ball has kinetic energy and other types of energy.

The ball does not have kinetic energy, but it does have other types of energy (e.g., HE, CPE, and EPE).

It's intuitive that a soccer ball flying through the air has energy — it's moving! It's a lot less obvious to think about the energy involved when the soccer ball is merely stationary. Even though the soccer ball is not moving, there is chemical potential energy and heat energy associated with the ball. Perhaps the idea that energy is only involved when there is motion stems from kinetic energy being the most familiar type of energy. However, energy results from an object moving, as well as the relative positions of objects. In truth, all systems contain energy even when the objects in the system are stationary relative to each other.

The definition "energy is the ability to do work" is hotly contested by some scientists and educators. In science, the term *work* traditionally has a very limited definition — the application of an amount of force over a given distance in the same direction as the force.

$$\text{work} = \text{force} \times \text{distance} = Fd$$

So it is very true that energy is the ability to do just that, apply a force over a distance. In fact, you likely used this relationship during the Science Investigation when you figured out that it required more energy to lift an object 1 meter than to drag it 1 meter across a table. A sample correct answer follows.

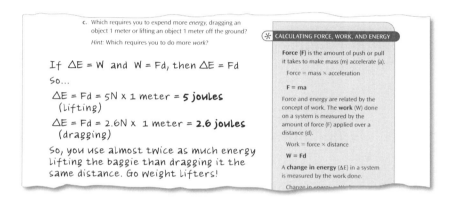

However, energy can also be defined as the ability to do work in a broader sense. For example, energy is also the ability to warm things, to apply forces in directions other than the direction objects are moving, and to break chemical bonds. None of these examples counts as work when thinking of it in the traditional, narrowly defined way (i.e., a force applied over a distance, W = Fd). Luckily, work can also be defined in relation to a change in energy (ΔE).

$$\text{work} = \text{change in energy} = \Delta E$$

If it is possible to calculate the change in energy (e.g., raising or lowering the temperature of an object), then it is also possible to know how much work has been done. While this is all true, it is not possible to do certain kinds of work, even when energy is clearly involved. For example, it is not possible to raise the temperature of an object (or system) if two touching objects are at the same temperature. So while each object may have heat energy, no "warming" work can be done. For these reasons, some scientists and educators feel it isn't entirely correct to say "Energy is the ability to do work." Another criticism is that the definition also misrepresents both the concept of work and the concept of energy to students.

More complete, accurate, and precise definitions

Given that energy is actually a construct created by scientists to describe how much change can happen in a system, it is most accurate to use a definition including the idea of energy being an amount or a quantity — a quantity that is conserved during interactions. Here are some definitions that highlight this critical aspect.

- Energy is a measure of how much change can happen in a system. It is a quantity that is conserved despite the many changes that occur in the natural world.

- Energy is the amount of work required to change the state of a physical system. The numerical amount of energy of a system diminishes when the system does work on any other system.

- Mathematically, energy is a quantity that does not change when an interaction happens in a closed system.

These definitions get at the heart of what energy is. While they may be more complex, they are also more complete, accurate, and precise because they incorporate the concept of conservation.

◉ Types of energy

Among scientists, there is no standard way to categorize energy, nor is there a single convention for naming the various types of energy. In these materials, we use two generally well-accepted categories of energy — *energy of motion* and *energy of position*.

ENERGY OF MOTION	ENERGY OF POSITION
Energy due to the motion of matter	Energy due to the relative positions of matter
Kinetic Energy (KE)	Gravitational Potential Energy (GPE)
Heat Energy (HE)	Elastic Potential Energy (EPE)
Light Energy (LE)	Chemical Potential Energy (CPE)
Sound Energy (SE)	Nuclear Potential Energy (NPE)
Electrical Energy (EE)	Electrostatic Potential Energy (ESPE)

Kinetic energy, heat energy, light energy, sound energy, and electrical energy are considered *energies of motion* because they all involve motion. Gravitational potential energy, elastic potential energy, chemical potential energy, nuclear potential energy, and electrostatic potential energy are considered *energies of position* because they are the result of the relative positions of objects.

It's often surprising how many types of energy are present in even simple situations. During the Science Investigation, you discussed the energy associated with a wind-up toy. A sample correct answer follows, showing some of the many possible types of energy involved.

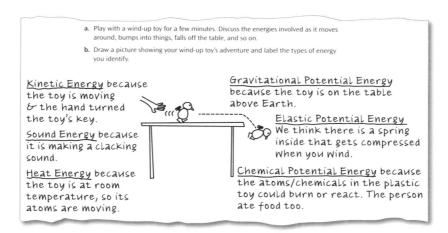

a. Play with a wind-up toy for a few minutes. Discuss the energies involved as it moves around, bumps into things, falls off the table, and so on.

b. Draw a picture showing your wind-up toy's adventure and label the types of energy you identify.

Kinetic Energy because the toy is moving & the hand turned the toy's key.

Sound Energy because it is making a clacking sound.

Heat Energy because the toy is at room temperature, so its atoms are moving.

Gravitational Potential Energy because the toy is on the table above Earth.

Elastic Potential Energy We think there is a spring inside that gets compressed when you wind.

Chemical Potential Energy because the atoms/chemicals in the plastic toy could burn or react. The person ate food too.

While the categories and types of energy used in this course are generally well accepted, they are not the only options. For example, some textbooks use *mechanical energy* when talking about the combined kinetic energy and various types of potential energies associated with mechanical systems (e.g., wind-up toys, bicycles, machines). We have chosen to talk about these energies separately because that is how they are commonly used by scientists and because kinetic energy, gravitational potential energy, and elastic potential energy can be described and understood in relation to the scientific formulas used to calculate them.

Other textbooks do not subdivide potential energy into specific types (e.g., gravitational, elastic, and chemical) as we do in this course. We use these more specific types of potential energy because sometimes it is very useful to make these distinctions. For example, engineers who design roller coasters care how much GPE the roller coaster carts have at different points in the ride, but they aren't especially interested in the carts' total potential energy (i.e., the sum of their GPE, EPE, and CPE), nor do they care about the amount of CPE because they aren't planning on setting the carts on fire. Lucky for all the thrill-seekers out there!

Still other textbooks suggest that renewable and nonrenewable are two types of energy, or they list them as examples alongside kinetic energy and chemical potential energy. This is incorrect! The terms *renewable* and *nonrenewable* describe two kinds of fuels (not energy). Renewable fuels are those that can be generated as fast as they are used. Nonrenewable fuels are those that cannot. Fuel is not energy. Fuels are objects, made of matter. Energy is not made of matter, nor does it come in these two kinds.

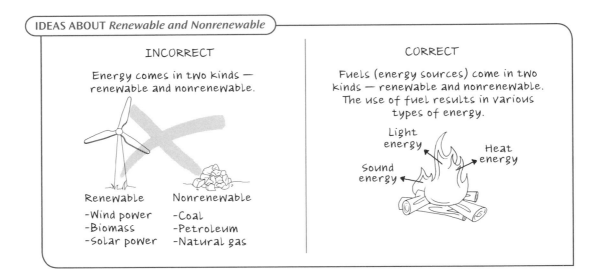

INCORRECT

Energy comes in two kinds —
renewable and nonrenewable.

Renewable
-Wind power
-Biomass
-Solar power

Nonrenewable
-Coal
-Petroleum
-Natural gas

CORRECT

Fuels (energy sources) come in two
kinds — renewable and nonrenewable.
The use of fuel results in various
types of energy.

Light energy

Heat energy

Sound energy

While it is incorrect to claim fuels are energy, they are closely tied in many peoples' minds. This is because we often use fuels to obtain the energy we need to run computers, light homes, and move cars. There is something logical about simply equating fuels to energy, even if that's not how things really are. Differentiating between fuels and energy helps us understand what energy is not. Energy is not any kind of matter that is stored inside objects.

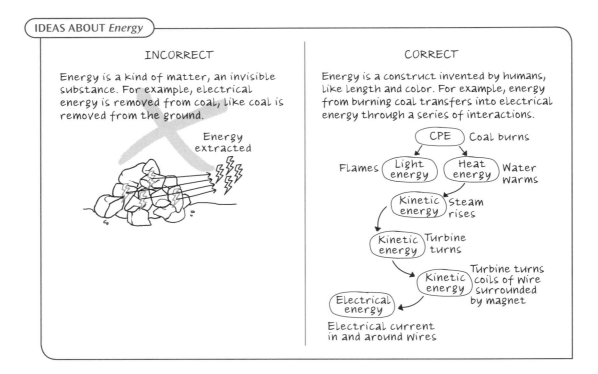

INCORRECT

Energy is a kind of matter, an invisible substance. For example, electrical energy is removed from coal, like coal is removed from the ground.

Energy extracted

CORRECT

Energy is a construct invented by humans, like length and color. For example, energy from burning coal transfers into electrical energy through a series of interactions.

CPE — Coal burns

Flames — Light energy — Heat energy — Water warms

Kinetic energy — Steam rises

Kinetic energy — Turbine turns

Kinetic energy — Turbine turns coils of wire surrounded by magnet

Electrical energy

Electrical current in and around wires

The origin of this incorrect idea may be our everyday use of the word *energy*. For example, we say, "Eat up! You need the energy in that food." Alternately the origin may be even simpler and be based on our knowledge that most things are made of matter. Early scientists also believed there was some invisible, undetectable substance passed between objects, so the idea is clearly logical to humans. Generations of scientific work have now established that energy is not made of matter, not even invisible matter. It is simply a measurement, represented by a number!

So if energy is in fact just a number, *a measure of how much change can happen in a system,* then it seems contradictory to describe energy as having different types. True. Whether we choose to talk about energy as a number or a type depends on what we want to explain or understand. Remember, energy is simply a construct, a made-up idea that helps us understand and explain interactions in the world around us. If an engineer is trying to reduce the amount of energy "lost" to friction in a car engine, it is helpful to think in terms of types of energy, such as when kinetic energy is transferred to heat energy. However, when an engineer needs to know how much change in energy a material is expected to withstand before breaking, then it may be most useful to think of energy as a number.

◉ Energy transfers

Every interaction involves a transfer of energy. Sometimes the interaction involves a *change in the type of energy,* such as a car engine transferring kinetic energy into heat energy as it moves. Other times there is no change in the type of energy involved, but there is a transfer or *change in the amount of energy* associated with an object. For example, when one car rear-ends another car, kinetic energy is transferred as the first car slows down and the second goes faster.

SCIENCE KEY CONCEPT

Every interaction involves a transfer of energy, and every energy transfer is evidence of an interaction.

In the Science Investigation, you used energy tree diagrams to track energy transfers resulting from interactions involving a wind-up toy. A sample correct answer follows.

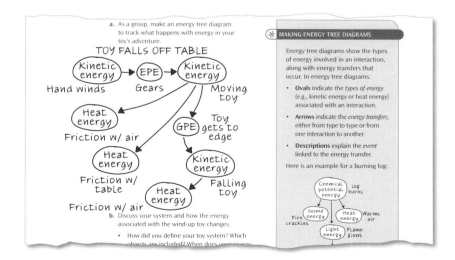

In this course, we use the term *energy transfer* to describe changes from one type of energy to another and to describe the same type of energy being moved to another location or object.

You may be familiar with other phrases for describing changes in energy. For example, *transformed* and *converted* are often used to describe what happens when energy changes from one type to another (e.g., in solar panels, light energy is transformed or converted into electrical energy). People who use either *transformed* or *converted* often reserve the term *transfer* to describe changes in an amount of energy when there is no change in the type of energy (e.g., one bumper car transfers kinetic energy to another). Each of these uses is correct and scientifically acceptable.

However, we chose to use the term *energy transfer* in all instances involving a change in energy. Using a single term for changes in energy reinforces the accurate mental model that "energy is energy" regardless of its type. In other words, because energy is merely a number quantifying how much change can occur in a particular situation, it is more important to keep track of how this amount changes than it is to keep track of what type of energy changes into what or the absolute amount of energy.

⦿ Defining systems

Typically, scientists define systems as a way of indicating what specific part of the universe they are thinking about, generally for the purpose of finding an answer to a question and to better understand how things work. For example, to understand what happens when we eat food, a scientist might focus on the human digestive system, but to understand the tides, a scientist might look at the Earth-Moon system.

SCIENCE ▸ **KEY CONCEPT**

Defining a system means naming the objects of interest and forces of interest that interact during a specific timeframe of interest. Different systems highlight different things.

If you are trying to understand something about energy or want to answer a question, it is especially helpful to define the boundaries of your system in order to limit what you are focusing on. In general, a system includes the *objects of interest* and the *forces of interest* within a specific *timeframe of interest*. A system doesn't describe every object, force, or period of time, rather it is a narrower selection related to your question or specific area of interest.

For example, during the Science Investigation, you looked at the energy transfers related to interactions involving a wind-up toy. A group might have been interested in exploring the question "What happens with energy when the toy collides with something?" If so, this group might have defined its system as shown in the following "System A" chart.

The boundaries for System A are quite narrow and focus on only two objects (the toy and the pencil box) and the forces related to the collision. Similarly, the timeframe would start just before the objects hit and likely end shortly after the interaction. As a result, the energy tree diagram for this interaction would involve two energy transfers.

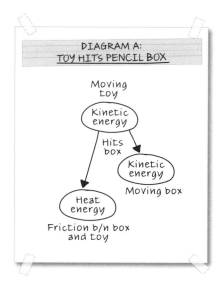

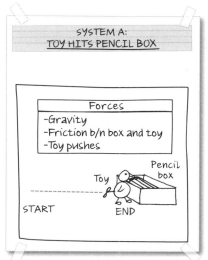

Another group might have been interested in exploring the question "What happens with energy from the time the toy is wound up until it falls off the table?" In this situation, the boundaries of the system would be defined differently, as shown in the following "System B" chart. Since the events of interest include the act of winding the toy as well as the toy falling, additional objects would be included in the system (e.g., the hand, the table, the air, and Earth). However, the pencil box is not involved in the interaction (even if it is sitting on the table), so it's not included in this system.

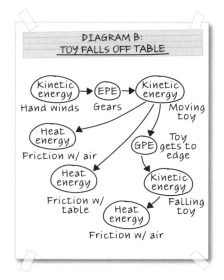

When thinking about various systems, it's likely people had different ideas about where the timeframe might start and end. This can be ambiguous because most systems are considered "open" with respect to energy, meaning there are "inputs" of energy into the system and "outputs" of energy from the system. We use a wide arrow (⟹) to show this transfer of energy into and out of systems.

In the example of System B, inputs of energy into the system include light energy from the Sun, chemical potential energy from food, and so on. The outputs of energy from System B include sound energy received by someone's ear and heat energy that warms the air beyond the boundaries of the system.

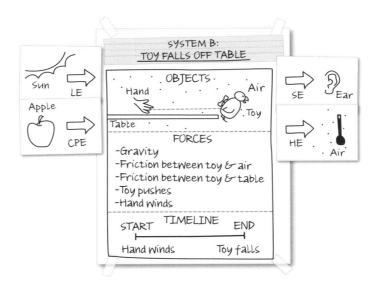

It's likely other groups were interested in exploring even broader questions. For example, a group may have been intrigued by the question "If the Sun is the source of most of the energy on Earth, what is the relationship between the Sun and the moving wind-up toy?" You would expect the boundaries for this system to be wider still, since it would need to begin months back in time with the growing of food and include all the objects involved in the chain of energy transfers beginning with the Sun. Some likely candidates would include vegetables, the person who eats the vegetables and eventually winds the toy, and the toy itself. You could also go into much greater detail at any of these points, for example, by thinking through the process of photosynthesis and the molecules involved, or the moving parts of the toy (e.g., twisting pin, gears, feet, and so on).

These examples point out that choices are made when a system is defined. Scientists do this frequently as a way of simplifying our complex, interconnected world in order to better understand a specific part. Often a physicist will say, "Assume there is no air resistance" or "Assume the surface is frictionless." By choosing not to include air or the atomic interactions between surfaces, a physicist can focus on the big picture and figure out the more general relationship between forces and moving objects. A chemist might say, "Assume there is no heat energy loss," or a geologist might choose to narrow the timeframe by looking at earthquake and volcano data for only the last 30 years. As with most things in science, the choices you make are driven by the questions you ask.

LEARNING OBJECTIVES

Energy and Energy Transfers

1.1 Energy is a measure of how much change can happen in a system (e.g., change in motion or change in conditions such as shape, temperature, or composition).

1.2 Energy is not a substance or an object, nor is it a force or power.

1.3 Energy is involved in every interaction.

1.4 Energy is a quantity that is conserved despite the many changes that occur in the world. It is often measured in joules, calories, and kilocalories.

1.5 The amount of energy associated with an object can change during an interaction.

1.6 When the amount of energy associated with one object goes down, the amount of energy associated with another object must go up.

1.7 The type of energy associated with an object can change during an interaction.

Types of Energy and Systems

1.8 Various types of energy result from objects moving or from the position of one object in relation to the position of another object.

1.9 In different parts of systems, energy is called by different names — kinetic energy, heat energy, chemical potential energy, and so on.

1.10 A system is defined by the objects of interest and forces of interest present in a timeframe of interest.

1.11 Thinking about energy as having different types helps us understand what is occurring in systems.

MISCONCEPTIONS

1.A It is incorrect to think of energy as something physical, made of matter or as some yet-to-be-discovered type of magical essence that is pulled out of one object and moved to another object during energy transfers. In fact, only the name and location of the energy really changes, and no physical substance moves object to object.

1.B It is incorrect to think energy is a force, similar to gravity or magnetic force, or to think of it as a nonscientific force (e.g., a magical force).

1.C It is incorrect to think the renewable and nonrenewable fuels used to power cars, homes, and businesses are energy. While humans use these natural resources in a variety of interactions that result in the presence of many types of energy, the fuels themselves are not energy.

1.D It is incorrect to think energy is involved only when objects are moving or things are changing. In fact, energy can also be involved when there is no visible change (e.g., holding a ball stationary in the air).

1.E It is incorrect to think energy transfers are perfectly linear, that one event triggers only one event. In fact, one event can trigger many simultaneous events and in turn involve many energy transfers.

In the past few days, it's likely you've zipped off an email, made a grocery list, written a birthday card, or jotted yourself some notes. But people have not always communicated through writing, and writing hasn't always been a part of our day-to-day lives. In fact, our civilization has its own writing history. We learned to write over thousands of years, with the earliest examples including symbols etched in a turtle's shell and images sequentially painted on a cave wall to tell a story. Centuries later, writing changed to hieroglyphics carved into wood and stone and elaborate symbols artistically painted onto tapestries.

LITERACY | **KEY CONCEPT**

Writing is not just an academic activity. It is personal and social too. Although we write using a range of common forms and conventions, no two people have quite the same life experiences with writing — writing is personal. We each bring a unique set of knowledge, skills, and mental dispositions to our writing. What we write is an announcement of how we think, it reflects who we are as individuals. Writing is also social. At its core, writing is an act of communicating ideas to others, and our ability to navigate the social aspects of writing can strongly influence our learning and success. Writing is complex — it involves a multitude of important skills, from spelling and grammar to organizing and refining ideas to understanding the expectations of an audience and conventions of the writing task.

LITERACY | **KEY CONCEPT**

Writing is neither an innate ability nor a skill mastered in the early grades. As writers grapple with new demands, they develop new skills. A host of things makes writing easier or harder for different people at different points in their lives. As the external demands and expectations of writers change over time, across grade levels in school, with life events, and with new jobs and technologies, writers develop and expand their abilities to meet these new challenges. As we each navigate this terrain, it is helpful to have support in four different dimensions — personal, social, cognitive, and knowledge-building.

The following Literacy Review summarizes important things about people's relationship with writing and the nature of writing. It includes things that likely came out of your group's discussion, along with commentary about related issues.

◉ Writing is many things

While writing has become integral to many people's daily lives, this does not mean everyone writes. It also doesn't mean writing is simple, even for expert writers. In fact, there is a huge variety in the kinds of writing people do, and writing means different things to different people. These and other truths about the nature of writing likely surfaced during the Literacy Investigation when your group pieced together its collective experiences with writing to say what "writing is…" A sample chart follows.

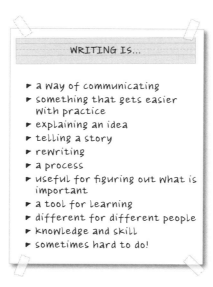

WRITING IS...

- a way of communicating
- something that gets easier with practice
- explaining an idea
- telling a story
- rewriting
- a process
- useful for figuring out what is important
- a tool for learning
- different for different people
- knowledge and skill
- sometimes hard to do!

Clearly, writing is complex. It is an advanced process of coding that takes place in our brains as we try to turn ideas and concepts into words, symbols, and images. This process requires a great deal of basic academic skill, which even accomplished authors sometimes find challenging. For example, F. Scott Fitzgerald, 20th-century American writer and author of *The Great Gatsby,* was described as "an idiosyncratic speller" who had his own ways of writing words and didn't much like the rigid structure of grammar. Yet writing goes well beyond knowledge of words, how to spell them, and how they go together. It is an intricate process of communicating, relaying our prior knowledge and personal experiences, and conveying our thoughts. In short, writing is an amazing act!

 LITERACY KEY CONCEPT

Writing is not just an academic activity. It is personal and social too.

During the Literacy Investigation, when everyone shared their writing histories, it's likely you noticed people's experiences were wildly different and profoundly personal. Maybe you heard stories of struggles and accomplishment, stories telling of encouragement and criticism, stories with strong feelings such as exhilaration, appreciation, or dread, and stories about experiences that changed with time. Maybe you heard stories like these.

"When I was a kid, I made comic books with fantasy drawings and the usual 'KAPOWs' and 'BLAMs,' but not many other words. My friends loved them."

"I've always hated writing. It makes me feel stupid. Sometimes it helps to remember what Ms. Lee, my 8th grade teacher, told me: 'I am not such a good writer, but I got through college and now I love to teach.' She helped me see there's more to being smart than being able to write."

"I had a secret diary. On rainy days I would write and write about everything that was happening in my life, with my parents, my friends, my troubles. I still write every day, but mostly emails to friends."

"One reason I went into chemistry is because you work problem sets and you don't have to write essays or long papers. Later in life I found out I'm dyslexic, like my daughter. That helped me understand why reading and writing were so hard. One surprise is that I now write for a living, and most days I like it."

Writing is personal

Writing is revealing. What we say and how we choose to write reflect who we are as individuals. Conversely, who we are as individuals affects what and how we write. Whether our writing is read today or in the next century, what we have written announces how we think, and it puts a piece of ourselves out for public scrutiny. This makes writing personal. This personal dimension of writing is one we sometimes forget. It is easy to think that everyone approaches writing the same way. And yet it also makes sense that writing is different for different people. After all, there are a huge variety of people in the world, and no two people have the same life experiences, so it follows that each person brings different skills, knowledge, and mental dispositions to the task. However, the magnitude of our differences is often surprising. Even among a group of middle school science teachers who have many things in common, there are vast differences in writing.

Writing is also personal because we each make our own choices about writing. Just as people like music for different purposes (e.g., to relax, to connect with others, to get stoked), people also prefer writing for different purposes. For example, someone who grew up telling stories may especially enjoy writing to entertain, while a journalist may like to write to document what happens. A third person may simply hate writing for the purpose of expressing feelings (e.g., condolences, best wishes, congratulations), but like to write as a way to remember things, get organized, or figure something out.

Some people find certain *audiences* more appealing than others. For example, people's stories may have revealed they prefer to write only for themselves. This makes sense because different readers come with different expectations and needs. Think about what it's like to explain the concept of energy to one of your students versus a scientist. In fact, how familiar we are with our audience greatly affects our writing. If you feel you can "sit in the shoes" of your readers, you're more likely to know how to connect with the audience, anticipate questions and reactions, and communicate effectively.

Writers also prefer certain *formats* and *styles*. For example, when people shared their personal writing histories, you might have heard "I'm fine when it comes to making lists and writing emails. Just don't make me write poetry" or "I like to play with fun, fanciful words, so science writing feels dry." There are many reasons people like or dislike specific kinds of writing. Sometimes it's as simple as having had one terrible experience. Sometimes it's about being more familiar with certain formats. Then again, writing likes and dislikes are sometimes simply a matter of personal taste.

In some ways, it feels logical that teachers would have lots of lovely things to share about writing and fond memories of learning to write. After all, aren't teachers the ones who "figured out school" and learned to succeed academically? While teachers are generally assumed to be good writers (experts so good they even teach children to write!), you likely heard that not everyone breezed through school, nor do all teachers consider themselves good writers or lovers of writing.

As our stories point out, people's personal identities are profoundly shaped by their experiences with writing. How we think of ourselves as writers often becomes integral to our individual social and emotional identities. This is especially true for people who feel they are somehow poor or inadequate writers. For example, people with dyslexia or other language-based learning disabilities may find it difficult to express themselves clearly in writing, which can lead to problems in school, in the workplace, and in relating to other people. People who struggle to write often end up feeling dumb and less capable than they actually are, even though they may be especially capable or gifted in areas that do not require strong language skills.

Writing is social

Intuitively, it feels like the *process of writing* is far from social. As adults, when we want to write, we often start by isolating ourselves from other people and their distractions. We grab a pen, or our computer, and close the door. But even with this "alone time," we aren't alone. This is because the act of writing is an act of communication. When we write, in essence, we are having an implied conversation with an audience (even if we are writing exclusively for ourselves). Through writing we explain our ideas and try to connect with another person's ideas. In a way, we figure out how our experiences and feelings fit, just as we do in a face-to-face conversation.

In addition, for elementary and middle school students, the *act of writing* is also often social. It is social not only because students at this age are especially influenced by their peers and learn from each other, but also because during these years, students are typically asked to share their writing with each other. Peer audiences and teachers usually respond by talking about what they liked about the writing, asking questions, and giving feedback to help the student-writer revise and strengthen the piece. At this age, being either "good" or "bad" at writing may be embarrassing and fodder for teasing. Whether being asked to write a single word (as in a spelling test) or write about an experience, the act of writing is social sharing and socially revealing. When we write, we give others a window into our life — our set of knowledge, experiences, and beliefs.

Perhaps the most obviously social dimension of writing is learning to write. We don't learn to write in a vacuum. Other people — peers, family, teachers, even television shows — help us learn to write and can strongly influence our success with writing. When sharing writing stories, you may have noticed a family member, teacher, mentor, friend, and even an author playing an important role. For example, someone in your group may have described an uncle who delighted in puns, a friend who wrote short stories, or an older sibling who read to them tirelessly. Still others may have been inspired by a particular author's work, the words of a powerful speech, a fabulous reading at a poetry slam, or the emotion in a song. All of these scenarios point to the ways in which we learn about writing through social interactions with others.

Sometimes these interactions are positive, as with a grandmother who always asked you to read your stories or a teacher who didn't write you off because you struggled. Other times peoples' influences can be unsupportive (or downright destructive!) — for example, a mean-spirited peer who teased you about your poor spelling, a teacher who acted as if writing was something that should have been mastered in the 2nd grade, or a professor who relentlessly assigned long writing assignments.

So although writing and learning to write are things individuals do, writing is, at its heart, a social activity — an activity that involves people we know and even people we don't know, such as audiences from future times and other walks of life. The importance of a supportive social environment for developing writers should not be underestimated, especially for middle school students. The nature of the social environment in which we learn to write is often a significant influence on the kind of adult writers we become.

◉ Writing skills and supports

When people share their personal writing histories, it is not uncommon for at least one person to say "writing is easy." While writing may be easy for some people, writing by nature is not. During the Literacy Investigation, when people talked about what makes writing hard, you likely heard a list of struggles such as these.

"Sometimes I just can't figure out what to write."

"I hear my dad's critical voice in my head and the words just stop flowing."

"Sometimes there are too many ideas milling around, and I can't decide what's most important or how to organize everything so it makes sense."

"My bad spelling and grammar always get in my way."

"When I write, it makes sense. Then I read it, and it's a mess."

"When I have to write something important, I write in my home language, then I translate to English."

This list points out how writing is like surfing — there are a lot of different specialized skills you need to master to experience success. Both surfing and writing present unexpected challenges and each takes a great deal of patience and practice. As you get better at each skill — paddling faster, reading the waves, and balancing — you experience less frustration and more exhilaration.

Changing demands

Perhaps the most important message that comes from people's personal histories is that learning to write is a lifelong process. People aren't born writers and nonwriters. Over time they learn different skills needed for different kinds of writing.

Writing is neither an innate ability nor a skill mastered in the early grades. As writers grapple with new demands, they develop new skills.

As people age and progress through school and careers, life brings new things to write and, with them, different expectations. From birth to kindergarten, children are not expected to write many words, but we do expect young children, even babies and toddlers, to scribble pictures and begin to communicate in symbols.

From the time we enter school until 5th grade, there is an emphasis on becoming "proficient" writers. K–5 students are expected to know and be able to spell more and more words as they progress through the grades. They are also challenged to learn to write sentences, followed by paragraphs, and to write increasingly difficult fiction and nonfiction tasks. At these grades, teachers expect students to make grammar mistakes, misspell words, forget punctuation, and write slowly.

By middle school and high school, students are expected to write longer and more complex texts and broaden their skill in writing a greater variety of texts, many of which have unfamiliar tones and language conventions. Perhaps the greatest change in writing expectations for middle and high school students is that they are expected to write all this fluently, meaning with great speed and accuracy.

In college, students are expected to write advanced texts from multiple subjects, some with very unusual language conventions, such as research journals. The amount of writing that's required also jumps significantly. It is not uncommon to hear teachers remembering their college writing as voluminous.

Even after school, our lives can be full of new writing demands and expectations. Many jobs require people to write professional emails, interoffice memos, and formal letters. Some professions require specialized writing, such as report cards, technical manuals, and detailed procedures. As technology and careers change, there are new things to write and new ways of writing. Even abbreviations, such as the "OMG" of text messages, and the hypertext of Web pages are some of the things we adults may need to learn to write.

Few people navigate these changing expectations smoothly. Those who self-identify as "good writers" may have no memory of struggles or encountering new writing expectations and challenges, even though they likely faced the same problems as everyone else. "Good writers" often developed the skills they needed quickly, perhaps without even being aware they were doing so. However, the vast majority of people, at one stage of life or another, can remember having difficulty meeting new writing challenges. Perhaps this is because it's difficult to adapt and improve one's writing skills seamlessly.

Writing supports

As the personal writing histories showcased, writing is personal and writing is social, but writing has two other important dimensions — the cognitive and knowledge-building dimensions. The *cognitive dimension* of writing includes the mental skills and strategies writers need in order to gather and organize information, focus their message, and write and refine drafts. The *knowledge-building dimension* includes developing a deeper understanding of a variety of purposes, audience expectations, and formats of writing in different disciples and genres.

Dimensions of a Writing Apprenticeship

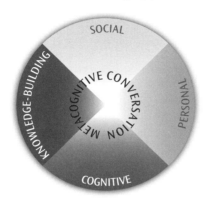

SOCIAL
- Discovering writer identity
- Building writer fluency and stamina
- Developing writer confidence and range
- Practicing and improving metacognition
- Getting into the habit of writing

PERSONAL
- Creating safety for public sharing
- Exploring the relationship between literacy and power
- Sharing author talk
- Investigating writing processes, problems, and solutions
- Noticing and appropriating others' writing strategies

COGNITIVE
- Getting the big picture
- Breaking down the text
- Learning writing strategies and when to use them
- Setting writing purposes
- Monitoring and adjusting writing processes

KNOWLEDGE-BUILDING
- Building knowledge of science
- Understanding the purpose of scientific writing
- Understanding the formats used by science writers
- Understanding the expectations readers of science have

During the Literacy Investigation, people may not have mentioned these dimensions of writing by name, but it is likely they talked about them. These four dimensions of writing often become obvious in people's writing histories when people talk about how their writing has been supported. The following examples show how writers might be supported in each dimension.

> "When I had to write every day for a new job, I found I got more confident about my writing and my writing got easier." (*Dimension:* **PERSONAL**)

> "My dad always read my school papers. He had a gentle way of pointing out places that didn't make sense. He also had good suggestions about how to make the words come alive." (*Dimensions:* **SOCIAL** and **COGNITIVE**)

> "In the third grade, my two best friends and I would sit around at recess and write stories together. We had a great time making up characters and figuring out what they would do." (*Dimension:* **SOCIAL**)

> "I have a couple of friends who are great writers, so I usually ask them questions when I get stuck. I learn a lot from them. They point out where I need to clarify an idea or rework a section." (*Dimensions:* **SOCIAL, COGNITIVE,** and **KNOWLEDGE-BUILDING**)

> "The first thing I do when I have to write something new is read examples of similar things other people have written." (*Dimension:* **KNOWLEDGE-BUILDING**)

Writing apprenticeships are one way to support writers in these dimensions. The model of support used in this course is based on decades of research and is in collaboration with the National Writing Project and WestEd's Strategic Literacy Initiative. A writing apprenticeship approach often begins as you began, by engaging people in conversation about their writing histories and writing processes.

As you progress through this course, you will become part of a science writing apprenticeship specifically designed to support you as an adult writer in science and as a teacher of students who are writers in science. The remaining Literacy Investigations focus primarily on the cognitive and the knowledge-building dimensions of science writing, as well as how to support students in becoming better science writers through metacognitive conversations and a process of review and revision that includes responses from peers.

POTENTIAL ENERGY

The word *potential* can mean something that is possible but not yet actual, while *energy* is a measure of how much change can happen in a system. Combining these two words sounds redundant, since energy is already a measure of what can happen or what is possible. So what exactly does *potential energy* mean? And what do the many types of potential energy — gravitational potential energy, chemical potential energy, elastic potential energy, electrostatic potential energy, and nuclear potential energy — have in common?

It's no surprise that students often have a lot of questions about potential energy and find the topic confusing. For example, when they see a candy bar sitting on a desk they will observe that "nothing is happening" and conclude there is no energy present — yet both chemical and gravitational potential energy are present. Unlike kinetic energy, which is the result of action or motion (e.g., a trumpet player blowing out a song or a jet flying through the air), potential energy is passive. With potential energy, the possibility for change comes not from motion, but from the position of objects in relation to each other.

A favorite way for students to explore potential energy is by doing the Food Calorie Lab. As described in the following Teaching Case, the scent of burning marshmallows and potato chips wafting through the hallways gets students really excited about chemistry. By combusting different foods under a can of water and measuring the increase in water temperature, students can calculate the potential energy of the various foods. In the process, their teacher discovers this classic lab isn't all sunshine and rainbows.

One challenge is that chemical potential energy is frequently calculated in calories. Yet a *calorie* to middle school students is often associated with nutrition or weight gain. That means it's no easy leap for them to think of a calorie as a scientific unit for measuring energy.

As you read this Teaching Case, think about the following questions:

- How are students thinking about chemical potential energy (CPE)?

- How is CPE like and unlike gravitational potential energy (GPE) and elastic potential energy (EPE)?

- What are the implications for measuring CPE in calories and measuring GPE and EPE in joules?

"THE POTENTIAL FOR PROBLEMS"

Before my students get to the famously popular Food Calorie Lab, they don't know much about potential energy. Earlier in our chemistry unit, they practice building molecules of hydrocarbons and simulate breaking them down into CO_2 and H_2O with a hypothetical release of energy. When they do this, I explain that because molecules can release energy during a reaction, we say they have chemical potential energy before the reaction. But that's about as far as we get with energy.

As a bridge between our larger units of chemistry and physics, I do a short nutrition unit. This year I plan to have my students study the new USDA My Pyramid Healthy Lifestyle Plan, discuss the chemistry meaning of the word *organic* versus the way the word is used in the food industry, and do the Food Calorie Lab — the highlight of the year for many of my kids. In fact, the excitement of burning food and smelling up the hallways is only rivaled by students' impatience to explore how roller coasters work in preparation for going to our local adventure park.

From the nutrition unit I want students to learn that food is actually made out of organic molecules and that when food is digested, it releases the energy we need in order to think, breathe, and move. The Food Calorie Lab gives them the opportunity to really see that foods release energy when they are broken down. The best part is that my students can actually measure how much energy is released and compare the amounts from different foods. Ideally, I want students to know the kilocalories they see on food labels are a measure of chemical potential energy. After they learn about chemical potential energy in the nutrition unit, I begin our physics unit by teaching about elastic potential energy and gravitational potential energy.

Monday: Chemical potential energy preassessment

I started the nutrition unit by asking for a volunteer to have her or his temperature taken. Pakuna, a bright girl who has trouble managing her weight, came to the front of the room and sat with a thermometer in her mouth while the rest of us measured the air temperature.

We determined that Pakuna's temperature was about 15°C higher than room temperature. I asked, "Where do you think Pakuna gets the energy to keep her body so much warmer than the air?"

A few students simultaneously called out "food" and then others started naming specific foods — cereal, chips, cookies, tacos, and soda. Then Viv spoke up in her typical authoritarian way, nearly shouting in her friend Pakuna's defense, "No! She likes healthy foods! At lunch she had salad."

I interrupted the discussion. "No matter which foods she eats, you are *all* on the right track. We get energy from food. When we eat food, the process of digestion releases energy when bonds are broken. Remember when we built long hydrocarbon chains and then 'broke' the bonds to make smaller molecules? Now it's time for us to figure out which foods provide more energy and which provide less energy." I asked table groups to talk for a few minutes about which kinds of foods they thought might give them a lot of energy.

Lingering near a group, I overheard a classic exchange. With a smirk and half-serious tone, Jason got them started. "You should have an energy drink and eat energy bars. You know, I heard two guys lived off energy bars for a month when they got lost! What's in those things anyway?"

Soft-spoken Marco challenged, "Don't you think we should drink water? You can only live three days without it."

Unable to resist, Perry, my perpetual joker, leaned in from a neighboring table to add, "Eat candy! It gives you a sugar rush!" Then seeing me, he attempted to contribute something serious to his own table. "Eat a double cheeseburger with tomatoes."

The two girls at the table — Viv and Pakuna — met these ideas with scorn. Viv asserted, "Well, you shouldn't eat anything with lots of fat if you want energy. Fat makes you sleepy and lazy."

Pakuna, who comes from a community that suffers from high rates of diabetes and heart disease, added, "My mom always says you shouldn't eat anything with lots of sugar, fat, or sodium. They're unhealthy."

I called for their attention. "I'm glad to hear so many different ideas. Now I'd like you to read page 157 in your book and then write down four things you would eat before a big athletic event to give you energy." They got right to work. The reading was more of a struggle than I expected, but I really shouldn't have been surprised. I've found our textbook has very little to say about a whole lot of things.

As I reread the section of text I had assigned, I noticed it mentioned organic compounds, carbohydrates, proteins, fats, and sugars, making and breaking bonds during digestion, and energy all in a single page! It even included the definition of a calorie — *the amount of energy required to raise the temperature of 1 milliliter (or 1 gram) of water by 1 degree centigrade.* At this point, I figured the definition meant next to nothing to my students, but I suspected the upcoming Food Lab would help them make the connection between calories and energy.

I looked over their shoulders as my kids wrote their ideas about what they would eat to give them energy before a big athletic event. Most of their work was very consistent with what I'd heard earlier. I was fascinated that so many students chose water as a good source of energy, even after the reading said it wasn't. Since the textbook reading didn't seem to make much impact, I capped off the period with a 5-minute lecture to reinforce some key points.

I started, "It's very hard to understand exactly what energy is because it's not a thing made of matter like most things we study. Instead, it's a measurement. Energy is a measure of the ability to make something happen. It is like other measurements — for example, temperature is a measurement of how hot something is and height is a measurement of how tall something is. Temperature can be measured in degrees Celsius and length can be measured in meters. What do you think energy can be measured in?"

Silence. Not a single eye met mine.

After a really long pause, I answered the question myself. "Energy is measured in calories. In our Food Calorie Lab tomorrow we'll get to measure the amount of energy available from different foods."

Tuesday: Calories, energy, and the Food Calorie Lab

Today was a double period, which I've found useful for completing the Food Calorie Lab in a sane manner. To get started, I wrote a "Do Now" prompt on the board and gave my students a few minutes to think and write in pairs. Then I pulled three popsicle sticks from a tin can and read the names of the "volunteers" who were to come up and post their response.

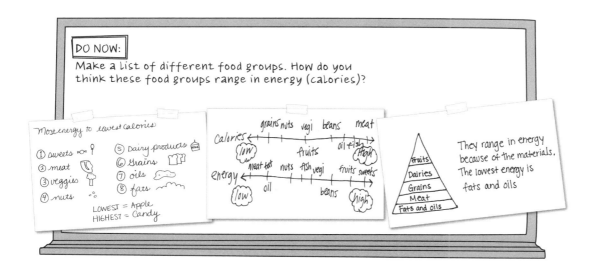

We started with the 1 to 8 list. I asked the pair who made it why sweets were on one end and fats were on the other. Perry shared a simple and matter-of-fact, albeit incorrect answer. "Candy has sugar, so it gives you lots of energy, but fats and oils are unhealthy, so they don't give you energy."

Then I moved on to the arrow lines. I asked that pair of students to explain their thinking. Marco volunteered, "Some foods have high calories, but give you low energy. Other foods have low calories, but give you a lot of energy."

I quickly realized these students were relating an energetic feeling to high-energy foods and a full, lazy feeling to low-energy foods. I told them that feeling energetic was not the same as how much chemical potential energy the food had. I explained that foods with a lot of calories, no matter if they were healthy or unhealthy, would give our bodies a lot of energy. I hoped the Food Calorie Lab would help them get this "calories are a measurement of energy" thing down.

Did I mention that I love the Food Calorie Lab?! I remember doing this same lab when I was a kid. Now I enjoy watching my students torch foods to warm water and figure out what it means. It's a good lab because it's quantitative and it gives me the opportunity to help students make sense of numbers and the importance of stressing accurate measurements. I make gathering the data into a competition so that the table with the least experimental error gets invited to a high-calorie root beer float party. One note: I *never* use nuts of any kind in this lab. Even if no student in my class has a nut allergy, I don't want the smoke from the lab to get into the hallways and potentially make other students ill.

To introduce the lab, I showed students the foods we'll be using — potato chips, corn chips, cereal, crackers, marshmallows, and even freeze-dried pineapple — and asked them to make a hypothesis about one food they thought might be higher in calories and one that might be lower in calories. Then I showed them the soda-can calorimeter, gave them time to draw it in their lab notebooks, and walked them through the procedure for burning the foods.

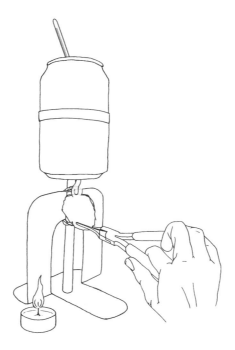

They couldn't wait to get started, so after I went over every aspect of proper safety, including using pliers with insulated handles to hold the food samples, not eating the samples, not burning anything but the samples, and not reaching across the flames of their candles, I let them dive in.

As I roamed the classroom, their excitement was fun to watch. I noticed Perry had a giant flame under his can. "Wow! That's a huge flame you've got there. What was the mass of that sample?"

"Huh?" Perry grunted.

"Didn't you even weigh the food?" Jason accused.

"My bad. Don't worry, I'll burn another one." Perry laughed and walked back to the supply station.

I laughed in return. "Looks like you got a bit too excited and forgot to record your data. That will certainly make it hard to write up your conclusions."

Wednesday: Making sense of the lab

Over the years, I've learned that very little sense making happens on the day students burn the foods, so the next day I showed my students a sample calculation for a marshmallow warming 100 ml of water. Then I gave them time to do their own calculations, discuss the data, and finish writing in their notebooks. In order to compare the amount of potential energy across various foods, students had to first calculate the calories it took to warm the water and then divide by the mass of the food to determine the calories/gram.

Food	Volume of water (ml)	ΔT (°C)	calories to heat water	Mass of food (g)	calories/g
Marshmallow	100	1.6	160	0.80	200

I've also learned there can be a great deal of variability across students' data such that it can be nearly impossible to have a meaningful class discussion using their results. So after students worked through their own calculations, I posted a sample data table for everyone to look at together. To begin the discussion I asked students to choose two pieces of data that showed them something interesting. Next I had each group write a statement on a sentence strip to summarize what they noticed and write the data supporting the statement on sticky notes. As a final step, I also asked students to record any questions they had.

Most often students compared similar foods, such as chips with chips, saying things like, "Hot Cheetos® have 300 calories per gram more than Ruffles®. Hot Cheetos® rule!" or "The marshmallows in Lucky Charms® cereal are pretty close to the regular ones — 250 for Lucky Charms® compared to 190 calories per gram for regular."

I found it surprising that students rarely looked across food groups, especially given that they'd watched grease drip from chips but not from marshmallows. To push the conversation toward broader generalizations, I offered a claim of my own. "I think fatty foods have more calories per gram than nonfatty foods. What do you think?"

We discussed the data and decided it supported my claim. To wrap up, I asked off-handedly, "Anything surprising about this lab?"

Hands shot up. I thought things were winding down, but apparently my students had a lot more to say. Perry didn't even wait to be called on and said, "Well, I thought these foods should have even more different calories, because they are really different foods."

"I thought that fruits and vegetables give you the highest energy and that fats and oils got all the calories," added Pakuna. "So I got surprised when even the pineapple had calories. All foods have calories, huh?"

Viv added in a very scientific voice, "Foods with lipids have the most energy *and* calories, and foods with cellulose, um, like pineapple, have less." I was impressed, but then she added, "The lower the calories, the healthier the food."

From the lab it was clear that my students now knew that *all* food had chemical potential energy and the amount varied from one type of food to another. I brought closure to the discussion by explaining the importance of eating enough calories to maintain proper body function. This naturally presented a chance to define anorexia and obesity.

For the last 5 minutes of class I gave a brief assignment. I asked my students to explain in their own words, first, what a calorie is and, second, how calories are related to energy.

I glanced at a few definitions and wasn't impressed, so I collected their papers to do a more careful read. Turned out nearly two-thirds of my students still couldn't accurately say what a calorie was. Ouch!

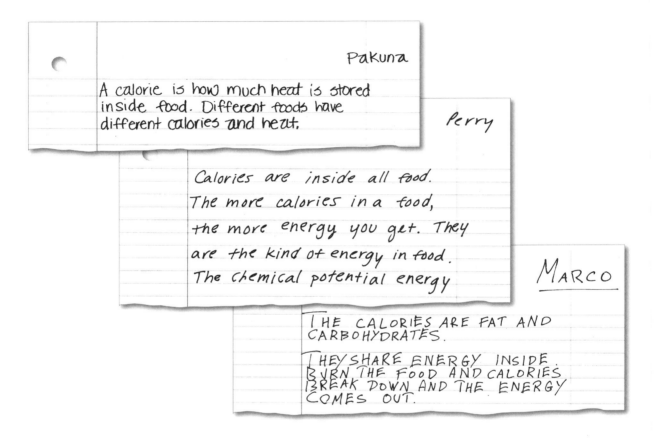

Pakuna

A calorie is how much heat is stored inside food. Different foods have different calories and heat.

Perry

Calories are inside all food. The more calories in a food, the more energy you get. They are the kind of energy in food. The chemical potential energy

MARCO

THE CALORIES ARE FAT AND CARBOHYDRATES.

THEY SHARE ENERGY INSIDE. BURN THE FOOD AND CALORIES BREAK DOWN AND THE ENERGY COMES OUT.

Viv was among the third of the class who did a good job accurately defining calories.

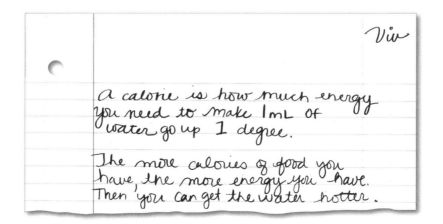

Viv

a calorie is how much energy you need to make 1mL of water go up 1 degree.

The more calories of food you have, the more energy you have. Then you can get the water hotter.

That same night, I also reviewed the questions they recorded during the Food Calorie Lab and their analysis of the data. Some questions were classic middle school wonderings and others really got to the heart of the science.

- "How can you compare calories in marshmallows to potato chips because one is soft and squishy and the other is hard and flat?"

- "What's more important, calories or calories in a gram?"

- "Does the air IN marshmallows have calories?"

- "Wouldn't it be better if not every food had to have calories?"

- "Do foods get more calories when you cook them hotter? They have more energy."

- "Why do Hot Cheetos® rule?"

- "Why do some foods have so many calories and not have good energy?"

Friday: Chemical potential energy props

Determined to help set my students straight about calories and energy, I decided to try another approach. Today they entered the classroom to see me standing at the front table surrounded by props. I'd planned an interactive lecture to get at some key points about chemical potential energy and calories.

My purpose was to clarify that energy is a measurement, a number, not a thing, and energy is a way to describe how much ability something has for making something else happen (like warming water). A calorie is just a unit describing how much energy there is.

Time to use my props. First I showed students two sugar cubes and asked, "Which of these has the most chemical potential energy?" They looked at me with inquisitive faces and eventually said the cubes should have the same amount. Then I smashed one sugar cube into little bits, inadvertently scattering it all across my table, and asked, "Now which one has the most chemical potential energy?" My students were laughing at the mess, but eventually managed to say the same amount of energy was still there.

"Yes," I said, "It doesn't matter what shape the food is in. Even if I dissolved this sugar in water, this amount of sugar still has the same number of calories — the same amount of chemical potential energy."

Next I showed them 1 slice of an apple and a whole apple. Students correctly said the whole apple had more chemical potential energy than a slice. Then I asked, "Which has more calories per gram, the whole apple or the slice?" This stumped them for a second, but then Perry worked it out: "Same apple. Same per gram."

Then I showed them 1 gram of potato chip and 1 gram of marshmallow and asked which had more energy. This got students flipping through their lab notebooks. With the help of their data, they determined the potato chip had more energy even though it looked like a smaller amount of food.

Lastly I showed them 1 gram of vegetable oil and 1 gram of cola and asked which had more energy. A few students called out the cola, saying it made them feel hyper, but most students called out oil. I sent them back to their data, and Viv was able to use it in her answer. "Well, we didn't test cola or oil, but cola is sugar like a marshmallow, and there was lots of fat dripping out of the chips. So the spoon of fat, I think, is like a potato chip and so it has more calories."

"Correct again," I smiled. "You are right on. The volume of the samples or the mass of the samples can be the same, but they can still have different amount of chemical potential energy, different amounts of calories, because they are made of different things."

Monday: Crossing the bridge — potential energy in physics

A new week, a fresh start. Because we were still talking about potential energy, students might not have realized that officially we began our physics unit today. I started by giving groups of three students a short reading assignment — a single paragraph from their text about either gravitational potential energy (GPE) or elastic potential energy (EPE) and another half page of information about either GPE or EPE that I'd gathered from Internet sites. I asked students to read and talk with their tablemates about the main ideas. Then I asked groups to draw a picture on a large piece of paper showing one example of their particular kind of potential energy and write a sentence or two explaining the picture in terms of energy.

The elastic potential energy posters were adorable. I especially liked that they all chose different examples.

The gravitational potential energy posters were not as impressive to me because they all looked a lot like the example in the textbook.

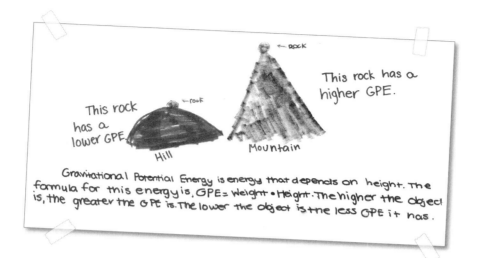

When the GPE tables shared their work, I tried to broaden everyone's thinking by asking for other examples. Marco came up with a car at the top of a hill getting ready to roll down. Perry reminded us of an apple hanging from a tree branch, ready to fall and "crack that scientist guy on the head" — he meant Sir Isaac Newton. I suggested a roller coaster because I knew those were coming up in our physics unit.

Tuesday: Calculating potential energy in physics

Just as I had wanted students to learn they could measure the amount of chemical potential energy, I also wanted them to see that they could calculate other kinds of potential energy. I modeled how to calculate GPE in joules using one of their rock-on-a-mountain posters and the formula

$$GPE = mgh$$

We talked about how the mass (m), the acceleration due to gravity (g), and the height (h) an object is from a potential resting place (or the distance between objects, such as a rock and Earth) all contributed to the amount of GPE. We also discussed that the more GPE an object had, the more ability it had to accomplish something.

Perry came up with a great way to explain this, building off his earlier apple idea. He said with a sly smile, "Okay, so there is a really heavy apple on the same branch as a regular apple. And, uh, Jason, yeah Jason, is sitting under the tree. Both apples fall and hit him in the head. The heavier apple will leave a bigger dent." The class erupted in laughter, even Jason, and we all agreed it was a good explanation.

With this background, I had students work together in table groups to solve several "challenges" related to potential energy that I'd set up at stations around the room. At each station students had to calculate how much GPE or EPE there was. Some students loved these "math" challenges, others struggled with the formulas.

Wednesday: Potential energy final assessment

The next day, I returned their work and reviewed the calculations for each challenge. As I did this, I let my students improve their own work by writing corrections and additions in a different colored pen. When I grade the second pass, all I evaluate is the quality of the improvements compared with what was possible to improve. I use this strategy when I have lots of variability in how well my students do with an assignment. For example, Marco had excellent drawings and clearly showed he knew where there was the most and least potential energy in different scenarios, but he got most of the calculations wrong. He corrected his math and added an explanation about why these new numbers made more sense with his drawings. He made 100% of the improvements he could, so he got 10/10. Viv did quite well with the calculations, earning 10/10, but her minimalist drawings did not put her numbers in context. She made some improvements to her drawings and earned a 7/10 on her second pass.

During this discussion and review, it seemed my students had a much easier time thinking about joules as a measure of energy than thinking of calories as a measure of energy. To help them make the connection, I showed students how to convert between calories and joules.

For this year's final assessment on potential energy, I had designed something new. I wanted my students to describe a scenario that had three types of potential energy — EPE, GPE, and CPE. I pulled a confiscated slingshot out of my desk and used it to shoot a walnut across the room. I asked students to draw at least three stages: (1) the slingshot pulled back with a walnut, (2) the walnut flying, and (3) the walnut on the ground. They needed to label all the parts of their diagram showing where they saw evidence for each kind of potential energy.

Perry's drawing was very typical. Like 90% of my class, he correctly described what was occurring in terms of GPE and EPE, but never mentioned CPE. In fact, only two students mentioned CPE anywhere in their drawing, and they drew food in the shooter's belly and labeled it CPE.

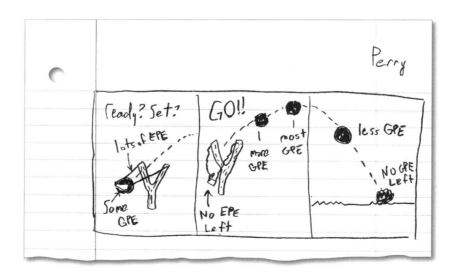

Thursday: Chemical potential energy revisited (yet again)

I drew a diagram like Perry's on the board and asked students to talk through examples of potential energy. The rubber band was easy. So was GPE in relation to the changes in height as the walnut flew through the air. To stretch their thinking, I pointed out how the arms of the slingshot bent too, indicating there was EPE contributed from more than just the rubber band.

Then I reminded them of the instructions for the assessment: "Show what is happening with all three types of potential energy — *chemical potential energy, elastic potential energy*, and *gravitational potential energy*." I asked if they felt we had done all that.

Pakuna raised her hand and said, "Yeah, I think so. We did EPE and GPE and there is no food in this." Most of my students nodded their heads.

I asked, "Really? What exactly is a walnut, then?" My class sighed like I had told a bad joke, and they agreed the walnut was food, so it had CPE.

When I pressed them about the amount of CPE, Perry added, "The walnut has the same amount everywhere, when it's in the slingshot and in the air."

I said, "I agree. Since the walnut isn't being burned or eaten, the CPE wouldn't change. Does anyone think this rubber band or this wood has CPE?"

Perry shouted out, "No way. Those are definitely not food. Not even for a chipmunk!"

The room erupted in laughter and I realized I had a room full of students who thought CPE was only in food. Logical in some ways, but far from correct.

When the laughter died down, I tried another approach. "Does anyone think there are calories available from the wood or rubber band?"

Pakuna answered, "No. No I don't think so. They aren't food. Only food has calories."

I pressed further. "If you burned little pieces of the slingshot and rubber band using your calorimeter, would the temperature of the water go up?"

Viv raised her hand and said, "Yeah, it would. But it would be from something else, not calories. What kind of energy do they have? Joules?"

Ugh. The concept of energy is just so abstract, and potential energy is the hardest. I used the last 15 minutes of class to explain the correct answers and reinforce the main points about potential energy.

As the bell rang, I couldn't help but wonder what my class really understood about potential energy after we'd talked about it, measured it, done calculations, drawn pictures, and talked about it some more. Unfortunately, I also started to wonder about my beloved Food Calorie Lab. What exactly had it taught my students about calories and potential energy? If I did the lab next year, I'd have to make some real improvements.

All objects — big and small, hot and cold, moving and stationary — have potential energy. Because objects can change position, there is always a possibility that the change will make other things happen. A stretched guitar string can be released to make sounds. Atoms in a marshmallow can rearrange during digestion and make it possible for us to move and think. A log can be dropped into a fire and make other logs fall and ash fly.

VOCABULARY

Potential energy (PE) is a measure of the possibility an object has of doing work, although the object is not doing so at the moment. PE results from the relative position of objects, even tiny objects, such as atoms and subatomic particles. Different types of PE result from different restoring forces that push/pull objects to more balanced, lower-energy positions.

Gravitational potential energy (GPE) is a measure of what could happen as a result of the force of gravity pulling masses toward each other.

Elastic potential energy (EPE) is a measure of what could happen as a result of elastic forces pushing/pulling masses back to a preferred shape.

Chemical potential energy (CPE) is a measure of what could happen as a result of electromagnetic forces pushing/pulling atoms into lower-energy arrangements (e.g., crystalline shapes and stable molecules).

Nuclear potential energy (NPE) is a measure of what could happen as a result of nuclear forces pushing/pulling subatomic particles into lower-energy arrangements in the nuclei of atoms.

Electrostatic potential energy (ESPE) is a measure of what could happen as a result of electrostatic forces pushing/pulling charged particles together or apart.

A standard unit for measuring energy is the **joule** (J). Energy on food labels is often reported in **Calories** (with a capital "C"), scientifically this is a **kilocalorie** (kcal). Energy can also be measured in **calories** (with a lowercase "c"). 1 calorie = 4.184 joules. 1000 calories = 1 kcal = 1 Calorie.

⊚ What is potential energy?

You can think about **potential energy** as the energy objects have "stored up" to do active work, even though they may not be doing any work at the moment. For example:

- A stretched rubber band has the ability to do work (e.g., fling a walnut).

- A compressed spring has the ability to do work (e.g., move a toy).

- A chemically bonded molecule has the ability to do work (e.g., rearrange atoms).

- An object held above the ground has the ability to do work (e.g., smash your toe).

Thinking about objects in this way helps partially account for why they have potential energy, but it raises another question: Why do these objects have this potential to do work?

Each of these objects has the ability to do work because of its position relative to another object and the presence of restoring forces, such as gravity, elastic forces, and electromagnetic forces. Restoring forces work to move objects to lower-energy positions or arrangements. Different restoring forces result in different types of potential energy.

Gravitational forces and GPE

If you lift a soccer ball from a resting position on the ground, you have transferred energy to the ball by doing work on it. The ball now has greater potential energy. More specifically, it has greater **gravitational potential energy (GPE)** because the ball has changed its position relative to Earth. The forces due to gravity, shown as arrows (⟶) between the ball and Earth, act as restoring forces between the raised soccer ball and Earth, working to pull the masses together and return the ball to a more stable, lower-energy position on Earth's surface.

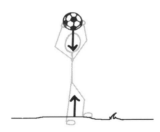

The ball has more GPE when held overhead because its position is farther from the ground.

When you let go of the ball, the force of gravity restores the ball to a more stable, lower-energy position. Now the ball has no GPE relative to the ground.

Elastic forces and EPE

If you compress a spring from its relaxed position, or natural shape, you have transferred energy to the spring by doing work on it. The spring now has greater **elastic potential energy (EPE)** because the elastic forces, shown as arrows (→) pushing outward, are acting as restoring forces on the spring, working to return the spring to its original shape.

The spring has greater EPE because it is in a compressed shape and its atoms are in a different position.

When you let go, the elastic force restores the spring to a more stable, lower-energy position. The spring has no EPE in its natural shape.

Electromagnetic forces and CPE

If you change the bonds between atoms through a chemical reaction, you can transfer energy to the substance by doing work on its atoms. The products of the chemical reaction will have a greater potential energy if the new molecule (or arrangement of atoms) is less stable than the reactants. More specifically, the new substance will have a greater **chemical potential energy (CPE)** if the atoms have rearranged in a way that requires more energy to hold them in their new position relative to each other. An example of this is an endothermic reaction, in which heat energy is transferred to the reactants from the surroundings, resulting in atoms that rearrange to form a new substance(s) with higher CPE. This stored energy (CPE) can be released, for example, in an exothermic reaction, when electromagnetic forces act as restoring forces between the atoms and rearrange the atoms to more stable, lower-energy positions.

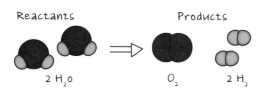

H_2 and O_2 have greater CPE because the arrangement of atoms in these positions is less stable than in water.

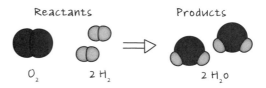

When hydrogen and oxygen atoms are arranged as water molecules, they have less CPE. The electromagnetic forces have restored them to a more stable, lower-energy position.

◉ Measuring potential energy

Potential energy is a measure of the ability to make things change or do work, and all measures have units. Energy can be measured in a variety of units, much like length can be measured in a variety of units. When you want to measure the length of something, you could use inches, centimeters, hands, yards, or nautical miles. Which one you choose to use depends on what you are measuring and what you want to use that measurement for. Picking a unit to measure energy is a similar process. Energy can be measured in calories, joules, BTUs, kilowatt-hours, electron volts, horsepower-hours, and other units, and each unit has its own utility.

Heat energy is often measured in **calories** (with a lowercase "c"). By definition, 1 calorie is the amount of energy needed to raise the temperature of 1 gram of water by 1°C. Unfortunately, the term Calorie (with a capital "C") is the unit commonly used on food labels to report the amount of energy released when the food is burned. A **Calorie** is equal to 1000 calories, or 1 **kilocalorie.**

Note: It is exceptionally easy to confuse calorie with Calorie, especially in discussions, and it is problematic given the huge difference in the scale of the units. Therefore, in this course, we use only calories (not Calories) for measurements.

While amounts of chemical potential energy are variously measured in calories, Calories, and kilocalories, other forms of potential energy are usually measured in joules. A **joule** is equal to a newton times a meter, because a change in energy is related to the amount of force (newton) applied over a distance (meter). A joule is described by the relationship

$$joule = newton \times meter$$
$$joule = (kg\ m/s^2)\ m$$
$$joule = kg\ m^2/s^2$$

One joule of energy is about the amount of energy involved in the following interactions:

- A human lifting a small apple 1 meter up from the ground
- The same apple falling back to the ground
- A human digesting 5 ml of wine
- A human moving at a speed of 18 cm/s
- A gram of air increasing in temperature by 1°C

While the calorie and the joule are the most common, other units for measuring energy are not obsolete, rather they are used for specialized fields. For example, British Thermal Units (BTU) are used primarily to measure the energy required by heaters and air conditioners; kilowatt-hours (kW-h) are used to measure the quantity of electrical energy leaving power plants; electron volts (eV) are used to measure energy on the subatomic scale and the photon energy of visible light; tons of TNT (tn) can be used to compare energy released from explosives; and horsepower-hours (hph) can be used to measure the energy of steam engines and other industrial machines.

Common Conversions
1 joule = 0.239 calories (cal)
1 joule = 2.39×10^{-4} kcal (or Calories)
1 joule = 9.48×10^{-4} British Thermal Units (BTU)
1 joule = 2.78×10^{-7} kilowatt-hours (kW-h)
1 joule = 6.24×10^{18} electron volts (eV)
1 joule = 2.39×10^{-10} tons of TNT (tn)
1 joule = 3.73×10^{-7} horsepower-hours (hph)

In the end, it really doesn't make much difference which units you use to measure energy because energy is energy is energy, just like length is length is length. One of the handiest conversions to know when working with energy is how to convert calories to joules.[1]

$$1 \text{ calorie} = 4.184 \text{ joules}$$

With the right conversion factor, you can convert between any units of energy, just like you can convert between inches and centimeters and miles. In fact, many computers and websites have applications that do these once-tedious conversions for you!

How is the energy of foods measured?

The unit of energy most people in the United States are familiar with is the kilocalorie (or Calorie) because it's the one used on U.S. food labels that dieters count diligently. The number of kilocalories that appear on these labels are calculated in a variety of ways.

Sometimes the number of kilocalories in a food is measured using a bomb calorimeter, which is similar to the soda-can calorimeter used in the Teaching Case but more advanced. A bomb calorimeter is a very strong metal container submersed in a water bath. Dried and pulverized food samples are inserted in the container, along with pure oxygen, and ignited. The result is a violent explosion, like a bomb (thus the name), which achieves nearly complete combustion of the food. The temperature increases of the container and the water bath reveal the amount of energy released during the combustion.

---

[1] To be precise, the amount of energy required to heat 1 g of water 1°C varies a little with pressure and temperature, so the conversion value between calories and joules also varies slightly (between 4.204 J and 4.182 J). However, the standard conversion is 1 calorie = 4.184 joules.

The following table shows the average potential energy of some foods and fuels in the bomb calorimeter system.

Food and Fuels	Bomb Calorimeter Values (cal/g)
Green wood	2,600 cal/g
Protein	4,100 cal/g
Oven-dried wood	4,800 cal/g
Coal	7,500 cal/g
Fat	9,300 cal/g
Kerosene	11,100 cal/g

It's important to remember the energy values for these substances are only true for a bomb calorimeter system. Any time the system changes, there can be variations in the amount of energy released from foods and fuels. The values calculated from a typical classroom calorimeter are not likely to match the values measured by scientists because the systems are different.

Just as the bomb calorimeter is a different system from the soda-can calorimeter, the human body is its own unique system. Burning food in a calorimeter is not the same as digesting it in the body. Typically, a bomb calorimeter value is the maximum caloric value of a food. The calories your body gets from digesting food are less, sometimes significantly less. For example, digesting whole-wheat bran in the human body releases only 50% of the calories whole-wheat bran releases in a bomb calorimeter.

For this reason, bomb calorimeters are not used in isolation for determining the calorie counts of foods. Scientists have determined we actually get about 4 calories for every gram of protein or carbohydrate we digest and about 9 calories for every gram of fat we digest. Therefore, some foods are simply assessed to see how much protein, carbohydrate, and fat they contain and then the number of grams of each is multiplied by the appropriate factor to determine the number of Calories.

Additionally, scientists sometime apply coefficients of digestibility, which report the percentage of food's potential energy actually released during digestion. These coefficients are used to reduce bomb calorimeter values, which may overestimate the efficiency of the human digestive system. This is particularly common with high-fiber foods, like whole-wheat bran. Even with all these options and adjustments, it's still difficult to make perfectly accurate food labels because the amount of energy released from a food depends on the system, and individual humans have slightly different digestive systems.

Science Investigation

60 MINUTES

 10 MINUTES **1** Exploring language

a. Individually write sentences using each of the following words in an everyday way:

- Calorie

- Energy

- Potential

b. In your small group, share your sentences and discuss how the words *calorie, energy,* and *potential* are used.

c. Discuss how these everyday meanings compare with the scientific definitions and explanations provided in the Content Notes.

2 Measuring chemical potential energy

a. As a group, use a soda-can calorimeter to determine the amount of energy a piece of food or a nonfood item releases:

- First put 100 ml of water in the can and measure its temperature.

- Then take a small (~1 gram) piece of food or other substance and find its mass.

- Next light the substance and hold it under the can until the substance is completely burned. For best results, the tip of the flame should touch the bottom of the can.

- Once the substance is combusted, measure the temperature of the water again.

- Find the ending mass of the burned substance.

b. Use your data to calculate the amount of energy (ΔE) released from the piece of food or other substance and to find the ratio of energy per gram (cal/g).

✳ CALCULATING ENERGY

The approximate amount of energy (ΔE) transferred from CPE to heat energy in a calorimeter system can be calculated by multiplying the mass (m) of the water in the can by the change in the temperature (ΔT) of the water and the specific heat capacity (C) of water.

change in energy = mass × change in temp. × specific heat capacity

ΔE = mΔTC

Using water in calorimeters is convenient because

1 gram of water = 1 ml of water
water's specific heat capacity = 1 cal/g°C

Specific heat capacity (C) is a measure of how much energy it takes to raise the temperature of 1 gram of a substance by 1°C. Different substances have different specific heat capacities, and the values are not constants — they vary with the substance's phase and temperature.

---

c. Add your data to the table and discuss what these numbers tell you about food, calories, and chemical potential energy.

Item	cal/g
potato chip	1,180
pineapple	250
cracker	730
corn chip	530
peanut	1,380
marshmallow	190
wood	1,250
napkin	1,000
white gas	1,420
sweetener	200
plastic bag	470

d. Write a couple of claims related to this Calorie Lab that are supported by evidence. Try to use some of the following terms: *energy, potential energy, chemical potential energy,* and *calorie.*

 WRITING SCIENTIFIC CLAIMS

Claims are statements you believe to be true and that answer a scientific question. For example, the statement "black cats are on average 10% heavier than other cats" is a claim that answers the scientific question "Does the weight of cats relate to fur color?"

Evidence consists of experimental data (e.g., observations, calculations, and measurements) or facts that contribute to the credibility of a claim. The evidence supporting the claim about cats might be, "Of the 12 cats we weighed, the black cats were 10% heavier on average."

The validity of claims is determined based on the quality and quantity of the supporting evidence. Therefore, our cat claim wouldn't stand up to much scrutiny!

3 **Tracking energy**

a. As a group, make a box and arrow diagram for a system that involves a chip and a calorimeter.

b. Discuss your system and how the energy associated with the chip changes.

- How did you define your chip *system*? What objects are included?

- In your system, was the chip the *energy source* or *energy receiver*? How did you decide?

- What are some ways to increase the chip's energy? And to decrease its energy?

Box and arrow diagrams identify energy sources and energy receivers in interactions. They are useful for tracking energy changes in a system. In box and arrow diagrams:

- **Boxes** indicate the *energy source* (an object experiencing a decrease in energy) and *energy receiver* (an object experiencing an increase in energy).

- **Arrows** indicate the direction energy is transferring (from energy source to energy receiver).

- **Descriptions** explain the event linked to the energy transfer.

Here is an example for kicking a ball:

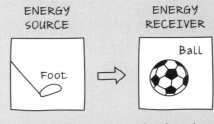

ENERGY SOURCE   ENERGY RECEIVER

Energy from the moving foot is transferred to the ball.

4 Comparing potential energies

 CALCULATING POTENTIAL ENERGY

a. A soccer ball with a mass of 0.43 kg is lifted 2 meters above the ground. Work together to calculate the amount of gravitational potential energy the ball now has.

A **change in energy** (ΔE) in a system is measured by the work (W) done.

> Change in energy = Work
> **$\Delta E = W$**

The **work (W)** done on a system is measured by the amount of force (F) applied over a distance (d).

> Work = force × distance
> **W = Fd**

b. A book weighing 2 kg was placed on an upright spring. The spring compressed down 6 cm. Work together to calculate the amount of elastic potential energy the spring now has.

Force (F) is the amount of push or pull it takes to make a mass (m) accelerate (a), where mass is measured in kilograms (kg) and acceleration is measured in meters per second squared (m/s^2).

> Force = mass × acceleration
> **F = ma**

The rate of acceleration for objects falling to Earth is a constant (g).

> $a_{gravity} = g = 9.8 \ m/s^2$

A standard unit for measuring force is a newton (N).

> $N = kg \ m/s^2$

c. Discuss how gravitational potential energy and elastic potential energy compare with each other and with the chemical potential energy from foods. In what ways are GPE, EPE, and CPE similar and different?

A standard unit for measuring work and energy is a joule (J).

> joule = newton × meter
> $J = (kg \ m/s^2) \ m$
> $J = kg \ m^2/s^2$

15 MINUTES **1** Exploring students' ideas about calories and energy

a. In your small group, take a few minutes to flip through the Teaching Case and point out things you each noticed about students' ideas related to calories and energy.

In particular, talk through the:

- "Do Now" whiteboard responses (p. 5)

- Class discussion following the Food Calorie Lab (p. 7)

- "What is a calorie?" writing assignment and questions (pp. 8–9)

- Potential energy posters (pp. 10–11)

b. Discuss what these students' words, images, and written work suggests about how they are thinking about energy generally, and potential energy specifically.

- What ideas do these students have about *energy*? What do they accurately understand? Where are their points of confusion?

- What ideas do these students have about *potential energy*? What do they accurately understand? Where are their points of confusion?

2 Analyzing instruction

    a. Look through the Teaching Case and identify the various things this teacher did to help students learn about potential energy. Make a timeline of these activities.

    b. Discuss what these students seemed to have learned from the various activities they participated in (e.g., "Do Now" prompt, Food Calorie Lab, and potential energy posters). Remember to point each other to the specific evidence you find in students' words and pictures.

Literacy Investigation

40 MINUTES

20 MINUTES **1** Surfacing our writing processes

a. Individually, take about 10 minutes to begin writing a brief story using the directions found on "Handout C: Memorable Teaching Story." Most likely, you will run short on time and not finish. That's okay.

b. In small groups, take turns sharing your approach to writing the story. For example, talk about:

- How you got started

- The choices you made

- What you did if you got stuck

- Changes you made, if any, and why

Use a Think Aloud routine and allow each person 2–3 minutes of uninterrupted time to share. As people share, listen carefully to what they did, felt, and thought about when writing. Make notes and write down what they said and did.

 USING A THINK ALOUD

A Think Aloud is a way to capture what goes on inside your head when you do something complex, such as reading or writing. The routine helps you think about your thinking. It also helps others "see" the process you use.

During a Think Aloud, it is important to:

- **Notice** what you do and how you are thinking as you write

- **Share** as much as possible about what you notice so others have a window into your writing process

c. Discuss what you noticed about each other's writing processes.

- Which strategies did people use (e.g., daydreaming to remember events, drawing a storyboard to get "unblocked," jotting notes to organize ideas)?

- What was similar and different about each person's approach to writing?

2 Surfacing our science writing processes

a. Individually, take 10 minutes to write an expanded definition for energy, using the directions found on "Handout D: Expanded Definition of Energy." Again, it is not likely that you will finish, and that is okay.

b. In small groups, take turns sharing your approach to writing the expanded definition of energy. For example, talk about:

- How you got started
- The choices you made
- What you did if you got stuck
- Changes you made, if any, and why

Use a Think Aloud routine and allow each person 2–3 minutes of uninterrupted time to share. As people share, listen carefully to what they did, felt, and thought about when writing. Make notes and write down what they said and did.

c. Discuss what you noticed about each other's science writing processes.

- How was writing an informational science definition the same as or different from writing a narrative teaching story?
- What strategies did people use this time?
- What feels different or unique about writing in science?

Classroom Connection

40 MINUTES

1 Reviewing key concepts

a. Individually, read the Science Review and Literacy Review on the following pages. Feel free to pick and choose the sections that are most valuable to you.

As you read, take notes and think about these questions:

- What is interesting or new to you?

- Which examples and images do you find especially helpful?

- What are you still wrestling with?

b. Individually, take a few minutes to think and write about your own big takeaways from today.

2 **Exploring the ideas of this session**

a. As a group, discuss the Science and Literacy Reviews. Use the questions on the previous page as a guide.

3 **Considering classroom implications**

a. Based on your experiences today, discuss implications for *what* and *how* you teach your students.

Session Review

SCIENCE REVIEW

No matter how many times you tell yourself that potential energy is simply a way of quantifying how much change can happen in a system, it is hard to let go of the mental model that energy is really more like an ingredient that is stored in foods and fuels, much like chocolate chips are tucked away in cookies.

SCIENCE **KEY CONCEPT**

While energy is not matter, all types of potential energy depend on the relative positions of matter. Matter is defined as something that has mass and takes up space, but energy does neither. Yet all the types of potential energy depend on the spacing and arrangement of matter. Chemical potential energy results from the structural arrangement of atoms and molecules that make up matter. Elastic potential energy depends on an object's position relative to its own natural position (e.g., expanded versus natural, compressed versus natural). Gravitational potential energy depends on an object's position relative to another mass, for example, relative to Earth.

SCIENCE **KEY CONCEPT**

Nearly all substances have chemical potential energy, not just foods and fuels. Foods are considered foods because they are made of the kind of matter that releases a lot of energy in the digestive systems of living things. Wood, coal, and gasoline are fuels because they are made of the kind of matter that releases a lot of energy during combustion. However, with very few exceptions, all matter when subjected to the right conditions can release energy.

SCIENCE **KEY CONCEPT**

Energy is energy, regardless of which unit it is measured in. Joules are a standard scientific unit for measuring energy. However, we often measure the potential energy associated with foods and fuels in calories, kilocalories, or Calories. Scientists in other fields sometimes use other units, such as the erg, the BTU, the kilowatt-hour, and the electron volt. Some units are historically embedded in a particular discipline. Others are simply handier for various calculations and comparisons. The thing to remember is that no matter which units are used, you can always convert back and forth between the units, and any measurement of energy can always be converted into joules because, in the end, energy is energy.

⊙ How is potential energy related to matter?

One of the hardest things to recognize about potential energy is that potential energy is not an attribute of individual things (e.g., soccer balls, springs, pieces of food). Instead, potential energy exists within systems because of the relative positions of objects within those systems. Another way of saying this is that the objects in the system are the matter, while the possibility for change — the potential energy — comes from the position, or placement, of those objects, along with the properties of those objects, such as mass and electrical charge.

 **SCIENCE ▸ KEY CONCEPT**

While energy is not matter, all types of potential energy depend on the relative positions of matter.

Gravitational potential energy (GPE)

In the Science Investigation, you calculated the gravitational potential energy for a lifted soccer ball, as shown in the following correct example.

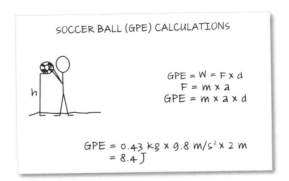

SOCCER BALL (GPE) CALCULATIONS

$$GPE = W = F \times d$$
$$F = m \times a$$
$$GPE = m \times a \times d$$

$$GPE = 0.43 \text{ kg} \times 9.8 \text{ m/s}^2 \times 2 \text{ m}$$
$$= 8.4 \text{ J}$$

At first glance it can seem like just one object is involved, the soccer ball, yet if potential energy depends on the relative position of two or more objects within a system, then there must be multiple objects involved. So where are the multiple parts in this system?

The soccer ball has GPE because of its relative position to Earth. The greater the distance between the ball and Earth, the greater the potential for change. If you are a soccer player, you know this intuitively because heading a ball that has fallen from a great height feels much different from heading a ball that has fallen from only a few meters off the ground. Similarly, a hail stone the size of a marble can really dent a car when it falls from great height, but dropping a marble from an inch above your hood should be just fine. There is a whole lot of GPE in the hail system because the hail is formed in the clouds a long way from Earth's surface.

When determining the amount of GPE, it turns out the amount of matter also matters. From the soccer-ball calculation, you can see that GPE depends on three things — the mass of the soccer ball, the acceleration due to gravity (abbreviated as either "a" or "g"), and the ball's distance or height from Earth (abbreviated as either "d" or "h"). This points out how the two equations most often used for calculating GPE are equivalent:

$$GPE = mad = mgh$$

Elastic potential energy (EPE)

With the spring example you used in the Science Investigation, there is elastic potential energy because of the relative position of the atoms when the spring is compressed compared with their positions when the spring is in its original shape. One way to visualize this is to think about atoms as charged particles that attract and repel each other, similar to tiny magnets. If two magnets repel each other and you push them closer together, you can feel you are having to do work by applying a force over a distance. If you let go, the magnets would slide away from each other because the potential energy makes it possible for change to happen.

Similarly, when a spring is compressed, the particles that make up the spring are pushed closer together, resulting in greater potential energy. This EPE comes directly from a change in the position of atoms that make up the spring. In the calculation of EPE with the spring, the force was applied as a result of the gravitational pull between the book and Earth. During the Science Investigation, you calculated the EPE resulting from the work of the force of gravity, as shown in the following correct example.

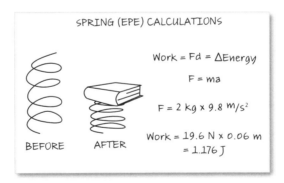

SPRING (EPE) CALCULATIONS

Work = Fd = ΔEnergy

F = ma

F = 2 kg x 9.8 m/s²

Work = 19.6 N x 0.06 m
= 1.176 J

BEFORE   AFTER

Chemical potential energy (CPE)

Foods, fuels, and other substances have chemical potential energy because of the relative position, or arrangement, of the atoms that make up the substance. When bonds are broken and new bonds are formed, the atoms rearrange. This change in the relative position of the atoms results in changes in energy.

During the Science Investigation you calculated changes in CPE indirectly by measuring how much CPE was transferred to heat energy to warm the water, as shown in the following correct example for burning a potato chip.

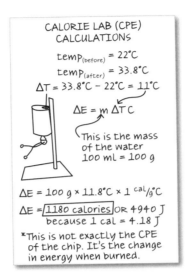

CALORIE LAB (CPE) CALCULATIONS

$temp_{(before)} = 22°C$

$temp_{(after)} = 33.8°C$

$\Delta T = 33.8°C - 22°C = 11°C$

$\Delta E = m \Delta T C$

This is the mass of the water
100 mL = 100 g

$\Delta E = 100 g \times 11.8°C \times 1 \ ^{cal}/_{g°C}$

$\Delta E = \boxed{1180 \ calories}$ OR 4940 J
because 1 cal = 4.18 J

*This is not exactly the CPE of the chip. It's the change in energy when burned.

Many chemical reactions, including combustion, require an input of energy to begin the process of breaking and reforming bonds. This is often true even if the overall end-result is a release of CPE. For example, when you burned the potato chip, you needed a small heat energy source, the candle, to start the reaction with oxygen. However, in the end there was an even greater change in the heat energy as a result of the rearrangement of atoms into more stable, lower-energy products, such as carbon (soot), carbon dioxide, and water.

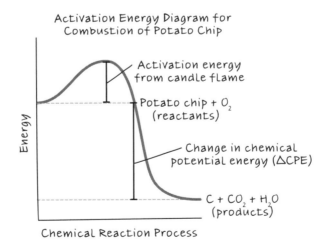

Activation Energy Diagram for Combustion of Potato Chip

Activation energy from candle flame

Potato chip + O_2 (reactants)

Change in chemical potential energy (ΔCPE)

C + CO_2 + H_2O (products)

Energy

Chemical Reaction Process

When you burned foods and other substances in the presence of oxygen, you were measuring the amount of CPE available for a *combustion reaction*. That is, you determined only how much energy could be released when the substance is combined with oxygen, resulting in the rearrangement of atoms to form soot, carbon dioxide, and water.

It is important to know that the resulting change in CPE would be different if a different chemical reaction took place. So it is not accurate to say the potato chip (or any other substance) has a given amount of CPE. All we can determine is the amount of energy gained or lost when atoms rearrange in various ways. If instead of burning a potato chip you burned sugar ($C_6H_{12}O_6$), the rearrangement of atoms would be identical to the process of cellular respiration that occurs in plants and animals when they obtain energy from the breakdown of glucose, as shown by this chemical reaction:

$$C_6H_{12}O_6 + 6O_2 \rightarrow 6CO_2 + 6H_2O + energy$$

Cellular respiration is the opposite reaction to what occurs during photosynthesis. During photosynthesis, plants and other photosynthetic organisms utilize light energy from the Sun to make sugar:

$$Light\ energy\ from\ the\ Sun + 6CO_2 + 6H_2O \rightarrow C_6H_{12}O_6 + 6O_2$$

These examples show that sugar is the *energy receiver* during photosynthesis and then the *energy source* during cellular respiration. Similarly, the potato chip can be both an energy receiver and an energy source during combustion, as shown in the following correct examples of box and arrow diagrams.

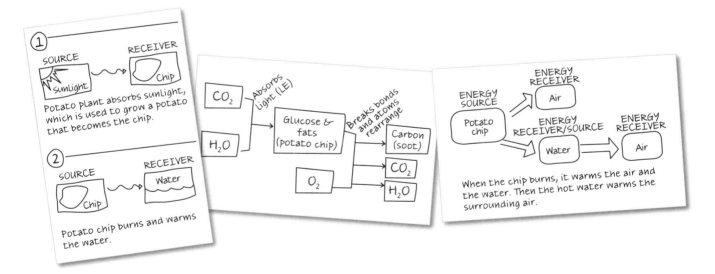

The linked, multistep box and arrow diagrams highlight the idea that potential energy does not just "appear" in a system — energy is always transferred from someplace else. For example, the CPE associated with a potato chip exists because the potato plant absorbed light energy, and the GPE in a system where a soccer ball is lifted above Earth's surface exists because of the kinetic energy a person uses to lift it.

⊙ Even rock has chemical potential energy!

We most often learn about chemical potential energy in terms of foods and fuels. This makes a lot of sense because the kinds of matter we call "foods" and "fuels" release lots of energy when they are digested or combusted. The reason we eat certain foods is because when we digest them, there is a lot of available energy. Matter that doesn't result in a lot of energy being released in our digestive process is not usually our food. However, not being food for us does *not* mean a substance is low in chemical potential energy.

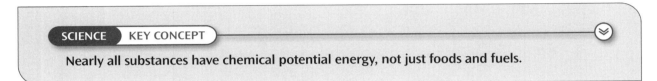

SCIENCE ❯ **KEY CONCEPT**

Nearly all substances have chemical potential energy, not just foods and fuels.

For example, there is a lot of chemical potential energy, and thus a lot of calories, associated with wood, but you have to put it in the right system. Wood is not food for us. It releases almost no energy in our digestive systems. However, wood is food for termites, beavers, and many bacteria, which have different types of digestive processes — ones that can break down the chemical bonds in wood. Additionally, when wood is burned, it releases large amounts of heat energy — heat energy that came from chemical potential energy.

During the Science Investigation, you looked at data showing changes in CPE associated with the combustion of different substances. In the process, you likely noticed that not all of the substances were things we would consider food.

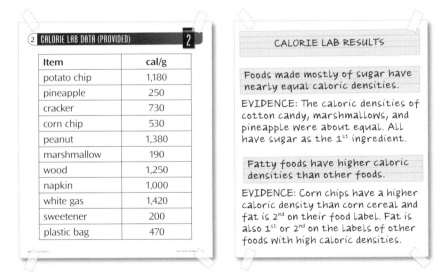

2 CALORIE LAB DATA (PROVIDED)   2

Item	cal/g
potato chip	1,180
pineapple	250
cracker	730
corn chip	530
peanut	1,380
marshmallow	190
wood	1,250
napkin	1,000
white gas	1,420
sweetener	200
plastic bag	470

CALORIE LAB RESULTS

Foods made mostly of sugar have nearly equal caloric densities.

EVIDENCE: The caloric densities of cotton candy, marshmallows, and pineapple were about equal. All have sugar as the 1st ingredient.

Fatty foods have higher caloric densities than other foods.

EVIDENCE: Corn chips have a higher caloric density than corn cereal and fat is 2nd on their food label. Fat is also 1st or 2nd on the labels of other foods with high caloric densities.

Nearly all matter (even plastic bags, paper towels, and rock) is made of chemically bonded atoms and, therefore, has chemical potential energy.[1] If a process exists whereby

---

[1] Monatomic gases, such as argon and neon, are the exception. They have no chemical potential energy associated with them because they exist as individual, unbonded atoms.

the chemically bonded atoms forming a type of matter can be broken and the relative positions of those atoms changed, then there will be a change in energy. How much change depends on which system the matter is in and the strength of the bonds.

There are many common, yet incorrect ideas about calories. One is that calories are a type of energy, when calories are actually a unit of energy like centimeters are a unit of length.

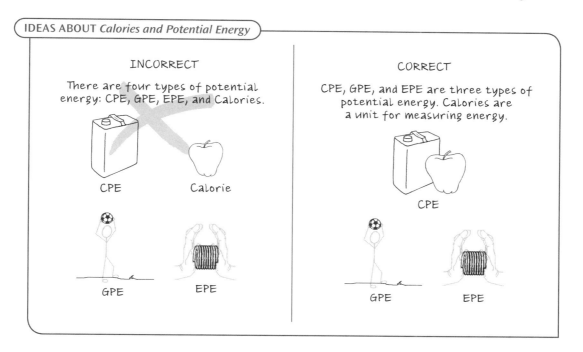

IDEAS ABOUT *Calories and Potential Energy*

INCORRECT

There are four types of potential energy: CPE, GPE, EPE, and Calories.

CPE

Calorie

GPE

EPE

CORRECT

CPE, GPE, and EPE are three types of potential energy. Calories are a unit for measuring energy.

CPE

GPE

EPE

Another common, yet incorrect idea is thinking calories are contained within foods. Again, calories are a unit of energy, and units aren't "contained" within anything.

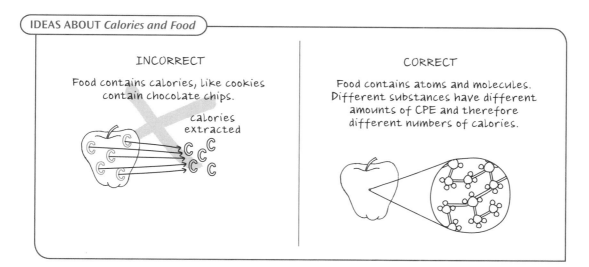

IDEAS ABOUT *Calories and Food*

INCORRECT

Food contains calories, like cookies contain chocolate chips.

calories extracted

CORRECT

Food contains atoms and molecules. Different substances have different amounts of CPE and therefore different numbers of calories.

While it is incorrect to think that foods contain calories, it isn't surprising that this idea is common. We hear about foods and calories nearly every day. Most things we eat have Calories listed on the label, just as the amounts of fat and fiber are listed.

In science, the phrases "high calorie" and "high energy" are interchangeable. For example, "cookies are high calorie" is equivalent to "cookies are high energy" and "gasoline is high calorie" is equivalent to "gasoline is high energy." However, the word *calorie* is not a synonym for the word *energy* — instead calories are to energy as centimeters are to length. Calories and centimeters describe how much energy and length, respectively, are present.

Calories are a measure of energy, a measure of any type of energy. So if cold soup is heated and gains heat energy, then you could say it has increased in calories. Hot soup has more total calories than cold soup, but it doesn't have more calories of chemical potential energy. The number of additional heat energy calories is not significant when compared with the number of chemical potential energy calories in hot soup. So those of you counting Calories, feel free to eat your soup hot!

◉ Joules versus calories

If you know how many calories, kilocalories, or Calories a food has, you can easily convert that to joules, for example, by using the conversion 1 calorie = 4.184 joules. When you did these conversions as part of the Science Investigation, it allowed you to compare the amount of energy associated with a raised soccer ball, a compressed spring, and a potato chip, as shown in the following correct example:

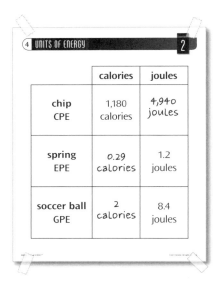

4 UNITS OF ENERGY		2
	calories	joules
chip CPE	1,180 calories	4,940 joules
spring EPE	0.29 calories	1.2 joules
soccer ball GPE	2 calories	8.4 joules

This comparison points out that you can measure CPE in joules, just as you can calculate GPE using calories. It is just like reporting distance in kilometers versus miles. People often incorrectly think calories are used only to describe the amount of CPE in foods, when really it's perfectly fine to use calories to describe the amount of any type of energy, and perfectly fine to use any other unit of energy to describe the CPE in foods.

INCORRECT	CORRECT
Specific types of energy must be measured with specific units of energy. For example, the amount of CPE in foods must be measured in calories or kilocalories.	Any type of energy can be measured with any unit of energy. For example, the amount of CPE in foods can be measured in calories, joules, or any other unit of energy, and the EPE in a spring can be measured in calories.

Vegetable oil
9.3 kilocalories/gram

Vegetable oil
9.3 kilocalories/gram
38,937 joules
36.9 BTUs

Spring
1.1 joules
0.26 kilocalories

It is not wrong to use calories as the units of energy for food and to use joules as the units for other types of energy — it's just an unnecessary distinction. This convention likely comes from the everyday use of the word calorie (nearly always in association with food) and the format of U.S. food labels (which use Calories with a capital "C"). Unfortunately, this distinction quickly turns into an incorrect association when people assume calories must be used for the CPE in foods and can't be used to quantify other types of energy.

It is true that certain disciplines of science or regions of the world prefer some units to others. But the ability to convert back and forth between units of energy proves that units are just units. Being able to use the same units for all types of energy also supports the correct idea that there is nothing intrinsically different about the types of energy — energy is energy.

SCIENCE **KEY CONCEPT** ⌄

Energy is energy, regardless of which unit it is measured in.

The same amount of potential energy can cause the same amount of change, but the type of potential energy determines the kinds of changes that can occur. For example, 500 calories of CPE released by burning a potato chip won't directly dent a car, but dropping a rock with 500 calories of GPE could.

Different types of potential energy can make different kinds of changes, and potential energy remains potential energy until the right circumstances or conditions occur in the system. The lifted rock may never dent a car — it all depends on what occurs in the system. Many scientists argue we shouldn't even talk about there being multiple types of energy for this very reason. If you can calculate every type of energy in the same unit and every type of energy can change into every other type of energy by some process, then why learn there are different types of energy in the first place? These scientists argue that the types of energy are an unnecessary distinction that leads to an incorrect idea that one type of energy is somehow meaningfully different from another.

Advocates of using types of energy point out the utility in helping us keep track of why energy is present. They also argue that because 100 joules of CPE doesn't have the potential to do the exact same things as 100 joules of EPE, the types of energy are useful distinctions. It's a debate that most likely will go on in the science and science education communities for years to come. But one thing is for certain — all the types of energy can be measured in the same units!

LEARNING OBJECTIVES

Potential Energy

2.1 Potential energy results from the relative position of objects, be they large or small (e.g., planets, atoms, and the smallest particles of matter).

2.2 Chemical potential energy (CPE) results from the relative positions, or structural arrangements, of particles of matter (e.g., atoms and molecules).

2.3 Elastic potential energy (EPE) depends on an object's position relative to its own natural position (e.g., an expanded or compressed position).

2.4 Gravitational potential energy (GPE) depends on an object's position relative to another mass, such as Earth. The amount of GPE is related to the object's mass, the acceleration due to gravity, and the object's distance from the other object (or height above Earth).

2.5 The amount of GPE can be calculated with formulas, such as GPE = mgh or W = ΔE = Fd, where F = ma.

2.6 If there is potential energy in a system, there is the potential for change. More potential energy means more change can happen.

2.7 Potential energy is not matter or a substance stored in objects.

2.8 Nearly all matter, when subjected to the right conditions, can release energy. For example, food releases energy in a digestive system.

2.9 Potential energy is a property of a system measured in calories, joules, or other units.

2.10 Potential energy does not just appear in a system. It transfers from other types of energy.

MISCONCEPTIONS

2.A It is incorrect to think the energetic feeling we get after eating certain foods means the food provided lots of energy. How a food makes us feel has little to do with the number of Calories of energy it has.

2.B It is incorrect to think Calories are a type of matter contained in food.

2.C It is incorrect to think Calories are "bad" for us. While too many Calories cause weight gain and being overweight does affect our health, all living things require a certain amount of energy to survive.

2.D It is incorrect to think that only food or only fuels can release energy, when anything with chemical bonds can release energy under the right conditions.

2.E It is incorrect to think that only the energy in food can be quantified with calories or that the energy in food must be quantified with calories.

Whether consciously or not, when we write we ask ourselves a slew of questions. Who's reading this? Is it clear if I say it this way? What will the reader know? Should I use the technical term or an everyday word? How should I explain this? Wait, does that make sense? Is that even a sentence? The fact that writing requires us to answer questions and figure things out means it is an act of problem solving. With writing, just like anything else, the more strategies you have, the more likely you are to come up with good solutions.

LITERACY   **KEY CONCEPT**

Writing is an iterative process of problem solving. At different stages writers solve different problems. People approach writing in various ways at different times depending on who they are, what they know, and what they are writing. In fact, there is no single, best approach or such a thing as "the Writing Process." Rather, writing has predictable stages — *prewriting, drafting,* and *revising.* Writers cycle through these stages often in nonlinear ways. At each stage, different writing "problems" crop up (e.g., what to write, how to organize ideas and communicate them clearly, the terminology to use, and which voice or tone is best suited for this purpose). Good writers have many good strategies to help them solve the various challenges of writing (e.g., brainstorming to gather information, graphical organizers to connect ideas, and getting feedback to hone the message).

LITERACY   **KEY CONCEPT**

The nature of science drives the conventions and style of science writing. Science involves collaboration of people across continents and time to better understand the world around us. So it follows that the purpose of scientific writing is largely to share information, explain, or persuade. The format of scientific writing is often "informational," containing elements such as claims, facts, observations, data, and interpretations. Scientific writing is organized in predictable ways, for example, to compare and contrast information or show connections among events. In science, as we gather information and challenge each other's ideas, our collective understanding of the world evolves. So it follows that scientists, learners, and skeptics are each other's audiences, as well as sometimes being one and the same person.

◉ Writing process

During the Literacy Investigation, people took turns talking about how they went about writing and what they were thinking about as they wrote. By hearing different people think aloud, you might have noticed that the act of writing is highly variable. Some people probably did a lot of thinking and talking to themselves before putting any words on the page. Others made lists, drew pictures, or wrote outlines before drafting a single sentence or paragraph. Then there were the people who dove right in and reorganized later. Regardless, everyone took on the challenges inherent in writing.

> **LITERACY** | **KEY CONCEPT**
>
> **Writing is an iterative process of problem solving. At different stages writers solve different problems.**

While people approached writing differently from each other and differently for various types of writing — the expanded definition of energy versus the memorable teaching story — the act of writing has recognizable stages. Stages of writing can be described in many different ways, but they usually include:

- *Prewriting.* As authors figure out what to write, they often do some form of prewriting, perhaps doing research, reading, outlining, or jotting notes. Prewriting is primarily a "thinking" stage in which authors start to prioritize and organize their ideas.

- *Drafting.* This stage is where "the rubber meets the road" and authors start getting their ideas into a written format, perhaps by stringing words and thoughts together, writing preliminary sentences, composing paragraphs, and selecting images. Drafting is primarily an "expressing" stage.

- *Revising.* The goal of the revising stage is to figure out what's unclear, missing, and extraneous and to refine the tone, structure, language cues, and key words for consistency. Revising is a "listening and refining" stage in which the author works to understand what readers may hear and makes changes to better communicate the intended ideas and feelings, perhaps by rereading drafts, reading drafts aloud, or asking others to read and respond to the drafts.

When you listened to others describe their *prewriting stage* for writing a memorable teaching story or a definition of energy, you may have heard authors struggling with what to write, how to get started, and which details to include. Perhaps you heard prewriting stories similar to these:

> "To write the teaching story, I closed my eyes and pictured what happened that day. I could see the students and even recalled what the weather was like. There were so many details, I had to figure out which to include."

> "At first I couldn't remember anything we'd been learning about energy. It was like I drew a big blank. Then I pulled out my Frayer Model and felt a sigh of relief. It spelled out four paragraphs I could write."

> "At first I had all these phrases and words floating around in my head, like 'energy is not a force' and 'the law of conservation of energy.' I just wrote everything I could think of. Then I started circling related ideas to help me get organized."

> "I wish my brother was here. Sometimes I talk in circles trying to figure out what I want to write. He teases me and says, 'Why don't you just say this and that?'"

It's also likely someone in your group didn't write a single word. Instead, the person spent the entire time thinking, perhaps reminiscing and deciding which of the several stories to tell. While this may initially sound unproductive, prewriting is essential. It takes time to gather information, think about what you already know, decide what you most want to say and how you want to say it, and basically get the lay of the land. In fact, the accomplished author Barbara Kingsolver spent 10 years researching and prewriting before actually drafting one of her recent books. Similarly, before writing a journal article, scientists do experiments, observe, and read other people's reports.

The *drafting stage* probably unfolded differently depending on the author and what was being written. Someone in your group may have described picking up a pen and the story just came tumbling out. Someone else might have drafted the punch line to the story first, then went back to chronologically fill in the events leading up to the punch line. For the definition for energy, it's likely many people started with a sentence something like, "Energy is…" and then followed by writing examples of various forms of energy. Another typical scenario is drafting a sentence, deciding it isn't right, scratching it out, drafting another sentence, going back to look at a note or another resource, then starting over. In fact, often the lines between drafting, prewriting, and revising are blurred.

The *revising stage* often takes place at multiple points and multiple times as a person writes. Some writers struggle to maintain the continuity of their thoughts because as they write they are constantly revising and perfecting. Other writers may have a hard time separating what's in their heads from what's written on the paper, making it hard to figure out what is confusing to another reader. From the Think Aloud sharing, you might have heard stories like these:

"I had this great professor in college who could explain anything. When I reread what I'd written for the energy definition, I tried to imagine her voice saying my words. This way I could 'hear' what was confusing."

"There is a constant chatter in my head when I write. 'Is that the word I want? I don't think that sentence makes sense. How did the Content Notes describe energy? What's another way to explain this? Do I need another example? That sentence is way too long.' This can make it hard to keep going with an idea."

"I just plow ahead when I write. After I blah it all out, I sometimes go back, like I did with my teaching story. Or maybe I don't pick my writing back up for several days."

Before hearing people's individual writing processes, it would have been easy to think writing happened in a predictable fashion, with authors moving linearly from one stage to the next. Yet this clearly is not reality. In fact, just as it is a myth to talk about "the Scientific Method" as if all scientists carry out research following an identical series of steps (e.g., posing a hypothesis, devising an experiment, gathering data, and so on), it's also a myth to talk about "the Writing Process," as there is no single such thing!

⊙ Writing strategies

During the Literacy Investigation you listened to what other writers did when they wrote, where they got stuck, and which strategies they used to help solve their writing problems. You may have noticed many of the strategies people used for writing the narrative story overlapped with the strategies they used for writing the scientific definition.

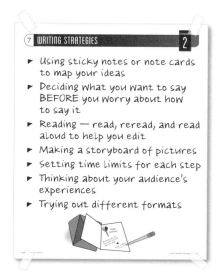

7 WRITING STRATEGIES — 2

▶ Using sticky notes or note cards to map your ideas
▶ Deciding what you want to say BEFORE you worry about how to say it
▶ Reading — read, reread, and read aloud to help you edit
▶ Making a storyboard of pictures
▶ Setting time limits for each step
▶ Thinking about your audience's experiences
▶ Trying out different formats

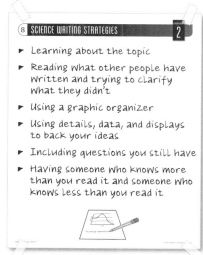

8 SCIENCE WRITING STRATEGIES — 2

▶ Learning about the topic
▶ Reading what other people have written and trying to clarify what they didn't
▶ Using a graphic organizer
▶ Using details, data, and displays to back your ideas
▶ Including questions you still have
▶ Having someone who knows more than you read it and someone who knows less than you read it

Despite using similar strategies, it's likely the science writing felt quite different. You may have noticed that at each stage — prewriting, drafting, and revising — writers faced a variety of challenges and drew on a range of strategies. Those that were most useful depended not only on what was being written, but also on whether the writer was brainstorming ideas, writing a first draft, gathering information, organizing ideas, clarifying, revising, or polishing words. Following are four common writing "problem spots" — getting started, managing complexities, overcoming writer's block, and clarifying — along with strategies some writers have found useful.

Strategies for getting started. It is nearly impossible to write when you don't know what you want to say, don't feel like you have anything to say, or don't know how you want to say it. Some people get ready to write by reading. Others prepare to write by talking, and some even prepare to write by writing. How strange is that?! Strategies that help you figure out what you could write include learning what other people have written on the topic, brainstorming by yourself or with others, interviewing experts or folks with different points of view, reflecting on your own experiences, observing, or doing an experiment.

Strategies for managing complexities. Another challenging aspect of prewriting involves planning and organizing your message, especially when it is complex. There are many strategies to help organize ideas before you write them out, for example, making an outline, drawing a storyboard, or using some kind of graphic organizer tool, such as a Frayer Model, Venn Diagram, concept map, or flowchart. Sometimes the hard part of prewriting is remembering to use these strategies. Another challenge is choosing a graphic organizer that is well matched to the specific kind of information you want to convey.

The following table summarizes some common graphic organizers and describes what they help writers do.

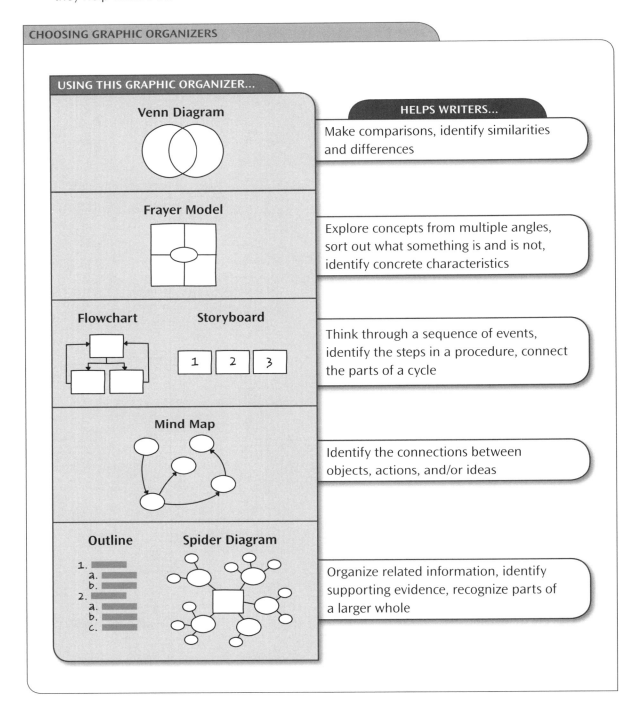

CHOOSING GRAPHIC ORGANIZERS

USING THIS GRAPHIC ORGANIZER...	HELPS WRITERS...
Venn Diagram	Make comparisons, identify similarities and differences
Frayer Model	Explore concepts from multiple angles, sort out what something is and is not, identify concrete characteristics
Flowchart **Storyboard**	Think through a sequence of events, identify the steps in a procedure, connect the parts of a cycle
Mind Map	Identify the connections between objects, actions, and/or ideas
Outline **Spider Diagram**	Organize related information, identify supporting evidence, recognize parts of a larger whole

Not only do these tools help writers organize different types of information, they also help prioritize what to include or what to omit. As an example, a writer might make an outline with information about different types of energy, but only choose to write in detail about the types that directly relate to potential energy.

Strategies for overcoming writer's block. Composing, the act of getting words on the paper, can be easy for some people and a beast for others. The difficulty of composing also tends to vary with the kind of writing we're doing — for example, it might be no problem for one kind of writing (e.g., emails, firsthand observations, lists), but it might be like pulling teeth for other kinds of writing (e.g., persuasive essays, conclusions). Here are some words of wisdom you might have heard from your group about ways to overcome writer's block:

- Start with something easy.

- Write the first sentence last.

- Set a timer for 5 minutes and just keep writing.

- Fill one small hole at a time.

These examples point out that composing a draft requires a certain amount of letting go so you can be creative and experience a flow of ideas. Other strategies for this include making your environment conducive to writing (e.g., eliminating distractions, putting on music) and practicing habits of good writers, such as persisting, writing often, prewriting, knowing that writing is revising, and asking others to read and respond to your writing.

Strategies for clarifying. Conveying just what you want to say in writing is a paramount challenge every writer faces at one time or another. When we write, there is often a lot more going on in our heads than we get on paper, and sometimes things get lost in the translation. This means a key aspect of writing is clarifying. A first step in clarifying is figuring out what is (or might be) confusing to your reader. One way to do this is to ask others to read what you have written and give feedback about what is confusing, what they see as the main point(s), where there are lapses in logic, and what is vague or lacking in detail. Another strategy is to reread your own writing and "get into the shoes" of the reader to try to identify those same things. One especially helpful way to get some distance from your writing and see the words as others might is to wait a couple of days before rereading what you've written.

Once a point of confusion has been identified, a writer might achieve greater clarity by reorganizing information so it follows a clear format (e.g., compare and contrast, chronological sequence, cause and effect). Another strategy to clarify an idea is elaborating by adding some details to more fully explain an idea or paint a fuller picture. Removing distracting information and off-point topics can also bring clarity.

◉ The nature of science writing

Contrast a research article with a novel, a scientific explanation with a persuasive essay, a data table with a blog, a definition for energy with a poem about love. While each represents a collection of words on a page, the juxtaposition of these text-types points out ways in which science writing is unique from other kinds of writing, yet at the same time not homogenous. During the Literacy Investigation when you wrote a story about teaching, followed by an expanded definition of energy, you experienced some of these differences firsthand. Through discussion, your group likely found ways of describing what makes scientific writing different. A sample chart follows:

Another way to understand the nature of science writing is to describe what it is *not*. Science writing might connect a series of events or paint a picture to describe something in detail, but science writing is *not* usually written as a narrative. Science writing does *not* generally contain characters, a setting, a plot, conflict, and a theme. Science audiences are *not* necessarily expecting to be entertained or transported to another place in time. The primary purpose for science writing is *not* to tell a story or raise a moral question to ponder. Does this mean science writing never does these things? No. In fact, science writers may use narrative techniques to convey sensory data, provide a metaphor to help readers understand an idea, or describe a situation to evoke an experience.

LITERACY KEY CONCEPT

The nature of science drives the conventions and style of science writing.

When you explored what makes science writing unique, it's likely your observations could be grouped into three main categories: the *purpose* for writing in science, the *format* for writing in science, and what a scientific *audience* knows and expects.

Purpose

The purpose for writing your expanded definition for energy was to "capture your thinking so far." This was a quintessential example of science writing because you were writing to explain an idea and share what you knew about an aspect of the natural world. Whether you are reading the science section of a newspaper, a science textbook, a scientist's lab notes, or a science book intended for popular consumption, the purpose of science writing is generally the same — to convey information and explain. This is why scientific writing is often called informational, or expository, text.

We also write in science to persuade people to think about the world in a new way. In Isaac Newton's revolutionary book, *Principia,* published in 1687, he describes why objects move the way they do based on his notion of gravity. As is often true in science, his thinking was unpopular because it flew in the face of the current Earth-centric way of thinking. This meant Newton had to do more than explain science ideas and convey information. He had to write to change people's minds. Today Newton's book is thought to be among the most influential in the history of science because it persuaded people to adopt an entirely different way of thinking.

If you are the audience for your own science writing, your purposes may be somewhat different from your purposes if you were writing for other people. For example, you might write to record your tentative thoughts or you might write to get clearer about how you are thinking. When drafting an expanded definition of energy, some people probably commented that they "finally figured some things out." Others may have said the writing pointed out what was confusing about energy. But whether you are writing for yourself or for others, the purpose of science writing is nearly always to convey information and explore ideas.

Format

When you wrote your definition for energy, the instructions suggested you use a format that is "typical of science writing used to convey information." This means you had to make decisions about how to *structure* the information, which *text-type* was best, and which *tone* was appropriate. Most science writing is structured in one of the following five ways, based on the nature of information being conveyed.

- *Cause and effect.* The cause and effect structure is used to describe a series of steps that lead to a given outcome, where the steps are sometimes sequenced parts of a larger process or cycle or related to certain phenomena.

- *Claim, evidence, and reasoning.* Scientific explanations often have a specific structure that begins with a claim or statement you believe to be true. The claim is then followed by evidence (e.g., factual information or data) that supports the claim and a discussion of the reasons the evidence logically links to and supports the claim.

- *Compare and contrast.* The compare and contrast structure is used to describe similarities and differences among two or more things, often according to categories that highlight likenesses or differences (e.g., comparing the types of energy by contrasting kinetic energy with potential energy).

- *Concept definition.* Conceptual definitions go beyond simple definitions. They name a certain word or concept (e.g., "energy") and then present attributes related to that word or concept, for example, "Energy is not a thing. You cannot see or hold it, nor is it a push or a pull. Rather, energy is a number that represents how much change might happen in a system."

- *Description.* This organizational structure is useful for sharing data organized around a specific experiment, object, or event. For example, the energy associated with a certain food can be described according to observations about what happens when the food is burned, measurements showing changes in a calorimeter's water temperature, and calculations that determine the ratio of calories per gram of food.

Just as there are well-established *structures* for science writing, the *text-types* for science writing are also distinct. Sometimes just by looking at a page without actually reading the words, you can tell it is about science. This is because text presentation in science has certain characteristics. Typically science writing includes the liberal use of headings in concert with bold and italicized words to help the reader follow the organization of information and recognize key points and is often full of images, tables, figures, and diagrams. The following example from the Content Notes for this session illustrates some of these characteristics.

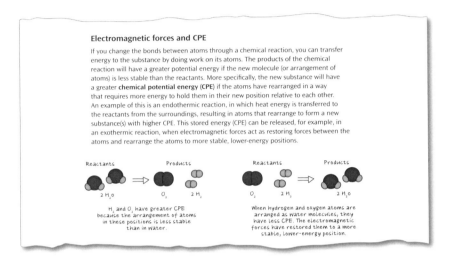

Electromagnetic forces and CPE

If you change the bonds between atoms through a chemical reaction, you can transfer energy to the substance by doing work on its atoms. The products of the chemical reaction will have a greater potential energy if the new molecule (or arrangement of atoms) is less stable than the reactants. More specifically, the new substance will have a greater **chemical potential energy (CPE)** if the atoms have rearranged in a way that requires more energy to hold them in their new position relative to each other. An example of this is an endothermic reaction, in which heat energy is transferred to the reactants from the surroundings, resulting in atoms that rearrange to form a new substance(s) with higher CPE. This stored energy (CPE) can be released, for example, in an exothermic reaction, when electromagnetic forces act as restoring forces between the atoms and rearrange the atoms to more stable, lower-energy positions.

Given that science values accuracy of information and nuanced ideas, the *tone* most often used in science writing is characteristically precise. In order to write with a scientific tone, writers often take great care in choosing words that convey just what they mean. They may also describe events or observations in factual, pithy ways that clearly separate data from inference and interpretation. Perhaps because scientists value an objective observer, science texts are often written in the third person with a tone that can sometimes be described as distant or removed.

While the preceding structures, text-types, and tones are common in science, there is also a great deal of variability in science writing. When a scientist writes for a professional journal, the tone of the article may be academic and formal with precise use of technical terms and specific headings prescribed by the publication (e.g., abstract, methods, and conclusions). A middle school science teacher might write about some of the same concepts or scientific principles, but will use a style that is more accessible to students, for example, a casual tone and everyday terms to describe or introduce science words. How we choose to present information in science really depends on our audience.

Audience

Think about what you'd expect if you were to read another teacher's expanded definition of energy. Would you want to learn something new? Or perhaps confirm if your own understanding of energy was "right"? Would you expect details and terminology at a technical level or a level more fitting for a layperson? Do you think you would likely agree or disagree with the author?

It turns out science audiences are a big part of what makes science writing unique. If the purpose of science writing is to convey information or explain, then it makes sense that science readers expect to learn from what they read. Given that science audiences read to learn, this undoubtedly means they bring some degree of prior knowledge to their reading. It also means science readers might be skeptical of new information and question what they read.

Just as science teachers benefit from knowing a great deal about their students, science writers benefit from knowing their audience. Writers are better able to communicate ideas and persuade audiences when they have a good handle on what their readers' likely know and can anticipate points of confusion and points of controversy.

In summary, one way to strengthen your science writing is to know more about the typical purposes, formats, and audience expectations in science. Another way is to increase the strategies you have for solving the writing-related problems that inevitably crop up during the various stages of prewriting, drafting, and revising.

HEAT ENERGY

In chemistry, students classify reactions based on whether they require or release heat energy. In geoscience, they study the role of heat energy in weather and plate tectonics. In biology, they explore the adaptations organisms have for controlling their body temperature. Understanding heat energy and its relationship to temperature and matter are important for many of the subjects students study in middle school, but heat energy and temperature are not easy things to understand.

In this Teaching Case, students refine and apply their thinking about temperature and heat energy to one of the mechanisms of heat energy transfer — conduction. At first glance, conduction seems pretty straightforward. Something hotter touches something colder, then the hotter thing cools down and the colder thing warms up.

However, conduction is a complex phenomenon that involves relationships between matter, energy, and temperature. In this Teaching Case, students work hard to determine what happens with energy, matter, and temperature in conduction. It's no surprise students find some aspects of these relationships particularly challenging.

- How do students think about the mechanics of conduction (e.g., the direction heat energy moves and when conduction stops)?

- How do students make sense of conduction involving ice versus conduction in other scenarios?

- How do students think about the relationship between heat energy and temperature?

Teaching Case

"COLD ON THE MOVE"

To start our thermodynamics unit, I reminded my students of our study of the phases of matter and how the atoms within each phase move. I then asked, "What do you think of when I say the word *temperature*?"

"Temperature is how hot something is," offered Toby. As usual, he was trying to challenge my question and get through the discussion as fast as possible. I pretended not to notice his impatience. "Good, Toby. Let's talk some more about what 'hot' means."

Students volunteered answer after answer to explain the meaning of the word *hot*. It was no surprise to me that they used the words *hot, cold, heat,* and *temperature* in some circular way. Toby finally spoke up again. "Hot is like ow!" and pantomimed touching a hot stove, "while cold is like ooooh." Toby had gotten another laugh from the class and proven once again that he has a unique ability to summarize concepts. The class spontaneously began to talk about the impact of hot and cold things on hands, feet, and tongues.

With their brains engaged, I put up two posters, one for temperature and one for heat energy. Developing these posters wasn't easy. It seems like every textbook and teaching resource talks about temperature and heat energy in different ways.

TEMPERATURE
Temperature is a measure of how hot or cold something is.

Hotter   Colder

- It's related to the motion of the molecules. The higher the temperature, the faster molecules vibrate and/or move.
- When molecules collide with a thermometer bulb, the fluid moves around more. As the fluid gets hotter, it expands and goes up the tube.

HEAT ENERGY (HE)
Heat energy is the sum of the kinetic energies of each individual particle in an object.

More HE   Less HE

- A cup of 150°F water has more HE than a cup of 70°F water because the molecules are vibrating faster.
- A gallon of 70°F water has more HE than a cup of 70°F water because there are more molecules vibrating.

Over the next several lessons, we talked a whole lot more about the difference between heat energy and temperature. We briefly investigated the concept of the total heat energy associated with an object. For example, Janie shared that "a rock in the classroom has a lower temperature and less heat energy than the same rock in the Sun," and Toby did a nice job explaining why "an inflated football has more heat energy than a squishy football, even if they're the exact same temperature." We also mapped out how different temperature scales relate to each other (e.g., 32°F = 0°C). We were now ready to look deeper into how heat energy moves.

Introducing Mountain Jim

I started the conduction unit with a preassessment that probed how my students were thinking about conduction. They read a short story about a camper named Mountain Jim who warmed up a container of soup by putting hot rocks into it. Jim warmed up rocks in his campfire, used a pair of sticks to pull the rocks out of the fire, and dropped them into his container of soup. He waited a few minutes, removed the first set of rocks, then added another set of hot rocks from the fire. He repeated this process several times. After adding and removing several sets of hot rocks, eventually the soup was hot enough to eat. The students were asked two questions about the science behind Mountain Jim's strange cooking method — "Why did the rocks get colder once they were in the soup?" and "When Mountain Jim took the first set of rocks out of the soup, they were cool. When he took the second set of rocks out of the soup, they were warm. When he took the last set out, they were hot. Why did the three sets of rocks have different temperatures?"

Many of my students were on the right track with the first question, but I was amazed at how many thought that heat energy transfer was dictated by what Jim, the soup, or the rocks "needed" or "wanted." Here is a summary of my students' responses to "Why did the rocks get colder once they were in the soup?"

- I don't know why the soup didn't get hot from the first set because it still gave them its cold, but the rest of the rocks gave up their heat and took in the soup's cold. (Elyse)

- The cold of the soup wore out the heat of the rocks. (Rico)

- The rocks aren't in the fire any more. (Lee)

- The soup absorbs the heat from the rocks because it needs to get hot. (Kira)

- The soup made the heat in the rocks die down, but not before the rocks released a good part of the heat into the soup. (Janie)

- The rocks don't have any heat to take out of the soup, so they can't stay warm. (Toby)

The second question was more challenging: "Why did the three sets of rocks have different temperatures?" A few of my students were able to surmise the reason, but found it hard to express their idea scientifically. However, most of my students had less clearly formed ideas.

- Maybe because the soup started giving back some of its heat to the rocks before Mountain Jim took them out. (Elyse)

- Soup takes a long time to get hot. When the soup gets hot, it needs less of the rocks' hotness to be hot. (Rico)

- The soup got hotter and so the rocks did too. (Lee)

- When the soup was hotter, the rocks didn't have to waste as much of their heat on the soup. They kept it for themselves. (Kira)

- The rocks help heat the soup, but at the same time they also get heat from the soup. Like give and take. (Janie)

- The soup didn't have as much coldness to share with the rocks. It didn't cool them down as much. (Toby)

Many students in my class shared Elyse's idea. These students seemed to think that once the rocks warmed the soup, the warm soup returned some heat energy back to the rocks. I dubbed this idea the "piggy bank" model. It seemed to work like this: The rocks added all of their heat energy to the soup (like depositing your whole allowance in the piggy bank), then took away some heat from the soup because they needed it back (like taking out just enough money from the piggy bank to buy a CD).

This preassessment proved to be especially difficult for the English language learners in my class. For example, Rico's responses showed me he was really struggling with putting his ideas about heat energy into words. I wish I had asked my students to draw what they thought was happening.

Frozen hands

My students typically have difficulty understanding the direction of energy transfers in conduction and what exactly is being transferred. The piggy bank model was new to me, but, like all my previous classes, this year's students also thought of the ever-mysterious "cold" being transferred. I decided to tackle the "cold moving" issue first.

The next day as the students entered the classroom, I handed each an ice cube and gave them the simple instruction "think and talk about what you notice as you hold the ice cube." After a few seconds, I heard, "It's melting! Oh, no! The water's getting all over the place!" Elyse was screaming and simultaneously apologetic for making a mess in the science room. Several students observed that their hands were getting cold. Some even went so far as to exclaim, "It's starting to hurt!"

I started to worry about the potential for a class-action frostbite lawsuit, but saw that most students were having a great time dripping water on each other. After collecting the now smaller ice cubes and offering paper towels to clean up the mess, I gathered everyone's attention. We made a list of observations on the board. Several students talked about cold moving from the ice to their hands.

Finally, Lee made a different kind of observation. He spoke very calmly and slowly, like he'd been thinking for a while about exactly how he might say this. Lee said, "My hand heats up the ice. My hand makes it melt." With Lee's carefully phrased observation as an introduction, I reminded students of the interaction diagrams we'd used earlier in the year by drawing an empty one on the board.

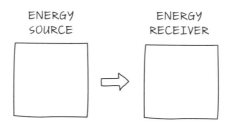

I asked my class what they remembered about these diagrams. They shared examples such as ball dents concrete, car smashes wall, and woman stomps ant. Last but not least, Toby volunteered, "fist hits jaw," mimicking delivering an uppercut to an invisible opponent.

Confident they hadn't forgotten how to use the diagrams, I asked the students to draw the diagram in their notebooks, then to write "ice" in one box and "hand" in the other, depending on which way they thought the heat energy was transferred.

One of my many classroom traditions is whenever we are faced with a situation that has a limited number of possible answers, the students vote to decide which they think is correct. I encourage them to vote even if they're on the losing side, joking that people vote on the losing side of political elections all the time. I called for a vote on the diagrams. About a third of the class raised their hands to vote for Ice ⇒ Hand. This group of students, hereafter known as the Ice-First Party, thought the *ice was the energy source* and the hand was the energy receiver. A few others, the Hand-First Party, thought the *hand was the energy source* and the ice was the energy receiver, so they voted for Hand ⇒ Ice.

This left half of my class not voting. I was surprised because my students know I don't allow them to abstain in our elections. I reminded them of the election rules and was grudgingly starting a second vote when Elyse interrupted. In her ever-helpful and apologetic tone, she said, "I'm sorry, but I don't want to vote for either one. Can't we vote for both?" The other abstaining students enthusiastically nodded. Almost half of my class pictured the hand-ice interaction as a two-way exchange of energy! They thought Ice ⇔ Hand.

Okay, well, even if they didn't vote, I at least knew what they were thinking. I had a three-way debate in the works, Ice-First, Hand-First, and Two-Way Street. I started the debate with the Ice-First Party. I asked the class, "Could someone who claimed ice was the energy source please explain the evidence or reasoning that supports your claim?"

Janie cheerfully answered, "The ice made my hand cold. You feel a difference in your hand. The ice is causing it." Several students nodded.

Another Ice-First member chimed in to help Janie sway the opposition. "Ice is water. It takes cold energy to freeze water to make it ice. When the ice melts, that cold energy comes back out and goes into your hand."

Janie, now brimming with confidence, added, "Yup, my hand is receiving that cold energy. The coldness flows right into my hand."

From the head nods across the room, I could see that the Ice-First Party had made a good argument. Time for the Hand-First Party's rebuttal.

Toby volunteered for the Hand-First Party. He was perched in his usual position, balancing his chair on its rear legs, and said, in a slightly annoyed way, "People, this whole unit is about heat, not cold. Your hand's hotter than the ice cube, so you're giving up heat."

Janie wasn't going to take this criticism lightly. "But even if you're not holding the ice cube, it will still melt!" The Ice-First Party was feeling strong again.

From the back of the room, Lee spoke up, again in measured tones. "Your hand must be giving heat to the ice. It's giving the ice the energy it needs to melt. The ice takes the heat out of your hand, and that's why your hand feels colder."

I could feel the energy of the room shift entirely. Suddenly the members of the Ice-First Party were silent, contemplating Lee's statement and not sure how to argue against it. Not one Ice-First voter volunteered to speak. I let them off the hook and pressed the Two-Way Street Party to share its thoughts.

Elyse still represented her constituency, although now she seemed uncharacteristically shy. "I wanted to vote the arrow went both directions because I knew that your hand was giving heat to the ice, but I also thought that the ice was changing your hand. But, um, Lee's answer makes sense. The energy is going into the ice. It just feels the other way."

The Hand-First Party had swayed the entire election. The Ice-First and Two-Way Street groups conceded. Consensus had been reached! I told the students the particles in cold things just are not moving very much. I explained that cold was a temperature, not a type of energy. I reminded my students that heat energy is the type of energy associated with the collective, random motion of particles. I also reviewed the basics of how to determine how much heat energy an object has. Specifically, I said that if we calculated the kinetic energy of every particle in an object and then added those amounts together, we'd know how much heat energy an object has. Then I offered two statements to define *conduction:*

- When two objects of different temperatures touch, the hotter object cools and the colder object warms. This is conduction.

- In conduction, the amount of heat energy in the hotter object drops and the amount of heat energy in the colder object goes up. No substance is transferred between the objects, just heat energy.

Whenever I give a definition, I try to come up with a way my students can use or test the definition right away — the real-world application seems to help the definition stick. Sometimes it's hard to come up with something applicable, but not this time.

I asked my students to touch something in the room that they thought their hand would conduct heat energy to. The answers came quickly and included binders, tabletops, pencils, and the board at the front of the room. Once again, Toby stopped all further touching with the perfect answer. "We can touch anything. It's all at room temperature!"

I confirmed Toby was correct. At this point someone asked, "If Toby's right, then how come the metal things are so much colder than everything else?" I gave them a wicked smile, which my students know means they've stumbled onto something neat to talk about. I asked my students why some people put cold sodas into neoprene koozies.

Rico explained, "It keeps them cold."

Janie added, "Yeah, they'll lose all their cold if you leave them out in the air."

No pun intended, I froze. We had just covered the idea that cold didn't move, that heat energy was transferred. Luckily Toby jumped right in saying, "Okay, people, we already agreed I was right. This unit is about heat, not cold. You put sodas in a koozie to keep the heat from your hand from going over to the soda."

I jumped in right on Toby's heels. "Heat energy is being conducted from your hand to the soda. Metal conducts heat energy very efficiently, so heat energy is able to transfer quickly out of your hand when you touch metal. This makes your hand feel cold. Neoprene is a poor conductor. It's an insulator, so it slows the conduction of heat energy from your hand, meaning your hand doesn't feel as cold."

I asked my students to identify other things that reduce the rate of conduction, other insulators. They volunteered things like oven mitts, hot pads, and shoes. Janie suddenly sat up with her back straight, almost rising out of her chair, and shoved her hand up.

Janie proudly said, "Sticks!" The whole room paused wondering what in the world she was talking about. She excitedly explained, "Mountain Jim! He used sticks to pull the rocks out of the fire, instead of touching them with his bare hands."

I asked the class what they thought of Janie's idea, and Lee said, "The sticks did keep the rocks from conducting heat energy into Jim's hands. They worked like an oven mitt, like an insulator." Janie was smiling ear-to-ear, pink-colored braces flashing.

Next I asked the class to imagine something they could touch that would conduct heat energy into their hands — something that would make their hands the energy receiver. Again, the answers were inventive, ranging from a bright light bulb, to a hot pan, to the surface of the Sun. My favorite came from Elyse, who chose black asphalt on a sunny day.

I sent my students home with an assignment to draw and describe a few more interaction diagrams for conduction. I was confident they understood the rules of conduction, and I was eager to see the creative ideas they might offer. When I reviewed their interaction diagrams the next day, I did find quite a few creative and accurate ideas, although I noticed a few students struggling with the nuances of conduction. For example, some students missed that for conduction to occur objects had to be touching and they had the Sun conducting heat energy to plants.

Janie's work was particularly interesting. Her diagram looked good. But was the piggy bank model surfacing again in her writing?

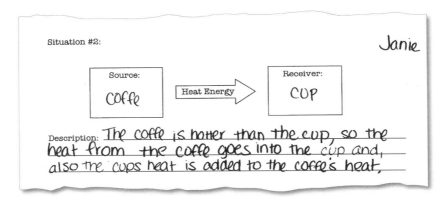

Rico's work brought up a misconception I see every year. The idea that mittens, hats, and clothes are sources of heat energy.

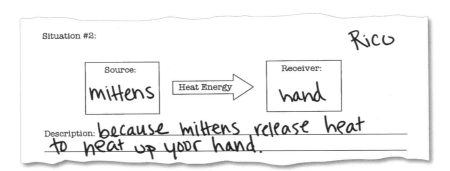

Beaker & Flask Lab

Usually when I teach about conduction, I do a demonstration using a variety of metal rods held over a Bunsen burner to see which heats up fastest. This helps students understand which materials are good conductors, but it doesn't help them understand the importance of temperature to conduction or the mechanics of conduction on a molecular level.

This year, I planned to have students observe conduction between two containers of liquid. This would demonstrate that conduction stops when two objects reach the same temperature — a concept I've never taught as clearly as I feel I should have.

The Beaker & Flask Lab was quite simple. A small Erlenmeyer flask was filled with 100 ml of hot water, while a larger beaker was filled with 100 ml of cold water. The flask was placed inside the beaker, and students measured the temperatures of the water in both containers over the course of 10 minutes. They then made a graph of their results. As students made their graphs, I asked each group whether heat energy was still being conducted now that the temperatures had stabilized. Many correctly said it was not.

The lab went so efficiently that I had time to give an extra challenge. I encouraged my students to see if they could "come up with a way to make the water in the beaker even hotter *without* adding water directly to the beaker." I hoped they would notice the parallel to Mountain Jim's story — the flask of hot water had warmed up the beaker of cold water just like the rocks had warmed up the soup. Mountain Jim got his soup hotter by adding new hot rocks from the fire. Some students saw the parallel and decided to pour out the water in the flask, which was now lukewarm, and replace it with fresh hot water. Other students had ideas that bore no relationship to Mountain Jim, but were great nonetheless.

Toby wanted to get it over with quickly and suggested we just "put the beaker on the hot plate." Lee wanted to rub the beaker because "friction will heat it at least part of a degree." Rico thought he could increase the temperature of the beaker by putting the whole setup in a wool hat. Several students thought Rico had stumbled on a great idea. They begged to visit their lockers and retrieve their winter gear.

Going with the flow I picked up my stocking cap from my desk and grabbed a thermometer. Then I asked my students what temperature they expected the hat to be. Most guessed "warm" or "80–90 degrees." Only a few students guessed "room temperature," and those who did were met with quizzical looks from their peers.

When we read the thermometer, many students were shocked — my hat, which had been lying on my desk since morning, was at room temperature! After an intense discussion, I summarized the concept. "Clothes are not warm unless heat energy has already been transferred to them by the body. Clothes simply slow down the transfer of heat energy away from our bodies. Clothes are insulators." I'm sure my students had heard this before. I hoped it would stick this time.

Going back to their previous challenge, I called for one last idea about how to increase the beaker's temperature without adding hot water to it. Janie suggested pouring the flask's water into the beaker. I reminded Janie that the flask water and the beaker water were at the same temperature.

Janie said, "Oh, um, I guess that wouldn't make the beaker any hotter," but she looked very confused. I wasn't sure why, and she couldn't explain her thinking.

As I reflected on her idea that afternoon, I wondered if it was possible she was mixing up temperature and heat energy. Her idea would have been correct, in fact brilliant, if I had asked, "How could we increase the total heat energy of the beaker?" Adding the flask water to the beaker would have meant more water molecules in the beaker, and thus more heat energy in the beaker.

Meet in the middle

The next day, we analyzed the results together. I asked students to describe the shape of their temperature graphs. With the exception of a few graphing errors, everyone's graphs looked about the same.

I then drew a picture on the board of a flask inside a beaker and asked them to tell me about heat energy and conduction. All agreed the heat energy was transferring from the flask water to the beaker water. I drew an arrow as they instructed. Then Rico said there was also heat energy going to the air from the flask water and from the beaker water, so I added two more arrows.

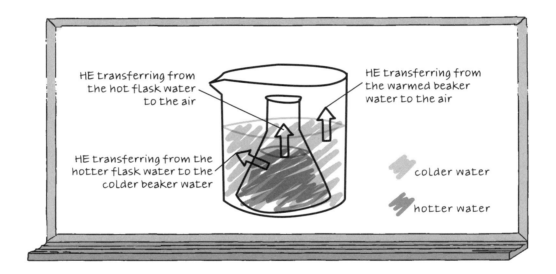

I then asked, "Why do you think the beaker didn't get as hot as the flask was at the start?"

Elyse was the first to offer an explanation. "For that to happen, the hot one would have to lose all its heat, and the cold one would have to gain all the heat. That can't happen."

Remembering the piggy bank model of heat exchange, I pressed a little further. "Couldn't the flask lose all its heat energy to the beaker, and the beaker could give a little bit back to the flask, so they ended up at the same temperature?"

Lee didn't fall for the ruse. "The temperatures would have to go past each other, but when they get to the same temperature, they don't conduct anymore." He held his hands up in front of him, one above the other, and moved them parallel like two elevators moving in adjacent shafts. When his hands got even with each other, he stopped them and said, "The conduction stops. They meet right in the middle of the two temperatures they started at. The graphs show it too."

I breathed a sigh of relief and hoped the results of the lab dispelled the piggy bank model. Confident the students understood the limits of conduction, I asked them to think of a way Mountain Jim could have gotten his soup even hotter with his first set of rocks.

Lee suggested using more rocks in the first batch, because they'd have more total heat energy to give. Elyse suggested instead that he use very little soup, because one rock would heat it up. Rico suggested, "Jim can put his hat over the soup after he puts the rocks in."

Oh, no! Not the warm hat again!

Rico must have noticed my single raised eyebrow and panicked look because he smiled triumphantly and said with confidence, "I know the hat will not make the soup get hot, but heat will not get out of the pot."

Touché.

Another day down, another major concept seemed to be clicking. I was confident students saw conduction was a one-way street that occurs only as long as there is a temperature difference between the two objects.

It was time to circle back to where we started — Mountain Jim. This time, I threw an icicle into the Mountain Jim story. I said, "Imagine Mountain Jim got his soup too hot to eat. He could blow on it or let it cool down on its own, but he was starving and wanted it to cool down fast, so he found an icicle and dropped it into the soup. Draw an interaction diagram and explain why the heat energy transfers the way you drew it." I wrote the prompt on the board as they got to work.

After they had finished drawing and writing about this in their science notebooks, I asked for a quick class vote on which object — the icicle or the soup — was the heat energy source. Shockingly, one-third voted for the icicle.

Janie explained her Icicle-First vote. "The soup is getting colder and changing. The icicle is going to make it cold because of the coldness going into the soup."

As if on cue, several students chimed in together in mock exasperation. "There's no such thing as coldness!" The bell rang, they burst out of the room, dropping off their notebooks in my basket. I was left to ponder their Icicle/Soup diagrams. I was pleased to see two-thirds of my students' work was correct and looked similar to Elyse's.

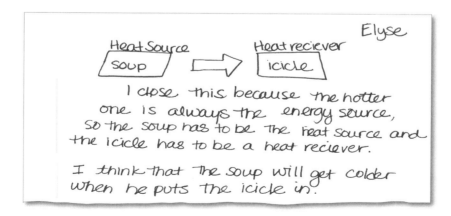

However, about one-third of the work looked like Janie's. Cold on the move!

Toby and a few others also drew the diagram incorrectly, but for a different reason. I think they were thinking that because even cold things have heat energy, adding a cold thing to a pot of soup would increase the soup's total heat energy. This is true — adding anything to a pot of soup adds molecules and thus adds heat energy. But adding something colder *still* lowers the temperature and means the soup is conducting heat energy to the colder thing.

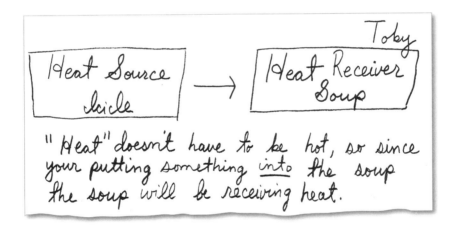

My students had learned a lot about temperature, heat energy, and conduction, so why did so many of them not get the direction of conduction correct for this task?

I was glad I came back to "cold transfer," asking about the icicle, on the last day. It was a good reality check for me. It made me realize just how easily my students could get confused by my prompts, the diagrams, and the vocabulary, not to mention the concepts at work. I felt like somehow the relationship between heat energy, temperature, conduction, and matter never became totally clear to them, even though I tried to parse it out into manageable pieces and gave them lots of different ways to interact with the concepts. I also think I somehow need to help them understand the mechanism for conduction so they could truly let go of the idea that some tangible substance is moving during conduction. I'll have to think a bit more about what I'll do differently next year.

Instinctively, we all know something about the term heat. We heat up our food in hot ovens. We know hot coffee left on a picnic table eventually gets cold. We put on clothes straight out of the dryer and relish the warmth on a cold morning. We can even tell how hot or cold the air temperature is by measuring it with a thermometer. But saying just what the terms *heat, heat energy,* and *temperature* are or how they relate to energy is more difficult. While scientists know a lot about what happens with matter as it gets hotter and with energy as matter gets hotter, even the most reputable sources sometimes define these three terms in contradictory ways.

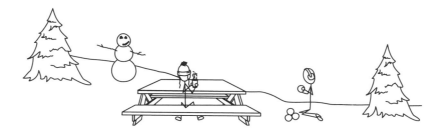

VOCABULARY

Heat energy (HE) is the type of energy associated with objects due to the random, unorganized motion of their particles. Heat energy is sometimes called thermal energy. It is the sum of the kinetic energy associated with each particle in an object. Only at a temperature of absolute zero would an object have no heat energy, because at absolute zero, particles do not move.

Temperature is a measure of how hot or cold something is. Temperature directly relates to the average kinetic energy of the particles within an object — a higher temperature means the particles have more kinetic energy on average.

The term **heat** by itself is most appropriately used as a verb to describe the action of getting something hotter. As an object is heated, its temperature goes up and so does its heat energy.

Specific heat capacity is the amount of heat energy 1 gram of substance requires to change 1 degree in temperature. The heat energy required depends on the nature of the substance.

Conduction, convection, and radiation are all mechanisms by which heat energy is transferred to new locations. **Conduction** is the spontaneous transfer of heat energy from a hotter object to a colder object through direct contact. **Convection** is the gravity-driven movement of hot and cold fluids. As convection moves a fluid, the fluid's heat energy is carried with it. **Radiation** is the emission of electromagnetic waves (e.g., radio, microwave, visible light, ultraviolet, X-rays, gamma rays). When an object absorbs radiation, the radiation's light energy is transferred into heat energy.

⊙ What is heat?

The word *heat* is perhaps the most vexing of the three terms because it is used in so many different ways, both in our everyday language and in scientific contexts. In fact, the term *heat* can be used as a noun, a verb, an adjective, and an adverb, depending on the context. For this course, we use **heat** only as a verb, meaning to make things hotter, as in "I want to heat the water to make tea." And for the most part we try to avoid using it altogether and use the word *warm* instead, as in "I want to warm the water to make tea."

When you see the word *heat* combined with the word *energy* in this course, it means something else. Heat energy is a type of energy resulting from the random, unorganized motion of atoms and molecules.

⊙ What is temperature?

We all have an intuitive understanding of temperature, but its scientific definition is more complex. For this course, we say **temperature** is an indication of the average kinetic energy of particles (e.g., atoms, molecules) that you can measure. Temperature is how hot or cold things are, and how hot or cold an object is depends on the average kinetic energy of the particles that make up the object.

Determining how hot or cold things are by touching them is rather imprecise (and sometimes even dangerous!). Thermometers provide a standard way to measure the hotness or coldness of things. As the particles from an object or fluid collide with a thermometer, they transfer some of their motion (and thus energy) to the molecules inside the thermometer. When the molecules in the thermometer bulb increase their motion, the fluid in the bulb expands and fills more of the thermometer tube. When a thermometer is put into a colder substance and particles from the thermometer collide with particles from the colder object or fluid, they transfer some of their motion (and thus energy) to the particles in the substance. When the molecules in the thermometer decrease their motion, the fluid in the bulb contracts and fills less of the tube. Thus the level of the thermometer fluid gives us an indication of the average kinetic energy of the particles in the object or fluid it is touching.

The reason we rely on temperature to tell us about the average kinetic energy of matter is because it's so difficult to calculate the average kinetic energy of all the particles in a substance. To do so, you would first need to measure the mass (m) and velocity (v) of each particle and then use the formula $KE = \frac{1}{2} mv^2$ to calculate each molecule's kinetic energy. Finally, you'd need to add each particle's kinetic energy value together and divide by the total number of particles. Whew! It's a lot easier to just stick the thermometer in the beaker and get an indication of the average kinetic energy.

Since temperature is just an indication of the average kinetic energy of the particles in a substance, it is *not* accurate, strictly speaking, to say "temperature is the average kinetic energy of the particles in an object." Unfortunately this definition is common — and somewhat misleading. If temperature really were "the average kinetic energy of the particles in a object," then temperature would be measured in units of energy such as joules or calories, not in units such as Celsius or Kelvin.

◉ What is heat energy?

Heat energy (HE) is the type of energy associated with random, unorganized molecular motion. Heat energy is present with any and all objects that are above absolute zero simply because the particles that make up the objects are moving. Heat energy, like all other types of energy, can be measured in joules, calories, kilocalories, or any other unit for energy.

Changes in heat energy

There are two ways to increase the total amount of heat energy associated with an object. You can either increase the object's *temperature* or increase the object's *mass*.

These are both options because total heat energy associated with an object depends on the *number of particles in motion* and the *average kinetic energy of those particles*. For example, to increase the amount of heat energy associated with 80 mL of water at 10°C, you can warm the water to 20°C. This increases the heat energy of the water because you have increased the average kinetic energy of the water's molecules, as shown in Example A.

EXAMPLE A
Warming the material to increase HE

BEFORE

AFTER

HE increases

The other way to increase the amount of heat energy is to simply add more water, as shown in Example B. This increases the amount of heat energy because you're adding molecules, all of which have heat energy associated with them.

EXAMPLE B
Adding material to increasing HE

BEFORE

AFTER

HE increases

It's fairly straightforward to describe and calculate increases and decreases in heat energy caused by warming or cooling. This calculation involves knowing the *mass* (m), how much the *temperature* has changed (ΔT), and the *specific heat capacity* (C) of the substance in that temperature range and using the following formula.

$$\Delta HE = m \times \Delta T \times C$$

Using this formula it's possible to calculate that the beaker in Example A gains 800 calories of heat energy when it is warmed from 10°C to 20°C, as shown in the following example.

$$\Delta HE = 80\ g \times (20°C - 10°C) \times 1\ cal/g°C = 800\ calories$$

Unfortunately, it is not as easy to determine the total heat energy associated with an object or amount of fluid at a given temperature. To do this you need to know the number of molecules in the object and the kinetic energy of each molecule. It seems like you should be able to use the preceding formula and say the initial temperature is absolute zero (–273°C). However, a material's specific heat is not constant across such vast temperature changes. Therefore the formula doesn't work. Not being able to use the preceding formula makes quantifying the change in heat energy in Example B difficult. What we can say about Example B is that there must be an increase in heat energy because the temperature does not change and there is an increase in mass. More specifically, the mass of the water doubled, so the heat energy associated with that water also doubled.

Specific heat capacity is the amount of heat energy 1 gram of substance requires to change 1 degree in temperature. The specific heat capacity varies among different substances, from one state to another (e.g., solid, liquid, and gas), and across temperatures (to varying degrees). It is dependent on the molecular makeup of the substance. The following table shows the specific heat capacities for a few different substances at 25°C.

Substances	Specific Heat Capacity (J/g°C)	Specific Heat Capacity (cal/g°C)
Hydrogen gas	14.27	3.41
Water	4.19	1.00
Air	1.02	0.24
Glass	0.84	0.20
Iron	0.44	0.11
Sand	0.29	0.07
Gold	0.13	0.03

Water, air, glass, and other materials with high specific heat capacities will not warm up (or cool down) very quickly, even when large amounts of heat energy are transferred to (or away from) them. By contrast, materials with low specific heat capacities, such as sand and gold, will get much hotter (or much cooler) with an equal transfer of heat energy.

To get a sense of how specific heat capacity relates to warming and cooling, let's compare water and gold. In order to warm 80 grams of water (roughly a cup) by 10°C, you'd need 800 calories of energy (as shown in the preceding calculation). If you transferred 800 calories of heat energy to 80 grams of gold, it could go from 10°C to a whopping 323°C, as shown in the following calculation.

$$\Delta HE = m \times \Delta T \times C$$
$$800 \text{ cal} = 80 \text{ g} \times (T_{final} - 10°C) \times 0.03 \text{ cal/g°C}$$
$$323°C = T_{final}$$

The high specific heat capacity of water makes it especially useful in regulating our body temperature, as well as in regulating Earth's climate. This is because a large change in water's heat energy results in a relatively small change in temperature. By contrast, the low specific heat capacity of gold and most other metals means even a small change in their heat energy results in a large change in temperature.

⊙ Why do objects change temperature?

Anytime something warms up, it means the amount of heat energy associated with it increases. Anytime something cools down, it means the amount of heat energy associated with it decreases. There are three main ways to warm or cool something — conduction, convection, and radiation. Conduction, convection, and radiation are often called "forms of heat energy transfer," but it is more precise to refer to them as *mechanisms for heating and cooling* because only conduction and convection actually move heat energy. Radiation moves light energy. Only when this light energy is absorbed by matter does it become heat energy.

Conduction

Conduction is a mechanism by which heat energy is transferred to new locations. **Conduction** is the spontaneous transfer of heat energy that occurs whenever two objects of different temperatures come in direct contact with each other. The direction heat energy is transferred depends on the temperatures of the objects involved. Heat energy always transfers from a hotter object to a colder object. Even the slightest temperature differences between objects will be equalized through conduction.

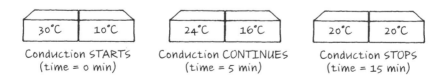

| 30°C | 10°C | | 24°C | 16°C | | 20°C | 20°C |

Conduction STARTS
(time = 0 min)

Conduction CONTINUES
(time = 5 min)

Conduction STOPS
(time = 15 min)

When objects reach the same temperature, we say conduction stops. This is because at equivalent temperatures, the average kinetic energy of the particles that make up each object are the same. Even though particles continue to move and collide, the average motion within each object remains unchanged, so the transfer of energy reaches an equilibrium.

Convection

Convection is a mechanism by which heat energy *and* matter are transferred to new locations. **Convection** is the spontaneous transfer of heat energy and movement of matter that occurs whenever a volume of fluid (gas, liquid, or plastic solid, such as parts of Earth's mantle) has an inconsistent temperature. In other words, when part of a fluid (often called a parcel) is warmer or colder than other parts, convection will occur. Colder, more dense parcels of fluids sink more than warmer, less dense parcels of fluids (due to gravity). As a result, convection pushes warmer, less dense parcels upward.

One example of convection is air currents. If a hotter, less dense air parcel is underneath a cooler, more dense air parcel, the hotter air parcel will rise and the cooler air will move to fill its place. This rearrangement, or movement, of the parcels means at any fixed location, the temperature will change. Convection literally moves parcels of matter. If those parcels are hot, then the location to which the hot parcel moves gets warmer. If those parcels are cold, then the location to which they move gets colder.

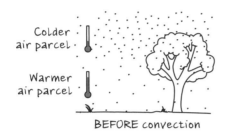
BEFORE convection

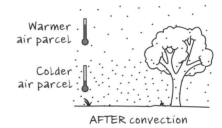
AFTER convection

Radiation

Radiation is a mechanism by which energy is transferred to new locations. It involves the emission of photons from matter. Photons (electromagnetic radiation) emitted from one object can be absorbed by another. For example, electromagnetic radiation emitted from the Sun can be absorbed by objects on Earth, such as trees, the ground, and people. In fact, any object that is not at absolute zero emits electromagnetic radiation that can be absorbed by other objects. This means electromagnetic radiation emitted by the ground can be absorbed by particles in the air. When electromagnetic radiation is absorbed by any kind of matter, this light energy (LE) is transferred to heat energy (HE) and the object's temperature increases.

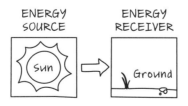
LE from the Sun is transferred to HE, so the ground gets warmer.

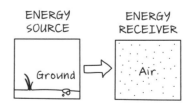
LE from the ground is transferred to HE, so the air gets warmer.

All matter that is not at absolute zero will spontaneously give off photons (electromagnetic radiation) because the particles that make up the matter are in motion. This means living things, nonliving things, large objects, small particles, hot things, cold things, and even snowmen emit electromagnetic radiation.

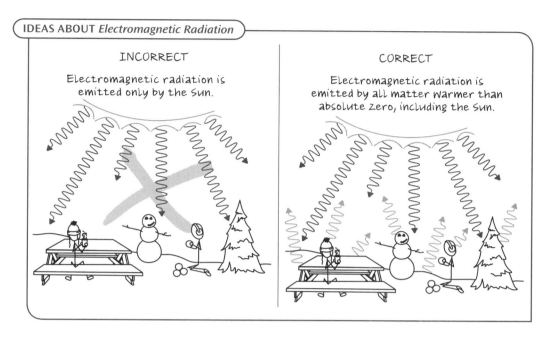

IDEAS ABOUT *Electromagnetic Radiation*

INCORRECT

Electromagnetic radiation is emitted only by the Sun.

CORRECT

Electromagnetic radiation is emitted by all matter warmer than absolute zero, including the Sun.

The amount of energy associated with the photons emitted by an object depends on the object's temperature. Hotter objects emit more higher-energy photons (i.e., photons with short wavelengths), while colder objects emit more lower-energy photons (i.e., photons with long wavelengths). Additionally, hotter objects emit more total energy than colder objects. The Sun and other objects with similarly high temperatures emit photons that have wavelengths of light in the ultraviolet (UV) and visible range. Objects that burn with blue flames (i.e., emit blue light) are hotter than objects that burn with yellow flames (i.e., emit yellow light). Humans and many other living and nonliving things on Earth are at a temperature such that they emit photons with wavelengths in the infrared range.[1]

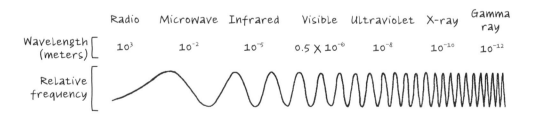

	Radio	Microwave	Infrared	Visible	Ultraviolet	X-ray	Gamma ray
Wavelength (meters)	10^3	10^{-2}	10^{-5}	0.5×10^{-6}	10^{-8}	10^{-10}	10^{-12}
Relative frequency							

---

[1] In reality, objects at any given temperature emit many different photons with a range of wavelengths. However, within this range there is a peak wavelength, or frequency, at which the majority of photons are emitted.

Science Investigation

55 MINUTES

---

 10 MINUTES **1** Talking to the Text

a. Take 3 minutes to individually review your Content Notes. Mark any text and images you find interesting or confusing. Record any questions you have and connections you make with the text.

b. Share your thinking about the reading with your group. Feel free to show the notes you made in the text. Discuss each other's ideas and questions.

Experimenting with the beaker and flask

a. Fill your beaker and flask with the designated amounts of cold and hot water, respectively, and measure their temperatures. Set the hot flask inside the cold beaker. Continue temperature readings every minute for 10 minutes.

As you conduct the experiment, discuss how much heat energy you think will transfer between the containers. For example, do you think the beaker and flask will see equal changes in heat energy or will one have a larger increase in heat energy than the other?

Beaker

Time	0	1	2	3	4	5	6	7	8	9	10
Temp (°C)											

Flask

Time	0	1	2	3	4	5	6	7	8	9	10
Temp (°C)											

b. Make a graph showing how the temperatures of the beaker water and the flask water change over time. Discuss what the graph shows.

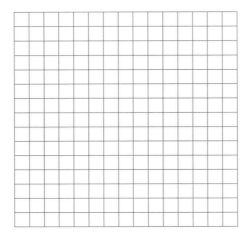

Thinking about conduction

    a. Discuss what the Beaker & Flask Lab temperature data reveal about:

- The direction of conduction

- The rate of conduction

- When conduction stops

Write a few summary statements that describe your findings.

    b. Work together to create a diagram that represents your thinking about how conduction causes the beaker water's temperature to increase and the flask water's temperature to decrease.

4 Calculating changes in heat energy

    a. Use the data from your lab to calculate the changes in temperature (ΔT) and the changes in heat energy (ΔHE).

	Beaker _____ ml	Flask _____ ml
Starting Temperature (°C)		
Ending Temperature (°C)		
ΔTemperature (°C)		
ΔHeat energy (cal/g°C)		

    b. What do these numbers reveal about conduction, heat energy, and temperature? Is there anything puzzling or surprising about the numbers?

✳ CALCULATING HEAT ENERGY

Heat energy is the type of energy associated with objects due to the motion of their particles. To calculate the change in amount of heat energy associated with an object, you need to know the object's mass, the change in temperature ($T_{final} - T_{inital}$), and the material's specific heat capacity.

$$\Delta \text{Heat energy} = \text{mass (g)} \times \Delta\text{temp (°C)} \times \text{specific heat capacity (cal/g°C)}$$

Specific heat capacity is the amount of heat energy 1 gram of substance requires to change 1 degree in temperature. The amount of heat energy required depends on the chemical composition of the substance. Water has a specific heat capacity of **1 cal/g°C.**

5 Connecting temperature and heat energy

a. With your group, develop a mind map using the following terms. Feel free to add more terms of your own.

- heat energy
- heating
- temperature

- matter
- convection
- conduction

b. Take note of any difficult spots you encountered while making your mind map and questions you have about the relationships among these terms.

 MIND MAPS

A mind map is a model that represents your current best thinking about a set of related terms. In mind maps:

- **Ovals** have a single term written inside each.

- **One-way arrows** show relationships between terms.

- **Linking verbs** describe how the terms are related.

Here is an example of a simple mind map made from four terms.

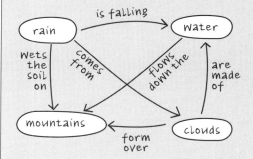

Note: Mind maps often go through many iterations. To make revisions easier, it's helpful to use a whiteboard or put the terms on sticky notes.

SESSION
3

1 ## Participating in a writers' group

a. Individually, take 5 minutes to prepare to share your writing with others using the directions found on "Handout G: Writers' Group Preparation."

b. Read the following tips for sharing writing and responding to writing in writers' groups.

c. Introduce yourself to your small group if you haven't worked together before. Decide the order in which you will share your writing pieces and who will be the timekeeper.

Note: The timekeeper's role is to make sure each author gets 5 minutes of focused attention from the writers' group, to give a 1-minute warning, and to call time when the 5 minutes are up.

d. Respond to each other's writing using the protocol found on "Handout H: Writers' Group Protocol."

✳ **SUPPORTING WRITERS**

Sharing writing

Share what you are currently thinking about your writing: What did you want to convey? What do you like? What's problematic in this draft?

Focus the discussion by posing a question and/or pointing to a part of the text you want help with.

Accept what your writers' group shares as a gift, one you cannot give yourself. Listen openly to understand different perspectives.

Question your writers' group about things you do not understand. Talk with them to gain clarity, not to defend your writing.

Thank your writers' group for sharing their honest reactions to your writing so you can learn from different perspectives.

Decide what you will do with the responses offered. Remember, you are in the driver's seat. It's your voice and your message!

Responding to writing

Listen with your full respect and attention, without interruption or judgment, to what the text and author are "saying."

Notice your reactions at various points. What voice emerges from the text? Where does it speak most to you? Where do you stumble, become confused, or get lost? What questions arise?

Decide what is most important to share with the author — it can be overwhelming to describe and/or hear all your thoughts. Be sure to respond to the author's focusing question directly.

Share your responses in a manner that is supportive and encouraging, not judgmental or challenging. Avoid input on spelling and grammar unless asked.

Thank the author for sharing the gift of the writing and enabling you to learn from the text and the author's writing process.

---

2 Reflecting on sharing and responding to writing

a. Take a few minutes to reflect on how it felt to be part of a writers' group, sharing your own writing and responding to another person's writing.

- What was easy and what was hard?

- What did you learn about writing by doing this?

- What did you learn about scientific explanations?

Teaching Investigation

25 MINUTES

1 Exploring student ideas about conduction

    a. Review the debate among the Ice-First, Hand-First, and Two-Way Street parties (pp. 6–7). What is logical about each party's stance?

    b. Analyze the students' initial box and arrow diagrams for conduction (p. 8). What do they seem to understand about heat energy and conduction? What *learning gaps* are you finding?

 IDENTIFYING LEARNING GAPS

A **learning gap** describes something students can't yet do or don't yet know, but if they could do it or did know it, their responses would be correct and complete. Learning gaps stand in the way of students reaching proficiency in their understandings. For example, many students do not know that air is made of matter and has mass. This is a learning gap that prevents them from accurately understanding air pressure — if they do not yet know that air is made of matter and has mass, then air pressure is an extremely difficult concept to grasp.

c. Analyze the last box and arrow diagrams students created (pp. 11–12). What do students now seem to understand about heat energy and conduction? What learning gaps are you finding?

2 **Thinking about tradeoffs**

a. Discuss the benefits and limitations of the following teaching tools. Start with the one that interests you the most, as you might not have time to discuss them all. For each tool, think about these questions: In what ways is this tool useful in understanding energy? In what ways is it potentially misleading? Would you use it with students? Why or why not?

- Using the phrase "meet in the middle" to describe what happens with conduction

- Box and arrow diagrams

- Energy tree diagrams

Classroom Connection

40 MINUTES

20 MINUTES **1** Reviewing key concepts

a. Individually, read the Science Review and Literacy Review on the following pages. Feel free to pick and choose the sections that are most valuable to you.

As you read, take notes and think about these questions:

- What is interesting or new to you?

- Which examples and images do you find especially helpful?

- What are you still wrestling with?

b. Individually, take a few minutes to think and write about your own big takeaways from today.

2 Exploring the ideas of this session

    a. As a group, discuss the Science and Literacy Reviews. Use the questions on the previous page as a guide.

3 Considering classroom implications

    a. Based on your experiences today, discuss implications for *what* and *how* you teach your students.

Session Review

SCIENCE REVIEW

Understanding heat energy requires an understanding of the nature of atoms. Atoms are in constant motion, even in solid objects, and because atoms are in motion, they can do work and they have energy — heat energy. Because all atoms are in motion, all matter has heat energy. Because heat energy is so common, it is no surprise that heat energy is constantly being transferred from place to place and that such transfers are important parts of understanding the world around us.

SCIENCE ▸ **KEY CONCEPT**

Conduction between objects stops when their temperatures become equal — even if the objects still have different amounts of heat energy. When two objects of different temperature come into direct contact with one another, conduction occurs. The hotter object will increase the temperature of the cooler object. Once the two reach the same temperature, somewhere between their initial temperatures, conduction ceases. This is true whether or not the two objects have the same amount of heat energy. For example, if a paper clip is dropped into a cup of hot coffee, the two will quickly reach the same temperature, but the coffee will still have more heat energy.

SCIENCE ▸ **KEY CONCEPT**

If the atoms and molecules of substances did not move, conduction would not occur. Conduction is a spontaneous form of heating that occurs when a hotter object's faster-moving particles collide with a colder object's slower-moving particles. In the collision, motion is transferred — causing the faster-moving particles to slow down and the slower-moving particles to speed up. This spontaneous transfer reaches an equilibrium (i.e., no net change) when the motion of all the particles in both objects averages out — in other words, when their temperatures equilibrate.

SCIENCE ▸ **KEY CONCEPT**

Heat energy and temperature both increase when an object is heated, but they are not the same things. On an atomic level, when objects are heated, their particles, atoms, and molecules move faster. This increase in particle motion means an object feels hotter (i.e., has a higher temperature) and the object can do more work, or cause more change (i.e., has more heat energy). Temperature relates to the average kinetic energy of the particles of a substance — faster-moving and/or more massive particles result in higher temperatures. Heat energy is the total kinetic energy of every particle in the substance. Therefore, it is possible for two objects at the same temperature to have different amounts of heat energy, just as it is possible for two objects with the same amount of heat energy to have different temperatures.

◉ Conduction and temperature

Conduction is the spontaneous warming of colder objects by hotter objects. This warming is caused by the particles (e.g., atoms and molecules) of matter literally bumping into each other and transferring motion. As a result of these collisions, the average kinetic energy of the colder object's particles goes up and so does the object's temperature.

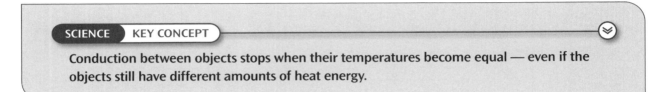

SCIENCE **KEY CONCEPT**

Conduction between objects stops when their temperatures become equal — even if the objects still have different amounts of heat energy.

During the Science Investigation, you observed the water temperature in two containers change until both reached the same temperature, as shown by the graphs below.

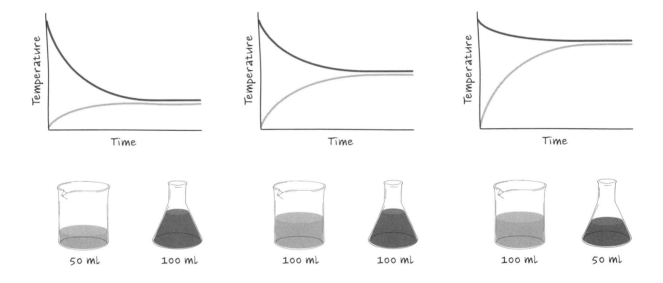

These graphs show conduction stops when objects reach the same temperature — the temperature at which one no longer spontaneously warms the other. Conduction stops when both objects' particles have the same average kinetic energy. This makes sense because if the particles in both objects have the same average kinetic energy, then there will be no overall change in the average kinetic energy when their particles collide. While individual particles may speed up or slow down as a result of collisions, the overall average kinetic energy remains the same. Therefore the temperature remains the same.

Often when students do similar investigations in classrooms, they see conduction stopping when the temperature of two objects (or liquids) reaches the average of their starting temperatures (or close to it). For example, you may have observed this in the Beaker & Flask Lab when the volumes of hot and cold water were equal. This resulted in the ending temperatures being roughly halfway between the starting temperatures.

While this "meet in the middle" result is accurate in this one instance, limited experience can contribute to the common, yet incorrect idea that conduction always stops at the average (or middle) temperature. However, this is only true when two objects are made of the same exact substance and have the same volume (mass). Reaching a temperature that is halfway between the starting temperatures is the exception rather than the rule.

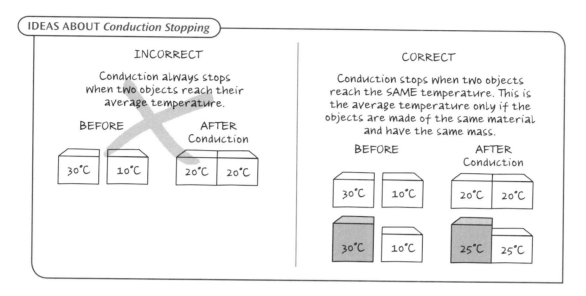

The origin of this incorrect idea may simply be that it's logical to think about conduction as "temperature sharing" and to think about sharing as splitting things in half. Another potential source of this incorrect idea is limited experience with conduction — for example, doing only investigations in which equal volumes of the same substances are used.

When equal volumes of the same substance in the same phase are used in conduction experiments (e.g., a beaker and flask that have equal volumes of water), conduction also happens to stop when the objects reach their average heat energy. Results like these can suggest that the reason conduction stops is because the two objects reach their average heat energy. However, sharing heat energy half and half is also the exception, rather than the rule.

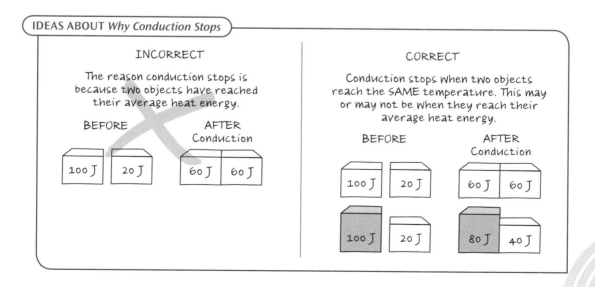

It feels logical that conduction would result in equal heat energies because heat energy is what is transferred in conduction, and it seems like the transfer should continue until both objects have equal amounts of heat energy. Yet this is true only in very limited circumstances.

Direction of conduction

Conduction spontaneously takes place whenever there is a difference in temperature regardless of how much heat energy each object has associated with it. Conduction doesn't always end with equal temperatures or with equal heat energies, but it always proceeds in only one direction — from warmer objects to cooler objects.

Conduction: a One-Way Street

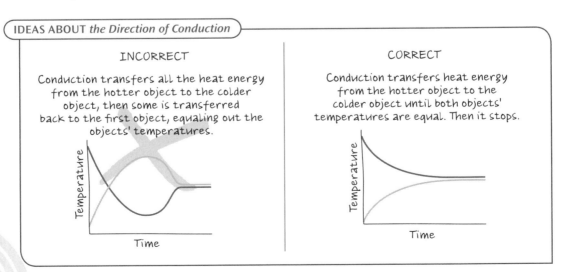

Conduction is a one-way street — hotter objects cool down and colder objects warm up until their temperatures become equal. Once their temperatures are equal, their temperatures don't change (unless other external conditions, for example, colder surrounding air, continue the process of transferring heat energy).

The data you collected in the Beaker & Flask Lab reflect this one-way-street nature of conduction. The water in the beaker got warmer and warmer, yet its temperature never got higher than the water in the flask. At the same time, water in the flask got cooler and cooler, yet its temperature never got lower than the water in the beaker. The temperatures always met somewhere between their starting temperatures.

Despite the one-way nature of conduction, it's not uncommon for people to think of conduction as two-way street — where all the hotter object's energy is transferred to the colder object and then some is transferred back, equalizing the two objects' temperatures.

IDEAS ABOUT *the Direction of Conduction*

INCORRECT

Conduction transfers all the heat energy from the hotter object to the colder object, then some is transferred back to the first object, equaling out the objects' temperatures.

Temperature

Time

CORRECT

Conduction transfers heat energy from the hotter object to the colder object until both objects' temperatures are equal. Then it stops.

Temperature

Time

Many people find the two-way-street idea logical because conduction is a kind of sharing, and often sharing can be considered a two-way street. For example, two working parents may deposit their entire paychecks into the same bank account and then take out what their family needs as they need it. Without understanding the mechanics of conduction, it is easy to think conduction works in a similar way, with both objects first "giving up" their heat energy and then taking some back.

⊙ Conduction at an atomic level

Conduction relies on particles (e.g., atoms and molecules) colliding with one another. In solids, this motion is *vibrational* — the particles oscillate and in the process bump into neighboring particles. In liquids and gases, the motion is *translational* — the particles move more like marbles rolling on the floor or balls on a pool table, colliding and ricocheting off one another.

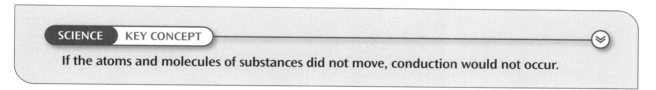

SCIENCE ❯ KEY CONCEPT

If the atoms and molecules of substances did not move, conduction would not occur.

In conduction, when faster-moving particles collide with slower-moving particles, two things happen — there are changes in motion *and* changes in energy. In terms of motion, the faster-moving particles slow down when they collide with slower-moving particles, causing the slower-moving particles to speed up. In terms of energy, the faster-moving particles transfer some kinetic energy to the slower-moving particles.

BEFORE collision   AFTER collision

Lots of KE   Little KE   Loses KE   Gains KE

During the Science Investigation, you simulated conduction using balloons. While not all balloons (water molecules) were moving in the same way and at the same speed, the balloons representing the hotter water should have been moving more rapidly on average. They had lots of kinetic energy. The balloons representing the colder water should have been moving slower on average. They had less kinetic energy.

In many ways, the balloon simulation is useful for understanding what physically happens during conduction, but like all models it has limitations. First, if the balloons were really water molecules, they would have translational motion (similar to balls on a pool table), plus rotational and vibrational motion. In the simulation, you likely remained in relatively fixed positions with your balloons vibrating (more akin to the motion of particles in a solid, less like balls on a pool table). Second, the balloons in the simulation experienced less-than-perfect transfers of kinetic energy from the faster-moving balloons to the slower-moving balloons. Some of this was a result of how people physically moved the balloons, but in addition, some of the balloons' kinetic energy was actually transferred into heat energy vibrating the balloons' own molecules. In reality, during conduction the particles (e.g., molecules) are the things colliding, so all the energy transfer happens at a molecular level, resulting in changes in the motion of the molecules themselves.

A related limitation of this simulation is in its application to the Beaker & Flask Lab. In the Beaker & Flask Lab, the hotter water is not in direct contact with the colder water because they are separated by the glass walls of the flask. Therefore, what actually happens is that the faster-moving water molecules collide with the glass particles of the flask, increasing the vibration of those glass particles. Then these faster-vibrating glass particles knock into the molecules of colder water in the beaker, making them move faster. In this way, heat energy conducts from the warmer water in the flask to the glass walls of the flask, then the glass walls of the flask conduct heat energy to the water in the beaker. This same process of conduction also takes place from the water in the beaker to the particles of glass in the beaker and then to the particles that make up the cooler surrounding air.

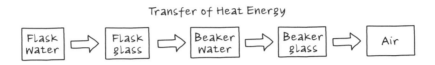

Transfer of Heat Energy

Flask water ⟹ Flask glass ⟹ Beaker water ⟹ Beaker glass ⟹ Air

In the end, the temperature of the beaker goes up, but *not* because "hot" is being transferred to the beaker or because "cold" is being transferred to the flask. Hot and cold are relative temperatures. They are indications of the average kinetic energy of a substance, not a "thing" or some kind of fluid or matter that can move from object to object. Although it's true that heat energy transfers from object to object, this is an exchange of motion, *not* the exchange of a physical thing.

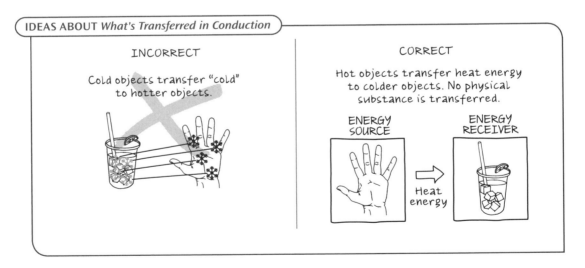

IDEAS ABOUT *What's Transferred in Conduction*

INCORRECT

Cold objects transfer "cold" to hotter objects.

CORRECT

Hot objects transfer heat energy to colder objects. No physical substance is transferred.

ENERGY SOURCE

ENERGY RECEIVER

Heat energy

The idea that "cold" transfers seems logical because of what we feel when we touch cold things. When you grab a cold drink, it feels as if cold is entering your hand. In reality, neither cold nor hot moves from place to place. Said in another way, no physical objects or substances move from one object to another during conduction.

Good conductors and poor conductors

Whether an object is a good conductor or a poor conductor (an insulator) depends on the type of material (e.g., glass, metal, air) and the density of the substance. The denser a substance, the better a conductor it is likely to be. Therefore, solids typically warm and cool by conduction faster than liquids and gases do. The following diagrams represent arrangements of particles in a solid and particles in a gas. In real life, these particles would all be moving. In solids, particles are packed closer together, increasing the likelihood a vibrating particle will collide with another particle. In liquids and gases, the particles are further apart, meaning they have a lower likelihood of banging into each other and transferring their motion to each other.

Particles in a solid

Particles in a gas

One reason materials such as snow, neoprene, wool, and dry wood do not conduct well is that they trap air inside them. Because air has a very low density, meaning the particles in air are quite far apart compared with the particles in a solid, the particles in air do not collide as frequently, so they can't transfer kinetic energy as quickly as a solid does. This is why people use neoprene koozies around their ice-cold drinks to slow the rate of conduction from their warm hands. Similarly, a cardboard sleeve around a hot drink slows the rate of conduction into our hands. This keeps our hands from getting burned and the drink from cooling as quickly.

The area of contact between materials is also important for conduction. If you pick up a cup of hot coffee and wrap your hand all the way around it, there is more conduction happening than if you pick up the cup of coffee with two fingers. This is because there is a smaller cross-sectional area of direct contact between you and the cup.

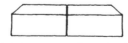

Larger area of contact, More conduction

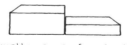

Smaller area of contact, Less conduction

◉ Comparing conduction, radiation, and convection

Conduction is just one of the ways objects are heated. Radiation and convection are also mechanisms for heating and cooling (less precisely known as forms of heat energy transfer). The three are similar in that energy is always transferred from hotter objects to colder objects, however the mechanisms are quite different.

In particular, conduction, radiation, and convection differ in terms of *where* they occur. Conduction can occur any time two objects — be they solid, liquid, or gas — come into direct contact with one another. Convection, however, occurs only in fluids (i.e., liquids, gases, and plastic solids, such as parts of Earth's mantle) and only when these fluids have inconsistent temperatures. Radiation is unique because it transfers energy through empty space. It does not need objects to be touching or fluids to be at different temperatures. With radiation, once matter emits photons (electromagnetic radiation), the photons can actually pass through a vacuum.

Conduction, radiation, and convection also differ in terms of what actually occurs. In other words, the mechanism by which energy is transferred in each is different. In conduction, objects are heated when they come into direct contact with matter of a higher temperature, yet the matter of the two objects does not mix. Instead the temperature (and heat energy) of the cooler object increases as a result of the random collisions with the hotter object's faster-moving particles. With radiation, photons are absorbed by objects. During this process, the photons' energy is transferred into heat energy, increasing the motion of the particles in the substance that absorbed the photons. In convection, the temperature in a particular region increases because a warmer parcel of fluid (e.g., air) moves into the region at the same time the temperature of another region decreases as a colder parcel moves in. This movement of parcels also results in the mixing of particles, so eventually conduction between the parcels can equalize the temperature between parcels and convection stops.

An important characteristic of convection is that it literally moves matter and, as a result, heat energy to new locations. By contrast, conduction only transfers heat energy. Matter does *not* move as a result of conduction.

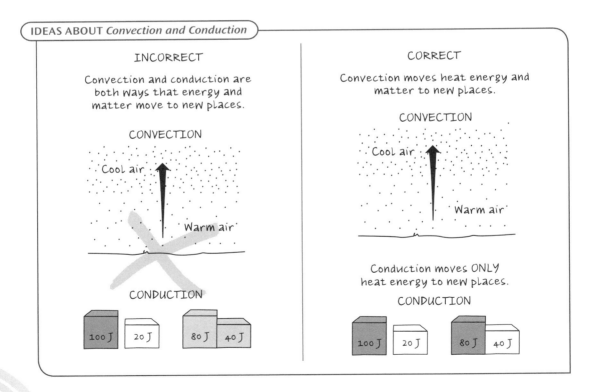

IDEAS ABOUT *Convection and Conduction*

INCORRECT

Convection and conduction are both ways that energy and matter move to new places.

CONVECTION

Cool air

Warm air

CONDUCTION

100 J   20 J   80 J   40 J

CORRECT

Convection moves heat energy and matter to new places.

CONVECTION

Cool air

Warm air

Conduction moves ONLY heat energy to new places.

CONDUCTION

100 J   20 J   80 J   40 J

This incorrect idea about convection and conduction likely arises from misconceptions about the important difference between matter and energy. We tend to think about energy as having mass and being some type of matter, but it is not. Conduction and convection both move heat energy to new locations, but by entirely different mechanisms. Convection moves heat energy because it moves matter.

In the Science Investigation, you explored the relationships between heat energy, conduction, convection, and temperature by constructing a mind map. A sample correct answer follows.

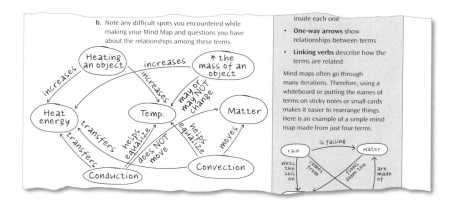

When constructing a mind map, your group may have spent time clarifying what is meant by the term *heat* and the term *cold*. It's often helpful to think about *cold* as being a range of temperatures, as opposed to a tangible thing as much of our everyday language suggests. For example, when we hear the phrase "close the refrigerator door, you're letting the cold out," we are talking about cold as if it is some sort of gas that can be "let out" of a refrigerator. More precisely, it is not *cold* coming out of the fridge as we stand there trying to decide what to munch on, it is air that has a cold temperature.

It is also important to note that a *cold temperature* means different things to different people. For example, a Canadian may think –10°F is cold, while a Floridian may think 30°F is cold. Using relative temperature words, such as hotter and colder, helps emphasize the difference in temperature rather than suggesting an empirical temperature. For example, the phrase "the hotter objects conduct heat energy to the colder objects" allows for both objects to be *hot* (e.g., 120°C and 100°C) or both objects to be *cold* (e.g., 0°C and –10°C).

A similar source of confusion for the term *heat* arises from a common, but incorrect definition. Very often, the term *heat* is defined as *the motion of particles*. However, upon closer inspection this definition is problematic. For example, if *heat* is defined as the motion of particles, we'd have to say, "hotter objects *the motion of particles* cooler objects by conduction." That doesn't make any sense!

A way to avoid this quagmire is to think about the term *heat* as a verb meaning *to increase the temperature*. Defined this way, *heat* is no more "the motion of particles" than *kinetic* is "the motion of an individual object." The motion of particles is the motion of particles, and the motion of an individual object is the motion of an individual object — motion is not energy! *Heat energy* is the type of energy associated with the random, unorganized motion of all the particles in an object, much like *kinetic energy* is the type of energy associated with the motion of an individual object.

◉ Differentiating heat energy and temperature

When warming a pot of water on the stove, you increase both the temperature and the heat energy of the water. Increases in temperature and heat energy both result from the molecules of water moving faster on average. When the water molecules move faster, they have a greater average kinetic energy and their total kinetic energy increases. The water's temperature is directly related to the *average* kinetic energy of the water molecules. The water's heat energy is the *total* amount of kinetic energy of all the water molecules.

SCIENCE **KEY CONCEPT**

Heat energy and temperature both increase when an object is heated, but they are not the same things.

Because temperature and heat energy quantify different things, it's possible for two objects to have the same temperature, yet different amounts of heat energy. It's also possible for two objects to have the same amount of heat energy, yet different temperatures. For example, an iceberg has more heat energy than a cup of hot tea. This is because the total heat energy associated with an object is based on the collective mass of its particles and how fast they are moving. An iceberg has lots and lots of slow-moving particles and that adds up to lots and lots of heat energy.

As you explored the Beaker & Flask Lab data, you probably made several realizations about heat energy. When you looked at the T-chart showing changes in heat energy (ΔHE) for water in the flasks and beakers, you may have noticed the amount of heat energy lost by the flask was often similar to the amount of heat energy gained by the beaker. In a perfect world, these numbers would be identical. However, in actuality heat energy is also transferred to the external environment, so the water in the beaker often gains less heat energy than the water in the flask loses.

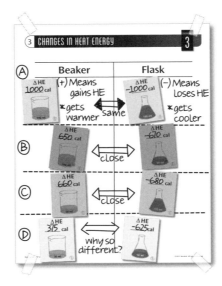

One way to reduce the transfer of heat energy away from a system (e.g., the Beaker & Flask setup or your head) is to use an insulator, like a wool stocking cap or Styrofoam cooler. Insulators work by putting a layer of air — a poor conductor of heat energy — between the object and its surroundings, not by providing heat energy to the system.

Our everyday experiences tell us wool hats, flannels sheets, and fuzzy clothes are warm, but they are not any warmer than the surrounding environment — not unless you, the dryer, or something else has warmed them. Instead, these objects are insulators. They reduce the rate at which heat energy is transferred away from your body, and this in turn keeps your temperature up. If high winds remove the warmed air trapped in your wool hat, you will still feel cold despite the hat because you are continually warming a new layer of colder air.

LEARNING OBJECTIVES

Conduction and Convection

3.1 Conduction is the spontaneous *transfer of heat energy* from a hotter object to a colder object. Conduction stops when the average kinetic energies of the particles in objects are the same.

3.2 Convection is a *movement of matter* driven by differences in density. As the matter moves, the heat energy it carries moves with it.

3.3 Conduction and convection can occur together (e.g., hot air rises by convection and then its heat energy can transfer to nearby colder air by conduction).

Heat Energy and Temperature

3.4 An object's heat energy is the sum of the kinetic energy each particle in the object has as a result of its random, unorganized motion.

3.5 Temperature is an indication of the average kinetic energy of the particles in a substance.

3.6 It is possible for two objects at the same temperature to have different amounts of heat energy. It is also possible for two objects with the same amount of heat energy to be at different temperatures.

3.7 Sunlight has light energy, not heat energy, associated with it. When objects absorb light, their temperatures increase (i.e., LE is transferred to HE).

3.8 Heat energy and temperature both increase when an object is warmed because its particles move more. This increase in motion means the object has a higher temperature *and* has more heat energy.

MISCONCEPTIONS

3.A It is incorrect to think of conduction as "cold" transfer. A cold temperature (a low average molecular motion) is not a physical "thing" that can transfer or flow between objects, nor is it the opposite of heat energy.

3.B It is incorrect to think that when objects are in direct contact, the hotter object gives all its heat energy to the colder object and then takes back however much heat energy it "needs." Conduction is a one-way street that stops when temperatures are equal.

3.C It is incorrect to think that conduction equalizes the amount of heat energy each object has (that's only true if the objects are exactly the same mass and composition and in the same phase).

3.D It is incorrect to think insulators provide objects with heat energy. Instead, insulators reduce the conduction of heat energy away from warm objects.

3.E It is incorrect to think heat energy and temperature are the same things.

3.F It is incorrect to think adding a cold object to a container of warm liquid lowers the total heat energy of the container. Instead, there is more mass in the container, thus there is more total heat energy, even if the overall temperature is lower.

3.G It is incorrect to think temperature is a physical "thing" that can be transferred during conduction.

The desire to make sense of the world around us starts with questions. What makes a double rainbow? Why did only some of my friends get sick? How do you get energy from a drink? Working to explain such things is the heart of science, so it makes sense that specific conventions have developed for writing scientific explanations. Such writing conventions anticipate that the audience might be a skeptical crowd that needs convincing and ultra-clear descriptions of new ideas. A good way to practice these science conventions and learn to write for an audience that demands a clear and compelling explanation is to share drafts of your writing with others. By listening to how people respond, where they get lost, and the questions they have, writers can improve their writing, and in the process, they also come to think more clearly about the science behind an explanation.

LITERACY KEY CONCEPT

Satisfactorily explaining an idea in science means writing a claim supported by evidence and describing the reasoning that links the claim and the evidence. Scientifically speaking, claims are statements that address a problem or question. Evidence is a description of the data that come from an investigation, an observation, and reports of research done by others. Reasoning is a description of the logical relationship between a claim and the evidence, which is often justified by using a scientific principle to point out the connection.

LITERACY KEY CONCEPT

Getting responses to drafts can improve your thinking and writing. Giving responses can do the same. The primary purpose for responding to another person's writing is to help the author recognize the strength of the written text and know more about what, where, and how to revise the writing to improve its message and voice. Sharing your responses (e.g., convinced, puzzled, overwhelmed, entranced) can push the author's thinking. At the same time, reading and talking about another person's writing can give you ideas for how to improve your own writing, not to mention that it stretches you to think, ponder, and question ideas in new ways.

◉ Writing scientific explanations

Although observing, documenting, and describing phenomena are critical aspects of science, they do not hold the same power as explaining. The drive to explain phenomena is at the heart of many scientists' work. In our everyday language, an explanation takes many forms. Compare the meaning of these examples: What is a logical explanation for your actions? Can you explain how I get to the nearest gas station? Is there a reason for that large jump in the stock price? In the world of science, the basic form of an explanation begins with making a claim or statement you believe to be true, followed by evidence (e.g., factual information or data) that supports the claim and a discussion that describes the reasons that form a logical link between the claim and the evidence.

Satisfactorily explaining an idea in science means writing a claim supported by evidence and describing the reasoning that links the claim and the evidence.

During the Literacy Investigation, people took turns sharing and responding to each other's written explanations of conduction. By reading and hearing several examples, you may have noticed that writers faced a variety of challenges. Some people struggled to write a clear, concise claim. Others were figuring out what counts as evidence so they could support or refute their claim. Most likely, reasoning was a bugaboo for nearly everyone.

Writing a claim

In science, claims are simple, proposed answers to scientific questions. Claims state a possible answer without going into the reasons people should believe the claim or how the claim fits with what is already known about the world. For example, the claim "Students prefer soda over juice" answers the scientific question "What beverages do students prefer?"

Notice a claim is different from a summary statement. A summary statement often just puts data into words. For example, "Nearly 63% of students prefer soda over juice" is a summary statement. A claim is broader and more general than a summary statement. Claims can be supported by multiple sources of related data. However, when writing a claim, it is also important to not overpromise and stretch beyond the scope of the evidence the claim can support. For example, saying "Students' favorite drink is soda" is an overstretch if the only data collected were about soda, juice, and milk.

In summary, good claims:

- Answer a scientific question

- Do not just summarize or restate the data

- Can be supported by multiple sources of data

Writing about evidence

Evidence includes data points and data summaries that can be used to support and justify the accuracy of a claim. Good evidence is compelling and logically connected to the claim. Good evidence makes you believe the claim. It tells you how the claim is known to be true. For example, good evidence for the claim "Students prefer soda over juice" might be "An overwhelming majority of students, 942 out of a sample of 1,000, consistently preferred soda over juice, even when offered a variety of juices."

Data are not the same thing as evidence. Data are what are collected during experiments, interviews, and direct observations. For example, if 1,000 students were asked if they prefer soda or juice, a piece of data would be "Sarah preferred soda over juice." Data summaries are generalizations about the data or descriptions of patterns in the data, for example, "More than 90% of students preferred soda over juice." Neither data nor summary statements explain anything on their own. They simply represent the facts using words, numbers, and graphs.

In summary, good evidence:

- Clearly and squarely supports the claim (i.e., it is not vague or only semirelated)

- Reduces doubt by addressing the most controversial or hardest-to-validate part of a claim

- Comes from multiple sources of data and different kinds of data

Writing about reasoning

While making claims and supporting them with evidence is difficult in its own right, it's even harder to craft full-fledged scientific explanations. This is partly because the reasoning aspect of scientific explanations is tricky, and most people have had little practice with it. In order to substantiate a claim with reasoning, a writer has to describe how the claim and its supporting evidence connect with what is already known about the world around us.

Reasoning includes things such as scientific principles, theories, and laws. It tells why the claim and evidence make sense. Reasoning fits the claim and evidence together with other things we know about science and the natural world. One strategy for doing this is to brainstorm a list of potentially applicable principles and then choose the ones that are best related to the claim and the most meaningful.

Good reasoning, like good evidence, must be logically connected to the claim. It should also offer an explanation of why the claim is reasonable. For example, supporting the beverage choice claim with ample compelling evidence might make you believe it, but you'd still want to know why students prefer soda to juice. Good reasoning helps to answer this *why* question and shows how the claim and evidence fit in with what else is known about the topic. An example of reasoning could be "Existing studies X and Y have found similar patterns in the beverage-choice data among students" or "Studies have proven (1) sleep-deprived people drink more caffeine than non-sleep-deprived people, and (2) students are often sleep-deprived. Therefore students may prefer soda over juice due to its caffeine content."

In summary, good reasoning:

- Makes a logical connection between a claim and supporting evidence

- Identifies existing theories and laws that link smaller events/experiments with larger phenomena or principles

- Offers a plausible explanation for *why* the claim and evidence fit

◉ Getting and giving responses

Throughout our lives we get advice (whether we want it or not) from many types of people. For example, parents might give advice about anything from table manners to what to do with our lives. A teacher might suggest how to go about completing an assignment or a doctor will describe what to do when recovering from surgery. Writers' groups offer something different. In a writers' group, the feedback is peer-to-peer, author-to-author.

Rather than giving advice on what to do (or not do), responders in a writers' group "try on" a piece of text for the author and share their reactions to it. Instead of the author being a passenger on someone else's journey (or vision of how a piece should be written), the author is the driver, the one who poses questions to guide the feedback, and ultimately chooses how to revise the text to convey the intended message. Such "test drives" with a supportive audience provide insights authors can't offer themselves. Over time, this kind of public reflection about writing helps writers become better at self-assessment, which in turn strengthens the quality of their writing.

LITERACY · KEY CONCEPT

Getting responses to drafts can improve your thinking and writing. Giving responses can do the same.

During the Literacy Investigation when you took turns getting and giving responses, you may have felt anxious about sharing your unfinished writing or concerned about telling other people how you reacted to their writing. But you likely felt other things too. Perhaps you were surprised by someone's perspective, relieved when others pointed out gems in your writing, frustrated that your words didn't convey the meaning you intended, or excited to find a solution to a writing problem. This makes sense, because writing is personal. Sharing your writing takes something about you and makes it public. This act of sharing required you to take a bold step and stretch your thinking. However, through this collaborative process, you likely learned some new things — new things about your own writing, about conduction and energy, and about working with others around writing.

Getting responses

Asking for responses from readers is acknowledging a truth about writing — that written text does not take shape all at once in fluent sentences and organized paragraphs. In fact, for complex tasks such as writing scientific explanations, the journey can be disorderly and unpredictable. While it is helpful to embrace the fact that writing is revising and that responses can strengthen the quality of writing, it is also helpful to know that it takes practice in order to get useful responses.

Figuring out what you're struggling with in a particular piece of writing is an important step in getting useful responses. Another important step is asking productive questions of your responder(s). During early drafts, productive questions are more likely to focus on content, organization, and clarity.

Content questions. Questions about content encourage responders to speak about the topic of the writing, for example:

* Am I missing something important? Is it complete?

* Do these feel like the right points? Are they accurate?

* Is there enough (or too much) detail? Is it precise enough?

Organization. Questions about organization encourage responders to speak about the structure and sequence of the writing, for example:

- Can you follow the flow of ideas?

- Where do you get lost?

- What are you noticing about how the ideas are organized? Do they follow a logical sequence? Are the ideas grouped in useful ways?

- In what ways does this organization work (not work) for you?

Clarity. Questions about clarity encourage responders to speak about how understandable the writing is, for example:

- Which parts made sense?

- Where did you find yourself getting confused?

- Could you imagine or visualize my intent with that part?

The questions suggested in the Literacy Investigation are aimed at the content, organization, and clarity aspects of the written text — the more *global* aspects of the writing. For example, they focus on how complete, accurate, and precise a scientific explanation is and how it is organized (claim, evidence, and reasoning). They also ask the responder to share information about which parts are more and less clear. You may have noticed that questions in the Literacy Investigation don't ask about small surface matters, such as spelling and grammar. This is because such *local* questions about sentence structure and mechanics encourage revisions of smaller matters — matters that pertain more to polishing a text than conceptualizing it.

While carefully choosing questions certainly steers responders in productive ways, you may have noticed that an author's stance toward receiving the comments and reactions of responders is also important. Listening without interruption is especially productive. In addition, authors get the most from responders when they work hard to understand the responders' perspectives and are prepared to think differently as a result. One way to maintain (or restore) a productive stance is for an author to invite comments about parts of the writing that worked well for the responders. This is a useful strategy, as there is often as much to learn from the gems of a text as there is to learn from the rust. Talking about the strongest parts helps writers visualize how to revise the weaker parts so they have sparkle and zing as well.

Giving responses

The primary purpose for responding to another person's writing is to serve as a *test audience* and *critical friend* for the writer. Responders can offer an outsider perspective the writer doesn't have. In return, responders are privy to the "gifts" of the text. They can learn from the unique strengths and challenges it presents.

A first step in giving productive responses is to understand the ways in which responding is different from evaluating, critiquing, or editing. To evaluate or critique means to stand in judgment of what is good or bad about the writing. And part of editing is identifying or fixing problems such as sentence structure and mechanics. In contrast, responding means sharing reactions to the words and images in the text. Responding involves providing comments and reactions related to the specific writing challenges identified by the author.

A second step in giving productive responses is making sure they are specific, descriptive, and relevant to the question(s) posed by the author. During the Literacy Investigation, you may have heard examples of productive responses such as these:

"Your first sentence felt clearly stated to me. It seemed like an opinion, but maybe it was a claim. I'm not sure because I couldn't figure out what question it might be answering."

"I know you wanted feedback about the evidence portion of your scientific explanation. I found this part especially strong. The way you showed a data table from your experiment and then described what it meant felt science-y."

"When I encounter statements in science that are written as *truths,* I expect supporting evidence, which I didn't find."

"I found myself feeling skeptical. Perhaps this was because all the evidence you presented was so convincing. This could be a good thing. But I know the world isn't so perfect, so it left me wondering if there was any evidence that refuted your claim or something you weren't sure about."

An especially useful stance for responders is to honestly share reactions to the writing and to serve as a collaborator who freely supports and encourages the writer without judging the writer. While a responder should avoid correcting writing errors, it is okay and good to bring up communication challenges you stumbled on or things you struggled to understand. It is also productive and helpful to identify the specific parts of the writing that are golden. Learning to get and give responses in productive ways takes practice. The next session's Literacy Investigation provides an opportunity to work again as a writers' group and build on this experience.

CONSERVATION OF ENERGY

Middle school students are often expected to learn about the law of conservation of energy and come to grips with the fact that energy is conserved within our vast universe. Yet our everyday language and experiences confound the issue. It is common for students to hear about energy getting used up or the need to conserve energy (really meaning energy resources) so we don't run out, as in: "Please turn off the lights, we need to conserve energy," "The ball stopped rolling because it ran out of energy," "It's time to change the batteries, those are all out of energy," or "I've about run out of energy, time for bed!" With these phrases in their minds, how do we move students toward thinking about the law of conservation of energy in the scientific meaning? How do we help them sort out when the law does and does not apply?

The teacher in this Teaching Case draws on a variety of approaches and scenarios to help students think about what happens with energy in the world around them. Students build and launch soda-bottle water rockets, discuss the effects of air resistance, explore resonant pendulums, and calculate energy associated with big rig trucks, motorcycles, speeding bullets, and soccer balls. They also contrast theoretical scenarios with real-world examples as they explore the law of conservation of energy.

As you read this Teaching Case, think about the following questions:

- How do students interpret the phrase *energy is never created or destroyed*?

- What do their calculations and conversations point out about what makes the law of conservation confusing?

- What do the real-world rocket launches show that students understand about energy? What about their calculations of the theoretical rocket launches?

Teaching Case

"LAW OR LIE"

Earlier this year my eighth graders had their first encounter with energy as they studied heat energy transfers in the context of global warming. Now they get to revisit energy as part of our rocket science curriculum. The rocket curriculum consists of five rocket launches focused on different physics mini units. I use the first rocket launch to assess my students' understanding of reference point, velocity, and acceleration. The second launch focuses on friction, gravity, and balanced/unbalanced forces. The third launch gets at Newtonian mechanics, and the fourth homes in on work and pressure. The fifth and final launch requires my students to analyze the rocket flight through the lens of energy.

My students make and launch their own soda-bottle water rockets constructed from plastic soda bottles and glued-on cardboard fins. To launch the rockets, students partially fill the bottles with water and use a bicycle pump to pressurize them with air. When the pump is removed, the pressure of the compressed air forces the water out of the bottle, propelling the rocket up and away in the opposite direction from the expelled water.

To determine the rocket's height at apogee, students use a homemade clinometer (a paper towel tube with a protractor attached to it) and a simple graphing tool. Then they use a stopwatch to measure the time from apogee to crashdown.

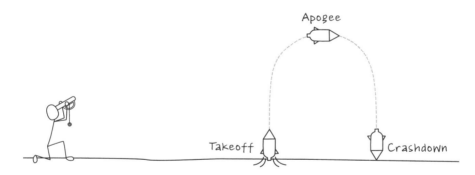

After collecting the data, students calculate different aspects of their rocket's flight, such as average velocity, acceleration, momentum, forces, and eventually energy. To help with these calculations, I have students use equation banks and a consistent format for solving problems called FSWAC (formula, substitute, work, answer, check). After each launch, they answer a series of questions requiring them to demonstrate their understanding of the concepts and numbers from their rocket's flight.

After the final rocket launch, my goal is for every student to be able to sufficiently answer the question "What makes my rocket move?" At the heart of this question lies a physics teacher's nemesis — the ungraspable, yet measurable energy. One day I hope my students understand energy as physicist Richard Feynman described it: "It is just a strange fact that we can calculate some number and when we finish watching nature go through her tricks and calculate the number again, it is the same."

Feynman's description of energy is straightforward and elegant. It's just perfect for physicists. However, I teach 8th grade. I've found kids have a hard enough time making sense of formulas related to energy and applying them, let alone wrapping their heads around the idea that energy is really just a numerical constant.

To understand conservation of energy, I believe my students must understand the quantitative nature of energy. But how can I teach the importance of energy being a measurable quantity if my students don't yet understand the law of conservation of energy? The two go hand in hand. Sometimes I feel like I'm trying to unravel the chicken from the egg.

Kinetic energy

We were partway into our rocket science curriculum. To get everyone focused on kinetic energy, a more graspable type of energy, I started class today by asking, "What comes to mind when you think about energy and motion at the same time?"

"I think of a bullet crashing through a car windshield while being chased by the police!" offered Raj, a big fan of action video games.

"Okay, that does have energy and motion in it, but can you think of something a little less violent?"

Mara, who dreams of being a professional soccer goalie, suggested, "Maybe someone kicking a soccer ball?"

"Yeah, and it smashes through a window!" interjected Raj.

Everyone burst into laughter. When they'd calmed down, I said, "Let's concentrate on the soccer ball before it hits the window. We know it's in motion. What other properties does the ball have?"

"It's round." "It's black and white." "It's filled with air."

"Aha!" I interrupted the flow of comments, "Now you are getting closer to a property that is important for energy. Can you think really scientifically?" I challenged.

"How about mass?" ventured Theo.

"Yes! The soccer ball has mass. Kinetic energy is the result of a mass being in motion, and how much mass there is really matters to how much kinetic energy, or KE, there is. Think of it this way. What if a motorcycle and a big 18-wheeler, traveling the same speed, hit each other? What is going to happen?"

"That's pretty violent…" Raj chided me.

"True, Raj. I stand chastised. But in the physics sense, what will happen?"

"The motorcycle will go flying!"

"Yes, the truck has a much greater *mass* — it has more kinetic energy and therefore more ability to cause damage, even though their speeds are the same."

Raj interjected, "So if I threw a ping pong ball at a window, it wouldn't break, but if I threw a…a…a…bowling ball, it would all be over."

"Indeed! In fact, we can relate the variables — mass and velocity — mathematically."

I wrote a definition and the formula for kinetic energy on the board, then continued, "Let's look at a different example in which the mass is the same but the speeds aren't. Against my better judgment, we'll go back to Raj's bullet. Say we threw a bullet at a glass window. It would bounce off, right? But if we give it more speed, say by firing it from a pistol, the bullet would go right through the window."

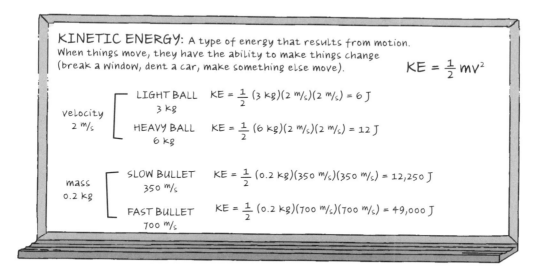

KINETIC ENERGY: A type of energy that results from motion. When things move, they have the ability to make things change (break a window, dent a car, make something else move).

$$KE = \frac{1}{2}mv^2$$

velocity 2 m/s

LIGHT BALL 3 kg $KE = \frac{1}{2}(3\ kg)(2\ m/s)(2\ m/s) = 6\ J$

HEAVY BALL 6 kg $KE = \frac{1}{2}(6\ kg)(2\ m/s)(2\ m/s) = 12\ J$

mass 0.2 kg

SLOW BULLET 350 m/s $KE = \frac{1}{2}(0.2\ kg)(350\ m/s)(350\ m/s) = 12,250\ J$

FAST BULLET 700 m/s $KE = \frac{1}{2}(0.2\ kg)(700\ m/s)(700\ m/s) = 49,000\ J$

Interestingly, students expected there would be a similar impact from changes in mass and changes in velocity. So they were really surprised when we worked the math and they saw that doubling the mass doubled the KE, but doubling the velocity quadrupled the KE!

After they practiced calculating KE for a few other scenarios, I had them work in pairs to make a Quick Tip with images and a few words to summarize the big ideas for the day.

When I looked at their Quick Tips, I felt most students had a good understanding of how mass and velocity affect KE.

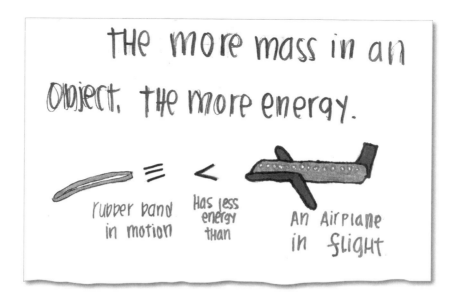

THE more mass in an object, THE more energy.

rubber band in motion   ≡ <   Has less energy than   An Airplane in flight

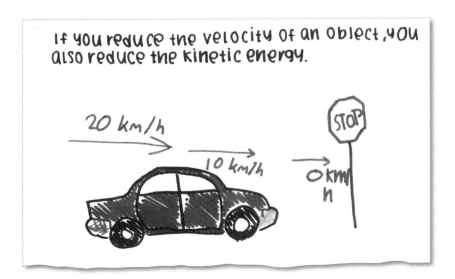

If you reduce the velocity of an object, you also reduce the kinetic energy.

20 km/h

10 km/h

0 km/h

STOP

With this understanding of kinetic energy and their prior work with gravitational potential energy, I felt my students were ready to embark on a journey to understand the law of conservation of energy.

Pendulum lab

We began with a classic experiment, the tried and true pendulum lab. Each group of 3–4 students arrived to find two ring stands connected by a string sitting on their table. I explained the pendulum setup and pointed out they would need to weigh down the ring stands to keep them upright. Stacks of books flew out of backpacks, and the strings between the stands tightened up. Then, I placed a pendulum "bob" made of a weighted film canister attached to a stiff coat-hook wire on each string. I also gave the kids a lab sheet with questions to guide their inquiry.

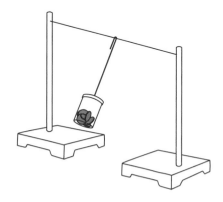

The questions were purposefully written to help students connect the changes in the pendulum system to the energy permitting the changes. For example, I asked, "What kind of energy does the velocity of the pendulum tell you about?" and "What kind of energy does the height of the pendulum's swing tell you about?" There were also questions prompting students to notice how the height and velocity of the pendulum swing changed over time.

Mara was the first to swing a pendulum and make a comment. "It's moving. See? There's kinetic energy."

I chuckled to myself, knowing she couldn't really see the KE, but I was glad to hear her practicing the new vocabulary and thinking.

Following her friend's lead, Collette jumped in. "It's getting lower and lower. Now it's wobbling. That must affect the energy."

Fidgeting turned into purposeful scientific inquiry (until someone realized tightening the pendulum string increased its elasticity, and a pendulum flew across the room).

I called out, "Hey, safety violation!" The class froze — I don't have to use the "safety violation" rule too often, but they know it means freeze. I continued calmly, "No launching pendulums, okay? Someone could get hurt." The guilty table apologized, and we got back to purposeful inquiry.

As they worked, I walked around. When I got over to Raj, Katie, and Theo's table, I asked, "What are you noticing about energy?"

Raj answered without taking his eyes off the pendulum. He pointed to where the pendulum was nearly parallel to the table and said, "It has lots of GPE here. It's like it's at its apogee. It has to have KE, too, because it's moving."

Theo nodded in agreement, but added nothing else to the explanation. Theo was writing ferociously in a worn black notebook. He's a quiet kid who never says much in class, but his writing is exceptional.

I overhead Mara telling Collette about how she knew the pendulum had KE and GPE because the pendulum had mass, velocity, and height. What I couldn't tell was whether she incorrectly thought the pendulum had equal amounts of each at every moment in time. Then I heard a disconcerting assertion behind me.

Katie was arguing the pendulum had the most energy at the lowest part of its swing because it had both KE and GPE, and the least energy at the top of the swing because it only had GPE. Her evidence was that the pendulum bob stopped for a split second at the top of its arc, so it didn't have KE at this point even though it had KE everyplace else.

Raj kept repeating, "You can't do that. You can't do that." But he didn't seem to know or be able to explain why.

"It sure does...look from the side. It stops right...there!" Katie belted out.

I leaned into the argument. "I know other students are thinking about something similar. In fact, I heard Mara and Collette compare their swinging pendulum bob to a falling ball. I think it helped them figure out what happened with velocity."

Raj, Katie, and Theo liked this comparison. "It's got to be a steady increase, like when you drop a ball. It's fastest...here," Theo remarks, pointing to the bottom arc of the swing.

"I guess," Katie admitted, a bit deflated, "I just can't see it. I know it stops at the top."

After 10 minutes of the class experimenting and writing, I called the activity to a halt and briefly introduced the law of conservation of energy. I said, "There is a famous law in physics that says energy can never be created or destroyed. Energy is conserved. This means the amount of energy that exists in the universe never changes. It can transfer from GPE to KE, or from KE to GPE" — I modeled the pendulum swing in slow motion — "or EPE to KE like with our rockets, but energy can't be destroyed. If it seems like energy is being destroyed or running out, or disappearing, then you need to look for the energy it's converted into." My kids wrote down the law dutifully in their notebooks. It seemed like an obvious no-brainer, so we moved on to resonant pendulums.

In a resonant pendulum, two pendulums transfer kinetic energy back and forth to each other. It's quite interesting. As soon as the first pendulum slows down and stops swinging, the second pendulum starts swinging. As soon as the second pendulum slows down and stops swinging, the first one starts up again. All you have to do to make a resonant pendulum is add another identical bob to the string about four inches away.

After a brief demonstration on the set up (and a rather lengthy student-centered discussion as to whether the plural form of pendulum was pendula, penduli, or pendulums), the investigation began.

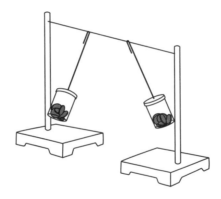

The "wow" factor was immediately apparent — Raj yelled, "Ah! Ah! Ah! That's so crazy! How do they do that?!"

After the initial surprise had subsided, I reminded the kids that they needed to finish their lab activity. "Alright, everyone use the See-Think-Puzzle routine on your lab sheet."

My thinking routines are scaffolds intended to develop a specific thinking disposition — in this case, inquiry. They are usually short and to the point, and if I use them often enough, my students internalize them. The routines that I use the most help kids separate observation from interpretation.

As usual, the most interesting question on today's routine was the puzzle question — *Puzzle: Given what you know about the law of conservation of energy, is there anything puzzling about the resonant pendulum?*

Most students, like Mara and Raj, were a bit confused about the difference between energy being destroyed and pendulum canisters stopping.

> Mara
>
> It's puzzling because the law states that energy cannot be destroyed, but the first canisters goes and stops, then the 2nd canisters goes then when it stops the first one goes. They create, destroy, create, destroy, over and over. But how can that be, when the law says you can't?

> Raj
>
> Yes, it is puzzling because the law of conservation of energy states that energy can't be created or destroyed but then how does it stop.

For homework, I gave a guided reading covering energy conversion, the conservation of energy, and friction converting kinetic energy into heat energy in pendulum systems. I hoped the reading would be meaningful — it directly addressed pendulums, which now fascinated my kids.

Defining the system

I began class today by going over their reading homework. It was clear from students' comments that everyone believed friction to be the reason the pendulums eventually stopped swinging. The reading had covered this and they had worked with friction on their second rocket launch, so I wasn't surprised that they surmised, "Friction did it." I also reviewed that the reason the bobs in the resonant pendulum system "took turns" swinging was because of energy transfers between them and the string.

I wanted to be sure my kids thought of friction as a force that did work on their pendulums, converting kinetic energy to heat energy. To reinforce this I had everyone rub their hands together while I described how friction works to convert the KE of their moving hands into the HE, raising the temperature.

"Alright, the law of conservation of energy states that energy cannot be created or destroyed in a system. However, it may be converted into nonuseful forms or transferred to nonuseful places. So in the pendulum system, heat energy is nonuseful because heat energy doesn't make pendulums swing. You are right to think KE is converted into HE in the air and then disperses around the room. Energy hasn't been destroyed, just transferred to different places and different types."

Theo was looking very puzzled and asked, "If all the air has energy in it from the pendulum, then couldn't the pendulum pick up some of that energy? Then it would keep moving even though it transferred energy to the air, right?"

To this comment many enthusiastic side conversations arose. Afraid we were diving into the abyss of perpetual motion, I interrupted them and directly addressed Theo's idea. I reminded them that energy is converted from KE to HE during the swing and explained that once the HE disperses throughout the room in multiple directions, it can't be pulled back into the pendulum and used for motion.

To demonstrate, I had one kid become a table-shaker, banging on the table, while others felt the vibrations. I explained the table-shaker's motion and the resulting motion of the table, classmates, and air molecules in the room could not be given back to the table-shaker to help the table-shaker continue shaking the table.

To help students think about the pendulum as moving within a system, I began a short lecture on systems.

First, I reminded my class about ecosystems and how they are composed of living and nonliving parts. From there I began to ask how we could similarly define the system of our classroom. After talking it through together, we concluded a physical system might be defined by the objects we see, plus things we can't see, such as forces and energy.

I drew a box on the board and said, "You know how I always tell you to think outside the box? When you define systems, it is really important to think *inside* the box." I drew the ring stands, string, pendulums, and a hand on the board and said, "If our view of the system is not very expansive, it could seem like energy is created or that it is lost. If you define the system as just the pendulum and your hand" — I drew a box around just my hand and the pendulum — "and you leave out the air, string, ring stands, and table, this might lead you to think that energy is lost. This is because you would be overlooking many of the places where energy is transferred."

As I erased the box I had drawn a moment ago, I said, "Now let's say you define the system as the pendulum, air, string, ring stands, and table, but leave out your hand." I drew a new box around these components and said, "In this system you might think energy was created because the pendulum just seems to gain energy out of nowhere."

I then went on to emphasize the role of forces in the system: "If you overlook unseen things like forces, then you are missing part of the story too. Say you overlook the force of friction between the pendulum and the air, and the pendulum and the string. Then you may forget how it converts KE into HE through work. Since HE is not useful for making a pendulum swing, it seems like energy is lost, but it's not. It just becomes HE that dissipates throughout the room in the air. Any time an object is moving through air, some of its KE is converted into HE in the air. The same is true if an object is moving through water — some of its KE is transferred to HE in the water."

My students were paying attention, speedily taking notes, and drawing diagrams. After the mini lecture, I had students practice defining systems. As a class we defined the resonant pendulum system. Then they worked in table groups to define the systems involved in the two labs we had done the prior week, one with bouncing balls and another with bows and arrows.

Launch in 24 hours

Our fifth rocket launch was scheduled for the next day, and students needed time to get everything ready, regluing fins and making last-minute design changes. They were excited about the launches and knew they would be collecting data to calculate their rocket's GPE at apogee and average KE at crashdown.

In preparation, I helped the class begin to define their rocket system. We brainstormed all of the objects and forces involved, but I left the discussion of energy out because this was part of what I wanted to assess in their lab writeups.

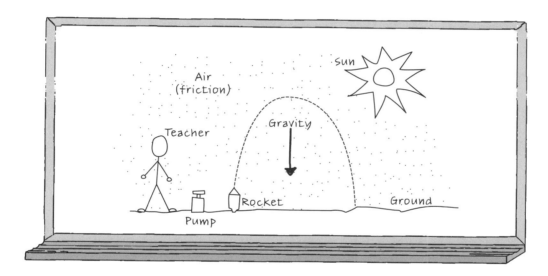

Real-world rocket launch

Today my students would need to use the equations for GPE and KE and make sense of their rocket flights. They'd done many other calculations with rocket data during previous labs (like speed, velocity, acceleration, force, momentum, and work), so I was confident they would be able to handle the algebra.

During this launch, one of my primary assessment objectives was to determine if the kids could correctly reason that the KE at crashdown should be much lower than the GPE at apogee because some of the KE was converted into heat energy by the force of friction between the rocket and the air.

I checked in with a few students before they began. Some predicted the KE and GPE should be equal when measured because energy will be conserved. Others said that GPE would be higher than KE because friction would heat the air.

I led the kids out to the field. The rocket launches were spectacular. At least three teams had flights of greater than 50 meters. As expected, a few crashed and burned, went way off course, or lost fins only to plummet toward the ground like birds of prey and leave dents the size of a fist in the soft dirt.

After cleaning up the intricate mess of scattered rocket pieces, we went back to class. The kids began to use the apogee angle data they collected to determine each rocket's maximum height. Then they used the mass of their rocket to calculate the GPE at apogee. While it was a less-than-perfect approximation of KE at crashdown, students used their stopwatch data to determine the average velocity and average KE. Every student correctly calculated that there was more GPE at apogee than KE at crashdown.

The last question on the Rocket Lab was telling — *Puzzle: Given what you know about the law of the conservation of energy, is there anything puzzling about your rocket flight? Why or why not?*

Nearly 75% of my students responded similarly to Raj, and I was glad to see most recognized the reason for the difference in the amount of energy at apogee and crashdown in their rocket launch.

Raj

There is nothing puzzling about my conclusion. The law of conservation of energy states that no energy can be created or destroyed, therefore none of the 91.14 joules of energy at apogee was destroyed. This mean that most of that energy was converted in to heat energy an un-useful form of energy due to friction.

Theo and the remaining 25% of my class firmly believed that the GPE and KE values should be the exact same for their rocket launch.

Theo

It is puzzling because the law of conservation of energy says that the amount of energy put into a system equals the amount of energy coming out. But the GPE was 104; and when it was converted, only 70.5; was present.

With a full quarter of the class showing some confusion about conservation of energy, I felt I needed to give them another chance to practice before we wrapped up. This time, as a contrast, I decided to leave the real world and dive into a theoretical example.

Theoretical rocket launch

When my students arrived, I handed out a reading assignment that described a fictional rocket launch in a *vacuum*. The reading had embedded data for calculating the GPE at apogee and the KE at crashdown. It also had many clues reinforcing that it took place in a vacuum, such as no sound, no wind, and a robot that didn't require air during the launch.

As students calculated the GPE at apogee and the KE a millisecond before crashdown, there was a lot of murmuring and rechecking of work. I was pleased because it made me think they were surprised the numbers for GPE and KE were equal.

Once students finished calculating the theoretical energies, I asked them to draw the system for this rocket launch and answer one final question — *Puzzle: Given what you know about the law of conservation of energy and rocket flights, is there anything puzzling about this rocket flight? Why or why not?*

I hoped my students would say it wasn't puzzling because in a vacuum there is no friction to convert KE into HE, and therefore the amount of GPE at apogee should equal the amount of KE at crashdown. I would have been nearly as happy if my students missed the lack of air in the system and said the flight was puzzling, because some energy should be transferred to HE during the flight.

It turns out about 50% of my students *were* puzzled that the numbers for GPE and KE were the same. Generally, their calculations were correct, but the logic was hard. Raj didn't draw air or friction in his system, so I expected he'd make sense of why the numbers were equal, but he didn't.

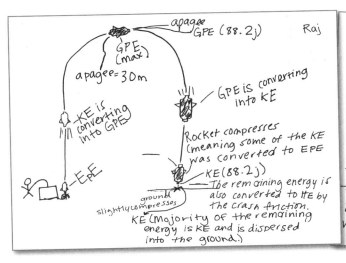

The other 50% of my students were not puzzled by the GPE at apogee and the KE at crashdown being exactly equal. I thought this was a good thing, until I realized many students were actually very pleased they *finally* had a rocket flight with the perfect conversions they'd expected since first hearing about conservation of energy. Theo thought the theoretical launch and calculations finally made perfect sense, even though he drew friction in his system (which there couldn't be) and talked about friction converting KE into HE.

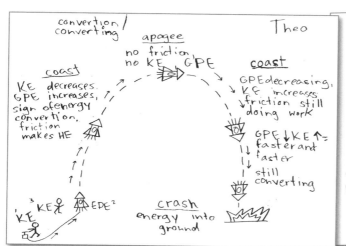

I guess the good news is that 25% of my students completely figured out the theoretical launch. Mara said, "There is nothing puzzling about this flight. There is no air, so there is no friction, so no KE is lost to HE when the rocket falls. The apogee GPE and crashdown KE should be equal." Collette said, "It's not puzzling, because why shouldn't the numbers match? There is no air in this system. No air. No Friction. No losing energy to HE."

The next day we reviewed all of the evidence in the story that pointed toward the system being a vacuum. Next, we compared the measured GPE and KE from their Rocket Lab with their values in the story. We also talked a lot about what friction is and isn't.

Unfortunately, I couldn't tell if this review made much difference to the students who believed this theoretical rocket flight *finally* showed a flight that *obeyed* the law of conservation of energy, when, in their opinion, no real rocket flights would.

Why is energy conserved? Many scientists, teachers, and students have pondered this very question. The answer is simpler than you might think. Energy is a numerical quantity that by definition is conserved within closed systems. Therefore, there is no other option but for energy to be conserved — it's defined that way. Before the child throws the bowling ball, there is just as much total energy present as after the pins go flying. It may be in different locations or in different types, but the total amount is equal.

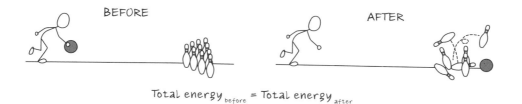

BEFORE   AFTER

Total energy$_{before}$ = Total energy$_{after}$

VOCABULARY

Kinetic energy (KE) is a type of energy that results from the motion of individual objects, be they large or small. The amount of KE depends on the object's velocity and mass according to the formula $KE = \frac{1}{2}mv^2$.

In physics, **work** is a measure of the energy transferred by a force that is acting over a distance. The amount of work, hence the change in energy, depends on the strength of the force and the distance it has been applied, according to the formula $W = Fd$, where $W = \Delta E$.

Friction (a.k.a. frictional force) is a pulling interaction between the atoms in two surfaces. The pulling force of friction works against an object's motion to slow it down or prevent it from moving. Drag is the equivalent of friction in fluids, such as air and water.

The **law of conservation of energy** states that energy cannot be created or destroyed because it is conserved within closed systems. **Closed systems** do not exchange matter or energy with any other systems. There are no inputs into a closed system, nor are there any outputs to other systems. In fact, "perfectly" closed systems only exist in theory.

A **scientific law** describes an observation of what occurs in nature and/or it describes a relationship that always applies under the same conditions (e.g., Newton's universal law of gravitation). Unlike theories, scientific laws do not attempt to explain *why* or *how* something happens, rather they describe *what* happens.

⦿ Does motion generate energy?

No. Energy is never generated, created, or made, not even when objects move. That's the law! This reality stems from how energy is defined — energy is a measurable quantity that describes how much change can happen in a system and is always conserved. Energy is an idea, a concept that has been invented by scientists to describe consistencies in what has been observed. The **law of conservation of energy** comes from scientists' conclusions that there was a certain amount of energy in the universe at the time it was created and that same amount of energy persists today — the energy is merely in different types as a result of the various interactions that have occurred between matter over the millennia. Scientists created the concept of energy as a tool to help understand these interactions between matter. The law of conservation of energy, like other **scientific laws,** does not explain *why* or *how* something happens, instead it describes what occurs in nature.

If the law says energy cannot be generated, then why is it so intuitive to think motion generates energy? Perhaps this is because we know something about windmills or water turbines being used to generate electricity. Perhaps it is because we have so many examples of something changing or happening as a result of moving objects. For example, moving air can push a sailboat, a moving car can smash and dent another car, and moving tectonic plates knock down buildings. However, just because things happen as a result of motion doesn't mean motion creates energy.

It is true that whenever any object moves, regardless of how large or small the object is, there is energy present. **Kinetic energy (KE)** is the type of energy that results from the motion of individual objects. The amount of KE depends on the object's velocity and mass according to the formula $KE = \frac{1}{2}mv^2$. For example, to determine the KE of a moving bowling ball (perhaps to determine how much damage it might do), substitute its mass (6.0 kg) and its velocity at impact (3.0 m/s) into the formula as shown in the following example.[1]

$$KE = \frac{1}{2}mv^2$$

$$KE = \frac{1}{2}(6.0 \text{ kg})(3.0 \text{ m/s})^2$$

$$KE = 27 \text{ J}$$

Knowing a bowling ball has 27 joules of KE is one thing, but understanding where that energy came from is another thing altogether. At first glance, it can seem like energy has been created in the ball. But energy can never be created (or destroyed), it can only be transferred from place to place and type to type. So if the moving bowling ball did not generate the energy, where did the energy come from?

---

[1] Technically, a rolling bowling ball also has some kinetic energy due to its rotation, which cannot be calculated using the formula $KE = \frac{1}{2}mv^2$. For simplicity's sake, all the upcoming calculations and examples involving the bowling ball ignore this amount of rotational kinetic energy.

One way to understand where this kinetic energy might have come from is to think in terms of systems. If the bowling ball itself is considered the system and there is no interaction (e.g., no push from a person and no collision with bowling pins), then there would be no change in the energy and no transfer of energy. However, earlier in time the bowling ball was at rest, so there must have been an input of energy to the bowling ball. One possibility is that a person's arm moved such that the KE of the arm was transferred to the KE of the bowling ball. Another possibility is that the bowling ball rolled from a higher height such that GPE was transferred to KE.

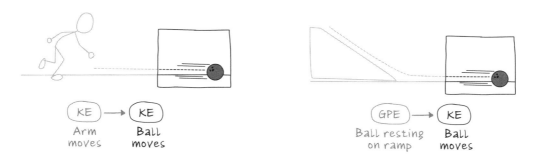

KE → KE
Arm   Ball
moves moves

GPE → KE
Ball resting Ball
on ramp   moves

◉ Do forces generate energy?

No. Energy is never generated, created, or made, not even when objects move. That's the law! That said, any interaction involving forces that are applied over a distance will result in a change in energy. This can make it appear as if forces generate energy.

Thinking about the rolling bowling ball in terms of forces is another way to understand changes in the kinetic energy. When a force is applied to an object, the motion of the object changes — for example, it speeds up, slows down, or changes direction. If the bowling ball had been at rest, then a force must have acted on the bowling ball to make it start moving. The change in the bowling ball's kinetic energy depends on how strong the force is and the distance over which it was applied to the ball. Intuitively, you may already know this. For example, if you barely swing your arm before releasing a bowling ball, the bowling ball won't go as fast as if you swing your arm in a large arc before releasing the bowling ball. The amount of work you do determines the change in energy for the ball.

In physics, the term *work* has a specialized meaning — it does not refer to just any kind of effort. For example, in physics, pushing with all your might against a stationary wall, thinking hard, or holding up the world are not considered work. Instead, in physics, **work** is a measure of the energy transferred by a force that is acting over a distance according to the formula W = Fd.

For example, to determine the work done by the force of your arm pushing a bowling ball, substitute the strength of the force (2 newtons) and the distance of the swing (0.5 meters) into the formula as shown in the following calculations:

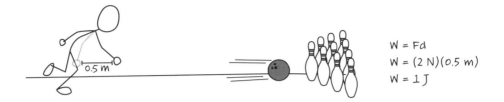

$$W = Fd$$
$$W = (2 \text{ N})(0.5 \text{ m})$$
$$W = 1 \text{ J}$$

Calculating the work also lets you figure out how much energy is transferred as a result of the force, as shown by the following formula:

$$W = \Delta E = Fd$$

◉ Is energy destroyed when objects slow down or stop?

No. Energy is never destroyed, nor does it disappear, not even when objects slow down or stop moving. That's the law! That said, how many times have you heard "The ball ran out of energy, so it stopped moving"? If objects do not stop moving because energy has been destroyed, how do we explain this change in motion? One way to sort this out is to think in terms of forces. Another way is to think in terms of systems.

Forces

Pushing and pulling forces often do the work of getting objects moving, and the force of friction often does the work of slowing down or stopping objects. **Friction** is a pulling force that results from other natural forces — namely, the electromagnetic forces that exist between charged particles (e.g., electrons, atoms, molecules). Any time matter touches other matter and the objects are moving or in the process of trying to be moved, there is a frictional force between them. The pulling force of friction works against the motion, either slowing the objects down or preventing them from moving. Friction is part of all real-world systems. It is involved every time two moving objects of any kind and any size touch. The kind of friction present depends on the kinds of objects and how they are touching. Two important kinds of friction are *static friction* and *sliding friction*:

- Static friction is the kind of friction that exists if the touching objects are not moving relative to one another. Static friction helps hold objects in place. Static friction is at work when a car sits still on a hill, a leaf remains unmoving on the ground on a windy day, and a stack of books stay put when you try to push them.

- Sliding friction is the kind of friction that exists if the touching objects are moving relative to one another. Sliding friction is present when a hockey puck slides across ice, a couch is pushed across carpet, a ball flies through air, and a boat cruises on the ocean.

One way to determine the strength of a frictional force is to calculate the change in kinetic energy (or the work done) when an object slows down. For example, if you rolled the

6 kg bowling ball down a carpeted bowling lane with an initial velocity of 3.0 m/s and the ball comes to a stop with a final velocity of 0 m/s, the change in KE for the bowling can be calculated as follows:

$$\Delta E = KE_{final} - KE_{initial}$$

$$\Delta E = \left[\frac{1}{2}(6 \text{ kg})(0 \text{ m/s})^2\right] - \left[\frac{1}{2}(6 \text{ kg})(3 \text{ m/s})^2\right]$$

$$\Delta E = -27 \text{ J}$$

If the bowling ball travels 10 meters before it stops and the only force acting on it was friction, then the force of friction can be calculated as follows:

$$\Delta E = W = Fd$$

$$-27 \text{ J} = (F_{friction})(10 \text{ m})$$

$$-2.7 \text{ N} = F_{friction}$$

The bowling ball slowed down and stopped because 27 J of work was done by the 2.7 N force of friction on the ball as it rolled. This resulted in a 27 J change in the bowling ball's kinetic energy. The minus sign (–) tells us this was a decrease in the bowling ball's kinetic energy.

Systems

So looking at the work done by friction can tell us what caused the bowling ball's change in energy, but where did the bowling ball's KE go? Friction is often the force that makes objects stop moving. It is not because friction destroys energy. Instead, the forces and objects within a system interact, and as a result energy is transferred from object to object and/or from one type to another type. For example, the bowling ball's kinetic energy is transferred to heat energy from rubbing with the carpet and sound energy from vibrations with the floor. As this transfer occurs, the ball slows down and eventually stops. Forces, including friction, can stop objects because they transfer the object's kinetic energy into other types of energy.

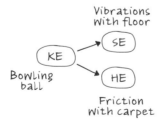

If the bowling ball system was a **closed system,** neither matter nor energy would enter or exit the system. The amount of SE and HE in the system after friction does its work would equal the amount of KE the bowling ball originally had. However, most systems are actually open systems, meaning energy and/or matter are transferred to other systems. For example, in the case of the bowling ball, there was an energy input to get the ball rolling. Other than the system of the universe, "perfectly" closed systems only exist in theory. Additionally, some systems might be closed systems with regard to matter, but open systems with regard to energy.

Science Investigation

50 MINUTES

20 MINUTES **1 Investigating energy in pendulum systems**

a. (SEE) Observe a swinging pendulum and discuss what you notice happening with energy.

b. (THINK) Work with your group to use the diamond diagrams to show the energy transfers that occur as the pendulum swings. Make notes in the space below.

Hint: Your first diamond card should begin with the pendulum bob pulled back just before it's released. Then think about the discrete steps that take place as the pendulum swings. Make a best guess about which energy types are involved and when there is more and less energy transferred.

 USING DIAMOND DIAGRAMS

Diamond diagrams show possible pathways and relative amounts of energy transferred in an interaction.

- **Diamonds** represent a discrete *step* of the interaction. Connected diamonds show the "flow" of energy in a sequence of steps.

- **Arrows** show the *pathways* of energy transfers from an initial type of energy (above the line) to later type of energy (below the line). Thicker arrows indicate relatively more energy.

Here is an example where ① a person kicks a ball and ② the ball whizzes up in the air, making a sound and encountering air resistance.

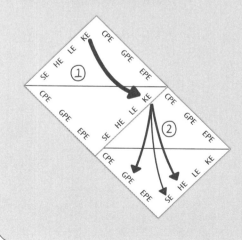

c. (PUZZLE) Given what your group noticed about the pendulum system, do you think it obeys the law of conservation of energy? Why or why not? How well does your set of diamond cards represent this?

d. (PUZZLE) Observe a resonant pendulum. Discuss what happens with energy as the bobs swing. Do you think the law of conservation of energy is obeyed in this system? Why or why not?

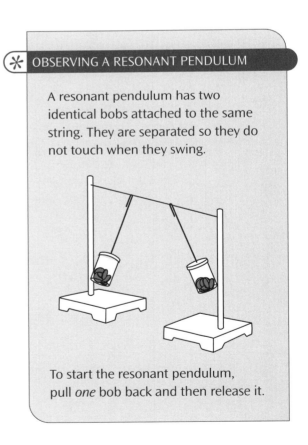

✳ OBSERVING A RESONANT PENDULUM

A resonant pendulum has two identical bobs attached to the same string. They are separated so they do not touch when they swing.

To start the resonant pendulum, pull *one* bob back and then release it.

2 Investigating energy in a rocket system

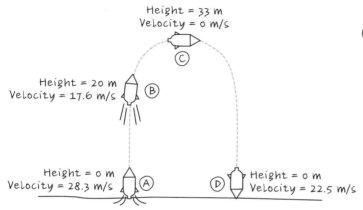

Height = 33 m
Velocity = 0 m/s
Ⓒ

Height = 20 m
Velocity = 17.6 m/s Ⓑ

Height = 0 m
Velocity = 28.3 m/s Ⓐ

Ⓓ Height = 0 m
Velocity = 22.5 m/s

Mass of rocket = 0.25 kg

a. As a group, calculate the GPE and KE at points Ⓐ, Ⓑ, Ⓒ, and Ⓓ. Label these values on the diagram.

b. Work with your group to determine how much *work* was done on the rocket between points Ⓒ and Ⓓ. What do you think is doing this work?

 CALCULATING ENERGY

Gravitational potential energy (GPE) can be calculated based on an object's mass (m), the acceleration due to gravity (g), where on Earth $g = 9.8$ m/s², and the height (h) or distance from another mass, such as Earth, according to the equation:

$$GPE = mgh$$

Kinetic energy (KE) can be calculated based on an object's mass (m) and its velocity (v), according to the equation:

$$KE = \frac{1}{2}mv^2$$

Work (W) is a measure of the energy transferred by a force (F) acting over a distance (d). A change in energy (ΔE) in a system equals the work done.

$$\Delta E = W = Fd$$

c. Together with your group draw two system diagrams:

- One that defines the rocket system such that energy is *conserved within the system*

- A second that defines the rocket system such that energy is *lost from the system*

Hint: A system is defined by identifying the objects of interest and the forces of interest present within a specific timeframe of interest.

3 Checking your understanding

a. Discuss what is both true and not true about the statement "Energy is conserved."

Literacy Investigation

45 MINUTES

---

10 MINUTES **Reflecting on images, symbols, and equations**

a. Individually, take 1–2 minutes to review the Content Notes and Session Reviews from previous sessions. Choose an image, symbol, or equation that helped you understand some part of the science.

b. Share your example with your small group. Talk about:

- Which image, symbol, or equation you chose and why

- What it helped you understand

- What, if anything, you found confusing about it

10 MINUTES **Revising scientific explanations**

a. Individually, take 10 minutes to revise and prepare to share your writing with others using the directions found on "Handout I: Explanation of Conduction – 2nd Draft."

---

3 Participating in a writers' group

a. Read the following tips for sharing writing and responding to writing in writers' groups.

b. Decide the order in which you will share your writing and who will be the timekeeper.

   Note: The timekeeper's role is to make sure each author gets 5 minutes of focused attention from the writers' group, to give a 1-minute warning, and to call time when the 5 minutes are up.

c. Respond to each other's writing using the protocol found on "Handout J: Writers' Group Protocol."

✳ **SUPPORTING WRITERS**

Sharing writing

Share what you are currently thinking about your writing: What did you want to convey? What do you like? What's problematic in this draft?

Focus the discussion by posing a question and/or pointing to a part of the text you want help with.

Accept what your writers' group shares as a gift, one you cannot give yourself. Listen openly to understand different perspectives.

Question your writers' group about things you do not understand. Talk with them to gain clarity, not to defend your writing.

Thank your writers' group for sharing their honest reactions to your writing so you can learn from different perspectives.

Decide what you will do with the responses offered. Remember, you are in the driver's seat. It's your voice and your message!

Responding to writing

Listen with your full respect and attention, without interruption or judgment, to what the text and author are "saying."

Notice your reactions at various points. What voice emerges from the text? Where does it speak most to you? Where do you stumble, become confused, or get lost? What questions arise?

Decide what is most important to share with the author — it can be overwhelming to describe and/or hear all your thoughts. Be sure to respond directly to the author's focusing question.

Share your responses in a manner that is supportive and encouraging, not judgmental or challenging. Avoid input on spelling and grammar unless asked.

Thank the author for sharing the gift of the writing so you could learn from the text and the author's writing process.

---

4 # Reflecting on the role of metacognition

a. As a group, discuss your metacognitive experiences, using these questions:

- When did you find yourself being metacognitive today?

- How did it contribute to your learning?

 USING METACOGNITION

Metacognition is thinking about your thinking — it is a process of stepping "outside" yourself to observe what you do, what you think, and how you behave during an activity (e.g., writing, reading, talking, doing experiments, driving the car).

When you share your metacognitive thoughts with others, it gives them a window into how and why you do the things you do.

b. Throughout this course, the Literacy Investigations intentionally used metacognition as a tool for learning. Pick *two* of the following literacy activities:

- Personal Writing History

- Think Aloud about your writing process

- Sharing your thinking (responding) as you read another writer's work

- Think Aloud about using images and symbols

As a group, talk about how metacognition was used in each activity and what it "bought" you as a learner.

Teaching Investigation

30 MINUTES

20 MINUTES **1 Analyzing student thinking**

a. Look at Raj's work for the *real-world* rocket launch (p. 12) and the *theoretical* rocket launch (p. 13)

- What is correct and not yet correct about his responses?

- What do you think Raj understands and does not yet understand about the conservation of energy?

b. Now look at Theo's work for the *real-world* rocket launch (p. 12) and the *theoretical* rocket launch (p. 14)

- What is correct and not yet correct about his responses?

- What do you think Theo understands and does not yet understand about the conservation of energy?

a. Would you use either real-world or theoretical rocket launches with students? Why or why not?

1 Reviewing key concepts

a. Individually, read the Science Review and Literacy Review on the following pages. Feel free to pick and choose the sections that are most valuable to you.

As you read, take notes and think about these questions:

• What is interesting or new to you?

• Which examples and images do you find especially helpful?

• What are you still wrestling with?

b. Individually, take a few minutes to think and write about your own big takeaways from today.

2 Exploring the ideas of this session

    a. As a group, discuss the Science and Literacy reviews. Use the questions on the previous page as a guide.

3 Considering classroom implications

    a. Based on your experiences today, discuss implications for *what* and *how* you teach your students.

The same amount of energy exists today as existed in years past as will exist in the future. Yet our everyday lives are full of talk about how Earth is "running out" of energy, and we frequently observe objects losing energy — our morning coffee inevitably cools before we drink it, children tire after a hard day at play, and our cell phone batteries die at the most inconvenient moments.

SCIENCE ▸ **KEY CONCEPT**

Energy is not created or destroyed. By definition, energy is a property that is conserved within a closed system. The same amount of energy exists in the universe today as existed in years past as will exist in the future. The universe is considered a closed system because it does not exchange energy or matter with any other system. This observation of the behavior of nature is known as the *law of conservation of energy*. This law isn't just something that governs energy, it is the basis on which energy is defined.

SCIENCE ▸ **KEY CONCEPT**

While energy is conserved within the universe and in closed systems, it is rarely conserved within a typical system. Because systems are defined with particular boundaries to highlight objects, forces, timelines, or energies of *interest,* it's possible (even likely!) for an individual system to violate the law of conservation of energy. This does not mean the system was incorrectly defined or that energy is not conserved in the universe. It simply indicates that energy moves between systems — systems have energy inputs and energy outputs. If one system gains energy, then another system must have lost energy. If one system loses energy, then another system must have gained energy.

SCIENCE ▸ **KEY CONCEPT**

Calculations of energy for theoretical, or "ideal," scenarios usually show that energy is conserved. Calculations of energy for real-world scenarios often suggest otherwise. In the real world, interactions always result in some energy being transferred, or "lost," to nonuseful types, such as heat energy, which are tough to calculate. Typically the nonuseful energy gets dispersed throughout the system (e.g., by warming the surrounding air) and then the nonuseful energy becomes an input of energy into another system. Because of this difficulty, many scientists assume more "ideal" conditions and thus their calculations ignore this phenomenon. In turn, theoretical scenarios result in very different pictures of what it means for energy to be conserved.

Energy is conserved

Nobel laureate physicist Richard Feynman said this about energy in his book *Six Easy Pieces: Essentials of Physics Explained by Its Most Brilliant Teacher*:

> There is a fact, or if you wish, a law, governing natural phenomena that are known to date. There is no known exception to this law; it is exact, so far as we know. The law is called conservation of energy; it states that there is a certain quantity, which we call energy, that does not change in manifold changes which nature undergoes. That is a most abstract idea, because it is a mathematical principle; it says that there is a numerical quantity, which does not change when something happens. It is not a description of a mechanism, or anything concrete; it is just a strange fact that we can calculate some number, and when we finish watching nature go through her tricks and calculate the number again, it is the same. (1963)

SCIENCE ‍ **KEY CONCEPT**

Energy is not created or destroyed. By definition, energy is a property that is conserved within a closed system.

The fact that energy is conserved is integral to many of the most scientific definitions of energy. For example:

- Energy is a measure of how much change can happen in a system. It is a quantity that is conserved despite the many changes that occur in the natural world.

- Energy is the amount of work required to change the state of a physical system. The numerical amount of energy of a system diminishes when the system does work on any other system.

- Mathematically, energy is a quantity that does not change when an interaction happens in a closed system.

The law of conservation of energy states that energy is always conserved and therefore cannot be created or destroyed. The law of conservation of energy does *not* say energy cannot be gained or lost by systems or objects. Systems and objects gain and lose energy all the time. With almost every transfer of energy, some object or system sees a reduction in its energy (i.e., it loses energy) or sees an increase in its energy (i.e., it gains energy).

There is a difference between losing energy and destroying energy, much like there is a difference between losing matter and destroying matter. You can lose your keys, but you can't destroy the matter that they are made of. Even if you blew them up with a bomb, the atoms that were once your keys would still exist.

For example, during the Science Investigation, you observed a pendulum swinging and eventually stopping. That event was filled with energy gains and losses, but the total energy associated with the pendulum and its surroundings before the interaction still equaled the total energy after the interaction. The total amount of energy was conserved. The pendulum stopped swinging not because kinetic energy was destroyed, but because the amount of kinetic energy decreased to zero in the pendulum bob and the amount of heat energy, sound energy, and kinetic energy in the rest of the system increased.

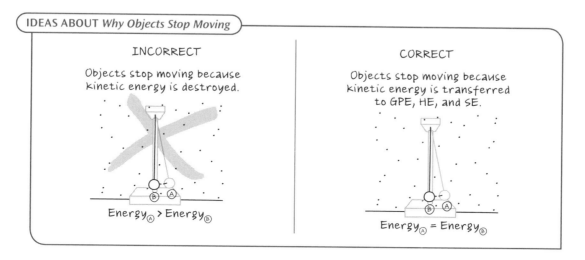

This incorrect idea may stem from our observations, our language, or both. For example, when we see a moving object slow down and stop or when we hear that our planet is "running out of energy," we can reasonably think that energy is being destroyed. Additionally, in everyday language the words *lost* and *destroyed* are sometimes used synonymously, as in "the boat was lost at sea" and the "boat was destroyed at sea." However, in terms of energy, the words *lost* and *destroyed* do not mean the same thing.

Sometimes our observations suggest energy is being created. For example, we think a cozy fire that makes us warm is generating heat energy. Similarly, the resonant pendulum you explored in the Science Investigation seemed to "get energized" when the second bob, initially at rest, began swinging, seemingly out of nowhere. As surprising as this was, all that happened was a transfer of kinetic energy from the first pendulum bob (Bob 1) to the string support and then from the twisting string to the second pendulum bob (Bob 2).

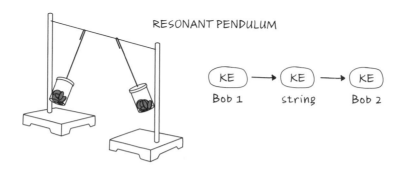

As Bob 1's kinetic energy transferred to the string, it slowed down and stopped swinging. Then when the string transferred kinetic energy back to Bob 1, it began swinging again. Eventually both bobs stopped swinging because the friction with air and the rubbing of the string resulted in all the kinetic energy transferring to heat energy and sound energy.

Nuclear reactions and energy conservation

Energy can be gained and lost by systems and objects, but it cannot be created or destroyed, not even by nuclear reactions. Nuclear reactions transfer nuclear potential energy into other types of energy. They do not create energy. There are two basic kinds of nuclear reactions — *nuclear fission* and *nuclear fusion*.

Nuclear fission. Nuclear fission is the splitting of heavy elements (e.g., uranium and thorium) into lighter elements. These heavy elements are rich in nuclear potential energy (NPE) and only form when very large amounts of energy are available in the right conditions. In fact, the only event powerful enough to create such energy-rich elements is the collapse of a supernova. In order to start the process of nuclear fission, a significant input of energy is generally required, but the output of energy resulting from the splitting of the nucleus is tremendous. This can make it seem as if energy is created. In truth, nuclear fission really just transfers incredible amounts of nuclear potential energy into kinetic energy.

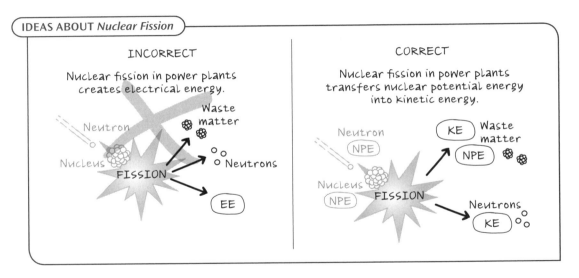

Perhaps because nuclear fission releases huge amounts of energy with seemingly little effort or because the media frequently says things like "nuclear power plants create enough energy to power entire counties," many people firmly believe nuclear fission creates energy. However, in nuclear power plants, the fission of uranium, thorium, and other heavy elements transfers NPE to KE, which can in turn be transferred through various interactions to the electrical energy we use to light homes and power computers, as shown in the following energy tree diagram.

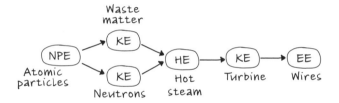

A related but more gradual process of nuclear decay also occurs in radioactive atomic nuclei, for example, those found in Earth's core. This decay provides energy for important geological processes such as tectonic plate movement, mountain building, and volcanic eruptions. However, neither gradual nuclear decay nor accelerated nuclear fission creates energy. These nuclear processes merely transfer nuclear potential energy into other types of energy.[1]

Nuclear fusion. Nuclear fusion is another nuclear process that is often thought to create energy, but does not. Nuclear fusion takes place in our Sun and other stars when the nuclei of tiny elements (e.g., hydrogen) fuse together to form heavier elements (e.g., helium). This process transfers the NPE of hydrogen atoms to NPE in heavier elements and into kinetic energy of these heavier elements and neutrons.

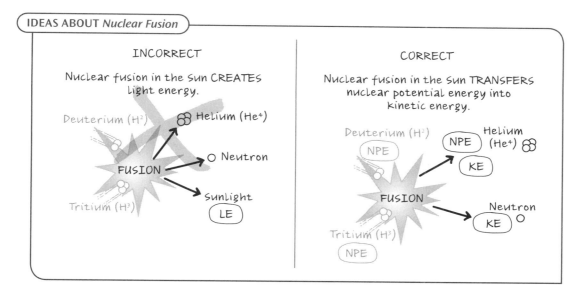

This incorrect idea is likely a logical extension of knowing the Sun is the primary energy source for Earth. Because the Sun provides the energy required to sustain life, to drive the hydrological cycle on Earth, and to generate winds, it's not a huge leap to incorrectly think the Sun creates the energy it provides. The Sun doesn't create energy, but instead releases light energy and heat energy that was once nuclear potential energy in hydrogen atoms, as shown in the following energy tree diagram.

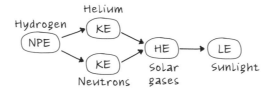

---

[1] This description of nuclear reactions is greatly simplified and does not get into an explanation of the fact that mass is also converted into energy during nuclear reactions. In truth, the mass of the products is measurably less than the initial mass. Scientists would say the law of conservation of mass-energy holds true in nuclear reactions because the sum of the mass plus energy *before* the reaction is equal to the total mass plus energy *after* the reaction. More information about $E = mc^2$ and this relativistic perspective is provided in the next section of this Science Review (and is optional).

E = mc² and energy conservation

This course describes the concepts of mass and energy as they are used in Newtonian mechanics, which is the way physics is taught in nearly all middle and high schools, and is sufficient for understanding many aspects of energy. However, if you want to know a bit about Einstein's revolutionary $E = mc^2$ formula, which is not part of Newtonian mechanics, read on, but do so knowing things get a bit complicated. Skip ahead if it's not for you.

Einstein's famous $E = mc^2$ formula is important to the progress of science because it unites the concepts of mass and energy. Under the frame of relativistic physics, mass and energy are interchangeable. They are two sides of the same coin. They are equivalent. The formula $E = mc^2$ tells us energy can be converted into mass and mass can be converted into energy. We know this actually happens in nuclear reactions because the initial mass is measurably more than the final mass.

This formula helps explain a surprising phenomenon that is measurable when it comes to very fast-moving objects. Here's the gist of things. If you apply a force to a moving object, the object's motion will change. For example, if you push on an object with 10 newtons of force, the object may speed up from 10 m/s to 15 m/s. However, if you push on an object that is already traveling near the speed of light with the same 10 newtons of force, the object's *speed doesn't change much at all!* At one level this makes sense, because objects cannot move faster than the speed of light, yet it is also confusing because energy was added to the object by applying a force over a distance. If this doesn't result in the object speeding up, what happened to that energy?

Since $KE = \frac{1}{2}mv^2$ and the object's speed doesn't increase, Einstein concluded the object's *mass* must increase. As objects move closer and closer to the speed of light, their mass increases without limit. In a relativistic way of thinking, mass that results from the transfer of energy to very fast-moving objects is called *relativistic mass* or *effect mass,* and the term *rest mass* is used to mean what we usually just call *mass* in Newtonian mechanics.

◉ Conservation of energy within systems and among systems

Even though energy is conserved and cannot be created or destroyed, it is common to find an increase in energy in one part of a system and not find a corresponding decrease in energy in another part of the system or vice versa. This makes it appear as though the law of conservation of energy has been violated.

SCIENCE KEY CONCEPT

While energy is conserved within the universe and in closed systems, it is rarely conserved within a typical system.

Whether or not energy appears to be conserved depends on how you define the system. In the following pendulum example, System A appears to violate the law of conservation of energy because initially the objects of interest (pendulum and Earth) are at rest relative to each other and at the end of the timeframe of interest the pendulum is swinging — yet the only force included in the system, the force of gravity, does not account for this change in motion. So in System A the pendulum gains energy, and there is no decrease in energy in System A to offset this increase.

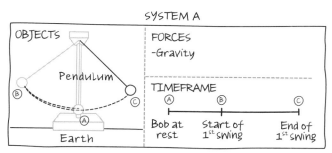

KE increased, but no other energy decreased
within the system. System A gained energy.

In this example, energy was *gained* by System A, but energy was not *created* by System A. Energy is never created! If a system sees an increase in energy, then another system must have an equivalent decrease in energy. A logical external system that might have provided the input of energy to System A could include a person's hand and the force pulling the pendulum back to make it swing. Another external system that might have provided the input of energy could include a second pendulum bob, as in a resonant pendulum.

The following box and arrow diagram shows a transfer of energy between an external system and System A, where the output of energy from the external system is an input of energy to System A (perhaps in the form of KE transferred from a person's hand). This example shows energy being *conserved among multiple systems,* yet *not conserved within each individual system.*

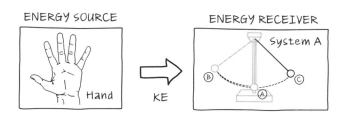

In another pendulum example, System B appears to violate the law of conservation of energy by destroying energy because initially the objects of interest (pendulum and Earth) are moving relative to each other as the pendulum swings and at the end of the timeframe of interest the pendulum is at rest — yet the only force included in the system, the force of gravity, does not account for this change in motion. So in System B the pendulum has lost energy, and there is no increase in energy in System B to offset this loss.

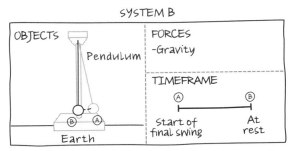

SYSTEM B

KE decreased, but no other energy increased
within the system. System B lost energy.

In this example energy was *lost* by System B, but energy was not *destroyed* in this system. Energy is never destroyed! A logical external system that might have received this output of energy from System B could include air and the force of air resistance that slows the pendulum down. The following box and arrow diagram shows a transfer of energy between System B and an external system, where the output of energy from System B is an input of energy to the external system (perhaps in the form of HE transferred to the surrounding air). Again, this example shows energy being *conserved among multiple systems,* yet *not conserved within each individual system.*

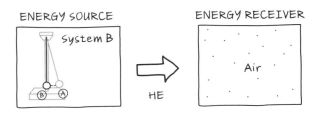

In yet a third pendulum example, System C appears to obey the law of conservation of energy. System C is much like System B, but it also includes the frictional force and the surrounding air. Therefore one part of System C loses energy (i.e., the pendulum slows down) and another part gains energy (i.e., the air warms up). In System C the energy differences offset each other, making it easier to see that energy is conserved.

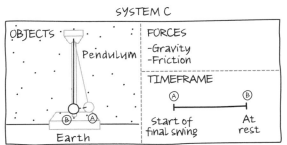

SYSTEM C

KE decreased in the pendulum while HE increased
in the air. System C has conserved energy.

System A, System B, and System C each highlight different aspects of the pendulum interaction and they all are correct systems. However, only System C highlights the most fundamental characteristic of energy — that energy is conserved within a closed system.

Theoretical versus real-world energy conservation

In theoretical examples, such as an "ideal" pendulum swinging in a frictionless system or a rocket launched in a system without air resistance, comparing calculations of KE and GPE is a powerful way to track what happens with energy. In such "ideal" scenarios, calculations clearly show energy being conserved. For example, in the "ideal" pendulum system, the total amount of energy present at any point during the interaction is equal, even as energy is transferred between GPE and KE.

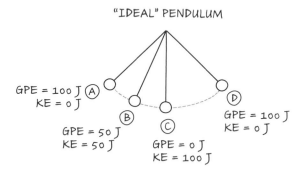

"IDEAL" PENDULUM

GPE = 100 J Ⓐ
KE = 0 J

Ⓑ
GPE = 50 J
KE = 50 J

Ⓒ
GPE = 0 J
KE = 100 J

Ⓓ
GPE = 100 J
KE = 0 J

SCIENCE ▸ KEY CONCEPT

Calculations of energy for theoretical, or "ideal," scenarios usually show that energy is conserved. Calculations of energy for real-world scenarios often suggest otherwise.

Although calculations do a nice job showing the conservation of energy in theoretical examples, in real-world scenarios they often tell a different story. Systems are far more complex in the real world, which makes it much more difficult to "see" that energy is conserved. When using data from the real world, calculations for GPE and KE do not show energy being conserved. For example, when a pendulum swings in the real world, friction does work on the pendulum, transferring some of the pendulum's kinetic energy to heat energy and sound energy, thus reducing the amount of energy associated with the pendulum by the end of the swing.

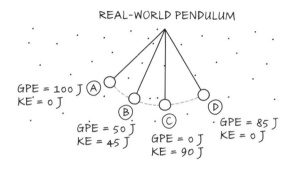

REAL-WORLD PENDULUM

GPE = 100 J Ⓐ
KE = 0 J

Ⓑ
GPE = 50 J
KE = 45 J

Ⓒ
GPE = 0 J
KE = 90 J

Ⓓ
GPE = 85 J
KE = 0 J

The same is true for data from a real-world rocket launch that you worked with in the Science Investigation — energy does not appear to be conserved. With the real-world rocket launch, the change in energy is a negative number indicating the energy associated with the rocket decreases. This decrease in energy is equal to the amount of work done by friction. A sample correct answer follows.

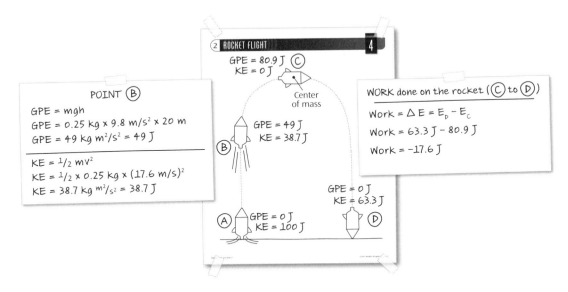

The fact that the calculations for GPE and KE don't show energy being conserved in the real world doesn't mean energy isn't conserved in the real world. Energy is always conserved. It's the law!

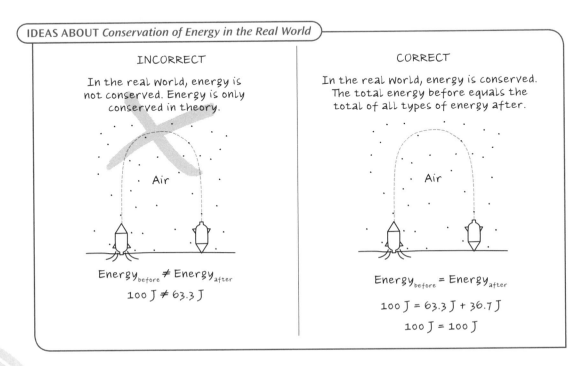

While it seems logical, especially in science, to rely on calculations, there is a lot more to the energy picture than simply GPE and KE. Real-world systems can be unbelievably complex. Often there are so many types of energy and energy transfers, it is impossible to either measure or calculate them directly. In order to "see" energy being conserved in real-world systems, you would have to track each type, some of which you can calculate and some of which you cannot. All real-world systems are less than 100% efficient. The rocket data you used in the Science Investigation shows an example of this.

$$\% \text{ Efficiency} = \frac{\text{Energy}_{final}}{\text{Energy}_{initial}} \times 100$$

$$\% \text{ Efficiency} = \frac{63.3 \text{ J}}{100 \text{ J}} \times 100$$

$$\% \text{ Efficiency} = 63.3\%$$

In reality, a 63% level of efficiency is pretty darn good. Perhaps too good to be true. Many real-world systems, such as solar panels and car engines, run with only 10%–30% efficiencies. Most systems are especially inefficient because much of the energy is transferred to nonuseful types during interactions. For example, the swinging pendulum you explored during the Science Investigation involved many energy transfers, several of which were not useful in keeping the pendulum moving. During the Science Investigation, you tracked the energy involved in a real-world swinging pendulum by linking diamond diagrams together and indicating estimates of the amounts of energy transferred along each path. These linked diagrams show that the amount of energy initially present in the system equaled the amount present at the end. However, the energy associated with the pendulum itself decreased, while the energy associated with other parts of the system increased. A sample correct answer with hypothetical amounts of energy follows.

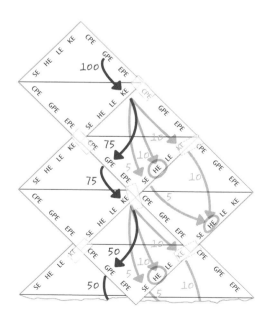

During the Science Investigation, some groups may have also used a box and arrow diagram or an energy tree diagram to track the amount of energy associated with a complex series of interactions. A sample correct representation of each type, again showing hypothetical amounts of energy, follows.

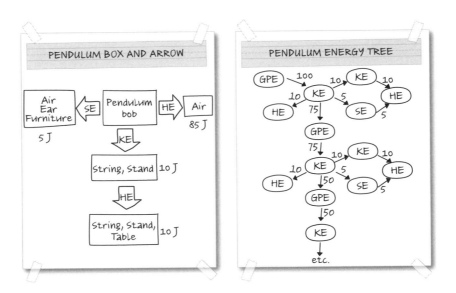

Diamond diagrams, energy tree diagrams, and box and arrow diagrams are all great complements to calculations of GPE and KE, especially for complex real-world systems, in part because they can show energy transfers that are not easy to calculate.

LEARNING OBJECTIVES

Conservation of Energy

4.1 Energy is not created or destroyed.

4.2 The same amount of energy exists today as existed in years past as will exist in the future.

4.3 Energy is conserved overall — it's the law — but energy is not always conserved within a single system.

4.4 Systems can gain and lose energy, depending on the forces and objects defined in the system.

4.5 If one system gains energy, another system loses energy. If one system loses energy, another system gains energy.

Kinetic Energy and Potential Energy

4.6 Kinetic energy (KE) depends on an object's mass (m) and its velocity (v). The amount of KE can be calculated using the formula $KE = \frac{1}{2}mv^2$.

4.7 A change in velocity has a much greater influence on KE than a change in mass. Twice the mass results in twice the KE, but twice the velocity results in four times the KE.

4.8 Gravitational potential energy (GPE) depends on an object's mass (m), the rate of acceleration due to gravity (g), and its height (h) or distance from another mass. The amount of GPE can be calculated using the formula $GPE = mgh$.

4.9 A change in energy (ΔE) in a system equals the work (W) done. Work is a measure of the energy transferred by a force (F) acting over a distance (d).

4.10 Transfers of energy between GPE and KE are never perfectly efficient. Some energy is always converted to heat energy during the process.

MISCONCEPTIONS

4.A It is incorrect to think the law of conservation of energy is obeyed only in theory and not in real-world scenarios.

4.B It is incorrect to think energy is created when an object moves and destroyed when it stops moving.

4.C It is incorrect to think forces create or destroy energy.

4.D It is incorrect to think energy is created in an interaction that generates heat energy or light energy (such as nuclear reactions).

4.E It is incorrect to think energy is destroyed in an interaction just because some types of the energy are difficult (or impossible!) to measure.

4.F It is incorrect to think energy is destroyed when calculations for the initial and final energies are not equal.

4.G It is incorrect to think energy is always conserved within every single system.

4.H It is incorrect to think a system (or object) cannot lose or gain energy.

4.I It is incorrect to think if a system loses energy then energy was destroyed and if a system gains energy then energy was created.

4.J It is incorrect to think energy transfers are 100% efficient.

4.K It is incorrect to think a large moving object always has more kinetic energy than a small moving object.

4.L It is incorrect to think all forms of energy can be readily transferred to usable forms. For example, it is incorrect to think dispersed HE can be readily converted to KE, resulting in the motion of objects.

If you've ever seen a fabulous movie or theater production, you know actors are expert communicators. Clearly, acting is about more than just memorizing lines. Actors meld highly visual expression with auditory expression to convey complex emotions and tell stories. Playing different characters requires learning specialized knowledge — for example, how to speak with a particular accent, how to walk like an elderly person, and which interactions are appropriate for a certain era or culture. Experienced actors do research, practice their skills, and get feedback from a director and others. Experienced actors are also metacognitive — they think about their performance in order to monitor and adjust their actions. Similarly, being a proficient writer in science is about more than just putting words on a page. It is about knowing the specialized formats for writing. It is about persuading and informing your audience. It is about incorporating visual elements such as charts, graphs, diagrams, and symbols into the text. It is also about being metacognitive in order to monitor and adjust your writing.

LITERACY **KEY CONCEPT**

Science writers communicate using images and symbols, not just words. Visual elements are plentiful in science writing, not present merely as eye candy (we hope!), but rather as effective communication tools. It may take more than a thousand words to convey what a single map, diagram, table, or photograph can show. Learning to incorporate images and symbols into writing helps writers communicate about complex science ideas, events, and processes with greater clarity and richness.

LITERACY **KEY CONCEPT**

Metacognition demystifies the invisible ways we write and helps us become better writers. Metacognition is thinking about your thinking — it is a process of stepping "outside" yourself to observe what you do, how you think, and how you behave. When writers use metacognition to analyze and reflect on their own writing, they can monitor and adjust their writing processes, persevere through difficult parts, and be strategic in solving writing challenges. When writers share these metacognitive thoughts with other writers, their conversations highlight sticking points, allow them to swap useful strategies, and give them a new way to interpret their own writing processes.

⦿ Images and symbols

Scan the science section of the newspaper, flip through a science magazine, open up a science textbook, or look at a scientist's working notebook and you will likely see the pages littered with graphs, diagrams, photographs, schematics, tables, and flowcharts, along with arrows, numbers, and equations. Images and symbols are inherent in the language of science. In fact, in an analysis of how scientists communicate (e.g., in scientific journals, textbooks, and presentations at professional meetings), Dr. Jay Lemke identified four distinct languages of science — words, actions, images, and symbols.

LITERACY KEY CONCEPT

Science writers communicate using images and symbols, not just words.

Although each of these four languages can be used independently to convey a particular idea, our deepest conceptual understanding comes from a layered communication involving multiple forms of expression, including symbols and images. In other words, when you read *"Energy is transferred back and forth between GPE and KE as a pendulum swings,"* these words do not convey the same thing as the action of a hand gesture used to show the swinging or a series of images such as time-sequenced diagrams illustrating the pendulum moving over time. Different still, symbols such as arrows and numbers in a diagram illustrate something new, as does an equation expressing the mathematical relationship between the relative amounts of GPE and KE. Taken together, these four languages communicate a great deal about the complex concept of energy transfers that occur with pendulums, more than words can achieve on their own.

Incorporating images

When done well, the use of images in written text is not merely gratuitous eye candy, rather the images add to our understanding of the ideas and information being communicated in ways that words don't. As a reader, you know an image is well chosen and well written when it helps clarify something complex, contributes to your interest, and adds to your "ah-ha" sense of what you read. As a writer, there are some useful conventions and things to know about how to effectively incorporate images into a text. During the Literacy Investigation, it is likely your group identified some helpful tips for incorporating images into science texts, such as using *captions,* adding *supporting text,* and including *legends and labels.*

Captions. A sentence or phrase written just above or just below an image is a useful support for reading the image. Well-written captions tell the reader the purpose of the image and briefly point out what's important to notice. In some ways, a caption is similar to the title of a chapter or the headline of a newspaper article, but it is typically more descriptive. Sometimes captions are italicized or in a smaller font size to set them off from the rest of the text.

Supporting text. While it may be true a picture is worth a thousand words, it is also true that images do not get their points across when they are merely plunked into a text or they stand alone. Images need supporting text — several sentences or paragraphs to introduce the reader to the image and to provide a kind of verbal tour. When writing supporting text, it can be helpful to think about what an expert tour guide might say. Tour guides situate what visitors are looking at in a broader context. They also point out important things to notice, something a first-time visitor might miss but would be enriched by seeing. Supporting text functions in a similar way. It can describe in words the overarching patterns presented in a graph or data table. Supporting text can also walk a reader through a complex process or series of events presented in a diagram or flowchart.

Legends and labels. Many images in science are not simple photographs — typically they include symbols (e.g., arrows, letters) or other visual elements that communicate abstract ideas in shorthand. Supportive science writers help their readers interpret images by including legends and/or labels. Legends define the elements used in an image, such as symbols, colors, and abbreviations. Labels identify the parts of an image and provide the reader with vocabulary for thinking more precisely about the information being shown.

In summary, well-chosen and well-written images:

- Add to a reader's understanding (and interest)
- Include captions that situate the image
- Are connected to supporting text
- Explain the meaning of symbols
- Are placed so they are easy to find
- Allow readers to go back and forth between image and text

Incorporating symbols

Writers use symbols as a form of shorthand to represent a variety of things, from actions to objects, and the relationships between variables. But symbols are more than simple shorthand. When ideas are conveyed symbolically, different things are revealed about them.

Symbols in science are much like some words — they are likely to have common everyday meanings and science-specific meanings that vary depending on the context in which they are used. For example, in a nonscience context, the word *energy* can mean *enthusiasm,* as in "he plays his guitar with great energy," or it can mean *a healthy capacity for vigorous activity,* as in "jogging requires lots of energy." *Energy* can also be used in a spiritual way, as in "the guru's energy permeates the temple." In contrast, in science the word *energy* might be defined as *a quantity that is conserved despite many changes with matter and forces.*

In a nonscience context, the symbol "V" might stand for peace when made by holding up your index and middle finger, but in science the letter "V" may represent the element vanadium. Similarly, on road signs across the country, a white arrow on a black rectangle indicates a one-way street. In science, arrows are found in abundance. In chemistry, arrows are sometimes used to show the products of chemical reactions. In physics, they often represent forces or motion. In the geosciences, arrows typically show the motion of objects, fluids, and gases (e.g., plate movement, Earth's rotation, ocean currents). For example, in the following diagram there are two kinds of arrows used to show the average global air currents, one an inline arrow in the subtropical and polar jets and the other the direction of the prevailing surface winds.

AVERAGE GLOBAL AIR CURRENTS

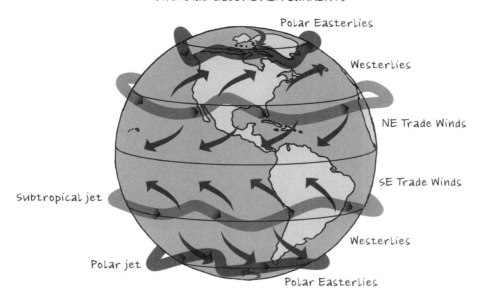

When symbols are used in equations, they can help express complex ideas and summarize interactions. They can also provide a shorthand way of precisely and concisely stating relationships. Perhaps the most common symbols used in equations are letters and arrows, although shapes are typical too. For example, chemical equations show the reactants that yield ($\longrightarrow$) certain products in a reaction. Chemical equations also use letters to show the elements (in this example, hydrogen and oxygen) that combine or break apart in a reaction. The numeric symbols serve as a shorthand way of expressing the proportions of atoms that combine. For example, 2 water molecules (H_2O) yield 2 molecules of hydrogen (H_2) and 1 molecule of oxygen (O_2).

Reactants $\longrightarrow$ Products

$2 H_2O \longrightarrow 2 H_2 + O_2$

Writers can be courteous to readers by describing the specialized use of symbols they include in text. This may mean including a legend or describing the meaning of a symbol the first time it is used. In summary, well-chosen and well-used symbols:

- Communicate abstract ideas in shorthand

- Might convey mathematical relationships

- Are defined in legends when associated with an image

- Are explained with words the first time they are shown

◉ Metacognition

As you think back on how you learned about writing during this course, you might notice that metacognition played an important part. In fact, it's not surprising if metacognition had a pivotal role in many of the things you learned about scientific explanation, incorporating images and symbols in text, and other science-specific ways of writing.

Metacognition, the act of thinking about your thinking, is a process of stepping "outside" yourself to observe what you do, how you think, and how you behave. Even everyday activities can cause us to be metacognitive. For example:

> "I notice my mind keeps wandering while I'm driving. It's at the point I don't feel very safe, but I have a lot farther to go. Maybe some coffee will help."

> "I like how it feels when I get my class planning done early. No last-minute rush and I'm more relaxed with the kids. I'll have to remember this for next week too."

> "Okay, I have too much to do. Last time this happened I decided instead of getting worked up, I'd just take a deep breath. Good. This is just what I wanted to do. Now, sit down, make a list, prioritize, and put the low-priority things on a do-later list."

Being metacognitive helps us monitor and regulate our own thinking and behavior. As the old saying goes, "The first step in fixing any problem is becoming aware of it." And metacognition helps us do just that. Metacognition also helps us learn from our successes. When we notice how we're thinking when we're successful, we have a better chance of repeating that successful way of thinking down the road. Metacognition turns our invisible thinking into something tangible that we can work with and learn from.

Being metacognitive can be very helpful for lots of everyday dilemmas, but this course emphasizes being metacognitive about your writing process. When writers are metacognitive as they write, they learn a lot about their own writing process. They discover problems that need to be solved, unhelpful behavior they want to stop, and good strategies they want to use more often. Here are a few examples of writers being metacognitive:

> "When I reread my claim, it felt right on this time. That revision makes it an answer to a question. Now does the evidence support this claim?"

> "I remember this feeling. It's like my brain is going around and around in a washing machine and I can't figure out what to say. I think it helps me organize my thoughts when I can talk with someone first. Who can I ask?"

> "When I was writing, I noticed I kept getting stuck trying to find the perfect words and I would lose my train of thought. Maybe when I'm writing a first draft, I can be okay with letting my mind go. Or maybe I should make a rule of no rereading until I get to the end of a paragraph or something."

LITERACY **KEY CONCEPT**

Metacognition demystifies the invisible ways we write and helps us become better writers.

Being metacognitive while writing helps writers learn what is giving them trouble, what they are doing that doesn't work, and what they are doing that does work. It helps them monitor and adjust their writing processes, persevere through difficult parts, and be strategic in solving writing challenges.

Being metacognitive about writing also makes writers better readers. Metacognitive writers are better able to navigate a range of texts, including those written with different formats, tones, and text-types. The process of being metacognitive while writing gives writers information about how to design text that works well for their readers, as well as how to read texts intended for a variety of audiences.

Metacognitive conversation

Sharing our private metacognitive thoughts opens up our writing process for the eyes of others. This allows others to help us improve our thinking and writing. For example, someone else might be able to provide suggestions for strategies we might try in order to clarify confusing text or point out key evidence we could include to strengthen our argument. Sharing our own metacognitive thinking also helps other people grow as writers. For example, they might learn from how we use images, write captions, structure text, handle data, and summarize multistep processes. Metacognitive conversations allow us to collaborate with others as we face the inevitable puzzles of writing.

Often the easiest and most effective way of encouraging metacognitive conversation is by doing public, real-time Think Alouds. There is just no substitute for hearing and seeing how people write. The realizations people make about writing after listening to another writer think aloud vary greatly, but it's likely someone in your group may have made important discoveries through metacognitive conversations, for example:

> "I was totally shocked by the big changes she made when she revised her explanation and how much better her second draft is. I need to be willing to do more than just fix the little stuff."

> "I never got around to the reasoning part, so I was super interested to hear my partner explain his process. Turns out I just needed to brainstorm a list of the things we'd learned about, then pick what matches the claim and describe it."

> "I didn't realize my scribble drawings are a form of prewriting, nor did I realize everybody else doesn't do something similar before starting to write. Seeing others struggle with organizing ideas pointed out just how important prewriting is."

While writers' groups and Think Alouds are very useful, they aren't always feasible to do, nor are they the only way to have metacognitive conversations. Sometimes there simply isn't time to get together or the amount of text is too long to read and respond to. This is when another type of metacognitive activity may be useful. For example, writers can reread their work and do a Talking to the Text in order to provide their own response and suggestions for revisions.

Supporting writers

Both metacognition and metacognitive conversations are important tools that can be used to support writers because they can be used to support the personal, social, cognitive, and knowledge-building dimensions in a writing apprenticeship. As a reminder, the *personal dimension* includes aspects of being a writer such as stamina, fluency, and developing writing confidence and range. The *social dimension* includes the ability of writers to learn from the writing processes of others and share their writing processes with others. The *cognitive dimension* includes the mental skills and strategies writers require in order to make sense of text. The *knowledge-building dimension* includes the knowledge of science-specific ways of writing (e.g., format, tone, text-type) and the background knowledge that's required in order to write about science ideas.

Dimensions of a Writing Apprenticeship

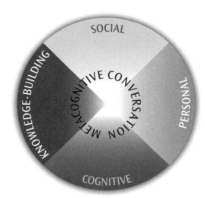

During the Literacy Investigation, you discussed how metacognition and metacognitive conversations contributed to your literacy experiences in this course. Often people mention aspects of personal, social, cognitive, and knowledge-building dimensions. Just as metacognition and metacognitive conversations were helpful to different writers in different ways during this course, they are helpful to students in different ways at different times of their lives. The following sample chart summarizes some ways the process of metacognition may have been useful to you or others in your group in relation to writing in science.

ROLE OF METACOGNITION IN
SCIENCE WRITING

► Showed me I use strategies &
  taught me new ones
► Was embarrassing at first, but
  everyone had trouble spots
► Showed me what I do, and now
  I can model for students
► Pointed out everybody does not
  write the same as I do
► Taught me things about science
  texts I did not know
► Made me feel more in control of
  my writing
► Made me feel less alone as a
  struggling writer

ENERGY IN ECOSYSTEMS

Students begin exploring ecosystems in elementary school. By middle school, most can rattle off simple food chains like "rabbits eat carrots, and foxes eat rabbits." Many middle school students can even describe and explain the interconnections of intricate food webs in which animals eat many other animals and plants. Nevertheless, knowing what different animals eat is not the same as knowing what happens with matter and energy in ecosystems. Understanding the matter and energy transfers that happen in ecosystems requires knowing what energy is and how it is different from matter. Central to understanding this is the concept of food. Consuming food is how matter and energy are transferred from one organism to another.

To help track, describe, and compare what happens with matter and energy in ecosystems, a variety of representations are helpful. Food chains and food webs help make visible the paths food takes in an ecosystem. Matter webs help make visible the paths that matter (not just food) take in an ecosystems. Energy tree diagrams help track the type and amount of energy that transfers in an ecosystem. Ecological pyramids (e.g., pyramids of energy, pyramids of biomass) are also common representations that help illustrate what happens with matter and/or energy in ecosystems.

This session explores each of these representations as a way to come to a complete, accurate, and precise description of what happens with matter and energy in ecosystems.

As you read the Content Notes, think about the following questions:

- Where do plants get the energy and matter they need to survive?

- What does food provide organisms? What do plants use as food?

- Which types of energy are involved in ecosystems?

All organisms require a source of chemical potential energy to survive. Food is the source of this energy. Plants use the sugars they make as food. Herbivores use plants as food. Omnivores use both plants and animals as food. Carnivores use other animals as food. Knowing what happens with food in an ecosystem tells you part of the story about what happens with energy in an ecosystem.

VOCABULARY

Food provides organisms (e.g., plants, animals, bacteria) with a significant source of chemical potential energy and the matter they need in order to grow and reproduce. Digestion breaks down food, making the energy and matter available for metabolic processes.

Producers (a.k.a. autotrophs) are organisms such as plants, algae, and some bacteria that synthesize their own food (glucose) from inorganic matter, most commonly using photosynthesis.

Photosynthesis is a chemical reaction that changes water and carbon dioxide into glucose.

Consumers (a.k.a. heterotrophs) are organisms such as animals, fungi, and some bacteria that cannot synthesize their own food from inorganic matter. Consumers must eat other organisms to obtain the matter and energy they need.

Food chains and **food webs** are models that represent a series of organisms eating each other. The number of steps an organism is from the start of the chain is a measure of its **trophic level.** Food chains start at trophic level 1 with producers, move to primary consumers at level 2, and move to secondary consumers at trophic level 3 and higher.

Pyramids of energy show the relative amounts of energy at each trophic level in a food chain.

Pyramids of biomass show the relative amounts of biomass — the amount of living matter — at each trophic level in a food chain.

◉ What is food?

Food brings families and friends together. It makes holidays memorable and helps us carry on cultural traditions. Food feeds us emotionally and physically. **Food** provides us, and all other organisms, with the chemical potential energy and the matter needed for growth and reproduction. Food is loaded with CPE as a result of the way its atoms and molecules are arranged. During digestion, the atoms and molecules of food are rearranged, releasing energy (CPE and HE) that is transferred to the consumer. Because organisms do not all have the same digestive process, organisms use different substances for food. Because organisms come in various sizes and do not have the same metabolic needs, different organisms require different amounts of CPE. On average, humans need about 1200–2500 kilocalories of CPE each day, while our canine companions need about 400–1000 kilocalories of CPE per day.

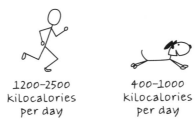

1200–2500
kilocalories
per day

400–1000
kilocalories
per day

Food is made of organic (carbon-based) molecules. Organisms require food to grow larger, generate new body parts, and produce offspring. While food provides a significant source of matter for organisms, it is only one of the kinds of matter organisms require to survive. Living organisms also require other kinds of matter — for example, some form of gas or mixture of gases (e.g., oxygen, carbon dioxide, sulfur), water, vitamins, and nutrients. What sets food apart from these other kinds of matter is that food also provides a significant source of CPE.

◉ Do producers need food?

All organisms, large and small, plant and animal, aquatic and terrestrial, need food. Yes, even plants need food! Algae and many photosynthetic bacteria that do not consume other organisms also need food. The special thing about these kinds of organisms is that they make their own food.

They are **producers,** or autotrophs. In Greek, *auto* means "self" and *trophic* means "nourishment," so autotrophs make nourishment for themselves. Autotrophs are the only living things able to synthesize organic molecules, such as glucose, from inorganic molecules. For this reason, producers form the base, or beginning, of food chains — producers are the first trophic level of ecosystems. Most often they use photosynthesis to synthesize organic molecules from inorganic molecules.[1]

---

[1] Not all producers use photosynthesis to make the organic molecules they need. Some producers make organic molecules using heat energy, rather than light energy, and use other oxidizing reactions, such as chemosynthetic reactions (a.k.a. chemosynthesis). Producers that use these reactions are known as chemoautotrophs and are often found near deep sea vents.

Matter and photosynthesis

In **photosynthesis,** producers combine water and the carbon dioxide found in air into a kind of sugar called *glucose.* In other words, they change inorganic material into organic material. The following equations illustrate the process of photosynthesis — the first in terms of the kind of matter (inorganic or organic), the second in terms of the reactants and products involved, and the third in the form of a balanced chemical equation.

$$\text{inorganic} + \text{inorganic} \longrightarrow \text{inorganic} + \text{organic}$$
$$\text{carbon dioxide} + \text{water} \longrightarrow \text{oxygen gas} + \text{glucose}$$
$$6CO_2 + 6H_2O \longrightarrow 6O_2 + C_6H_{12}O_6$$

It is remarkable that producers can make organic material from inorganic material. It is even more remarkable that the majority of the mass of this organic material comes from *air.* Yep, you read that right, air! In fact 93% of glucose's mass comes from carbon dioxide. Most of the molecular mass of glucose comes from its carbon and oxygen atoms, as shown by the following table and calculations. Of glucose's 180 atomic mass units, 168 come from carbon and oxygen and only 12 come from hydrogen.

Element	Atomic Mass (u)
Hydrogen (H)	1 u
Carbon (C)	12 u
Oxygen (O)	16 u

glucose ($C_6H_{12}O_6$)
carbon (12 u x 6) + hydrogen (1 u x 12) + oxygen (16 u x 6) = 180 u

All of the mass of glucose's carbon atoms come from air — they must because the only other reactant in photosynthesis (water) has no carbon atoms. However, it's harder to tell where the oxygen atoms in glucose come from — both reactants (carbon dioxide and water) have oxygen atoms. Based on experiments involving "tagged" oxygen atoms, scientists have proven the oxygen atoms in glucose actually originate in carbon dioxide.

Since all of glucose's carbon atoms and most of its oxygen atoms originate in carbon dioxide, the majority of its mass comes from the carbon dioxide pulled from the air. This phenomenon is sometimes called carbon fixation, as producers are taking carbon from the air and "fixing" it into a glucose molecule.

Energy and photosynthesis

Photosynthesis is a kind of work. Not in the "work equals force times distance" sense of work, but work as in the "work will not occur without an input of energy" sense of work. Photosynthesis is the work of rearranging molecules. Like all work, this process cannot occur without a change in energy.

The energy that permits photosynthesis to occur is light energy, usually associated with sunlight. The following equation shows an input of light energy on the reactant side of the chemical equation.

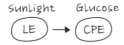

$$LE + 6CO_2 + 6H_2O \longrightarrow 6O_2 + C_6H_{12}O_6$$

In other words, during photosynthesis, light energy from the sunlight is transferred into chemical potential energy in glucose, as shown in the following energy tree diagram.

Sunlight   Glucose

LE → CPE

What's especially interesting is that the reactants for photosynthesis — carbon dioxide and water — are both low-energy molecules. Glucose, by contrast, is a high-energy molecule. So glucose may get its matter from carbon dioxide and water, but it gets most of its energy from sunlight, as shown in the following box and arrow diagram.

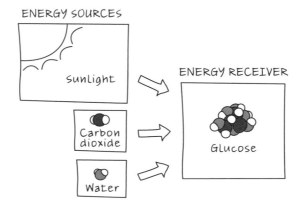

This CPE-rich glucose provides both the energy and the matter producers need to survive and grow. *Glucose is the food of producers.* After producers have made glucose, they break it down using other biological processes. These processes free up the molecular building blocks (e.g., carbon) that producers need in order to grow and repair damaged cells. These processes also result in energy transfers in which glucose is the energy source and the plant is the energy receiver.

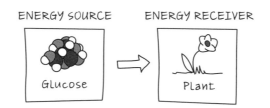

As producers live and grow, they transfer the CPE once associated with glucose to other places and into other types of energy. For example, some of glucose's energy is transferred into CPE in leaf tissues and seeds and some of glucose's energy is transferred into HE in the air, making it no longer available to the plant or its consumers.

◉ How do consumers get food?

Animals, molds, fungi, and some bacteria are **consumers** that eat producers or other consumers for food. They are also known as heterotrophs. In Greek, *hetero* means "other" and, again, *trophic* means "nourishment," so heterotrophs get nourishment from other organisms. Heterotrophs cannot synthesize the organic material they need from inorganic material like producers can. They must consume organic material to survive and grow.

Like producers, consumers get both the matter and the energy they need from their food. Consumers only get matter and its corresponding energy from the parts of their food they can digest (i.e., the parts of the food they can rearrange the molecules of). The indigestible parts pass through the consumer's body and are expelled as waste.

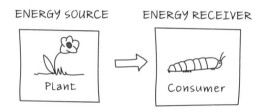

◉ What happens with energy and matter in ecosystems?

Ecosystems are large complex systems involving many *biotic* (living and once living) and *abiotic* (never been living) parts. Due to the scale and complexity of ecosystems, models are very helpful when trying to study ecosystems. There are many kinds of models that help us understand what happens with energy and matter in ecosystems. The most common ones are food chains and food webs, but matter webs, ecological pyramids, energy tree diagrams, and box and arrow diagrams are also useful and reveal different things.

Food chains and food webs

Food chains and **food webs** are models that show the links between consumers and their food. Both show what animals eat — something that is important to know if you are trying to track the energy transfers that occur in an ecosystem. Many, but not all, of the energy transfers that occur within an ecosystem have to do with what eats what. Food chains are linear, showing a one-to-one relationship between organisms. The following is an example of a food chain from a boreal forest:

FOOD CHAIN

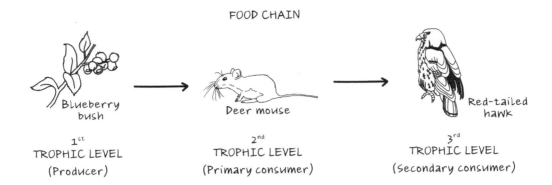

Blueberry bush

1ˢᵗ
TROPHIC LEVEL
(Producer)

Deer mouse

2ⁿᵈ
TROPHIC LEVEL
(Primary consumer)

Red-tailed hawk

3ʳᵈ
TROPHIC LEVEL
(Secondary consumer)

The number of steps an organism is from the start of a food chain is a measure of its **trophic level.** Food chains start at trophic level 1 with producers, move to primary consumers at level 2, and move to secondary consumers at trophic level 3 and higher.

By convention, the arrows in food chains and food webs are drawn from the organism being eaten to the organism doing the eating — that is, they go from the food to the consumer (food ⟶ consumer).

It can be difficult to remember which direction the arrows go. One useful tip is to think about what goes into the mouth of a consumer and draw the arrow to match that action. For example, getting into the habit of saying "X goes into the mouth of Y," as in "moose go into the mouths of wolves," is helpful. When said in this way, the flow of the phrase matches the direction the arrow should be drawn. Thinking of interactions using phrases such as "wolves eat moose" often results in backward arrows that suggest there is a carnivorous moose on the loose!

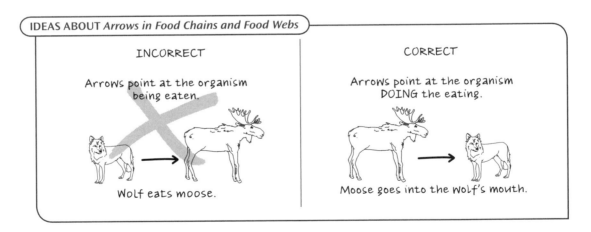

IDEAS ABOUT *Arrows in Food Chains and Food Webs*

INCORRECT

Arrows point at the organism being eaten.

Wolf eats moose.

CORRECT

Arrows point at the organism DOING the eating.

Moose goes into the wolf's mouth.

Food webs are much like food chains. The difference is that food webs show more of the complexities that occur in nature. They show relationships among *many* organisms. For example, the following food web shows more primary and secondary consumers than a food chain can.

FOOD WEB

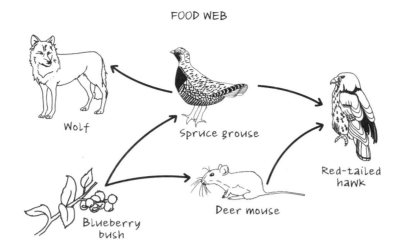

Matter webs

Matter webs are less common models, but they are especially helpful for tracing many different kinds of matter involved in interactions that occur in ecosystems, not just interactions involving food. For example, the following matter web shows much of the matter involved in the interactions that occur between a dog and its environment over the course of a day.

MATTER WEB — A Dog's Day

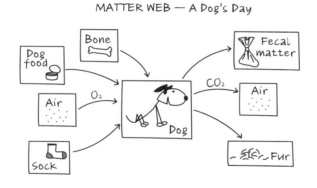

While matter webs track matter, they are also helpful tools for thinking about what happens with chemical potential energy. For example, the more matter (e.g., food) consumed by the dog, the more CPE is transferred to the dog. The more matter lost by the dog (e.g., fecal matter, fur), the less CPE is associated with the dog's body. And in the unfortunate event that the dog is eaten by a predator, the predator can obtain the CPE associated with the dog's body only and not with any matter that has left the dog's body.

You may be familiar with matter webs being used in the geosciences to track a single kind of matter through various interactions. For example, matter webs are often used to track the movement of carbon in ecosystems and the movement of water around the planet. In the geosciences, matter webs are often called *cycle diagrams* (e.g., the carbon cycle, the water cycle) as they show matter cycling within the large ecosystem of Earth. Here is a matter web (a carbon cycle) that shows some of the paths carbon can take through an ecosystem.

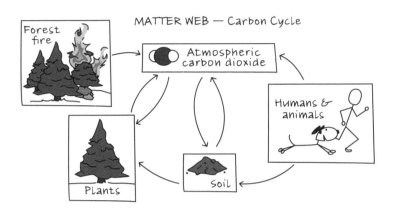

Ecological pyramids

Another tool that helps us understand what happens with energy and matter in ecosystems is an ecological pyramid. Ecological pyramids are similar to food chains and food webs as they show relationships among the trophic levels in an ecosystem. Ecological pyramids go one step beyond food chains to quantify the relationships among trophic levels either in terms of the *amount of biomass* or the *amount of energy* present at each trophic level.

The most helpful pyramid for understanding what happens with energy in food chains is a **pyramid of energy,** which shows the relative amounts of energy at each trophic level. The shape of the following pyramid of energy is classic. Only about 10% of the energy associated with any given trophic level is passed up to the next trophic level. This pyramid of energy shows this 10% transfer using hypothetical amounts of energy (i.e., 100 J, 10 J, 1 J).

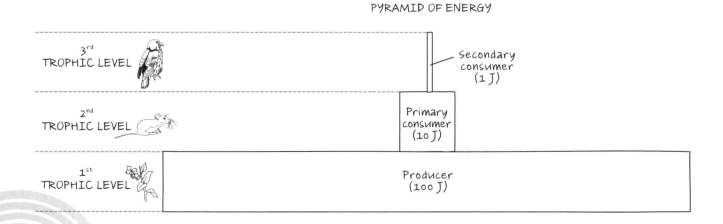

The most helpful pyramid for understanding what happens with matter in ecosystems is a **pyramid of biomass,** which shows the relative amounts of biomass at each trophic level. The shape of pyramids of biomass tend to be very similar to the shape of pyramids of energy. This is because most of the organic matter (i.e., the bodies of organisms) in an ecosystem have similar amounts of chemical potential energy. So if each trophic level has about 10% of the energy of the previous trophic level, it stands to reason that each trophic level has about 10% of the biomass of the previous trophic level. The following diagram shows a classic shape with hypothetical masses.

PYRAMID OF BIOMASS

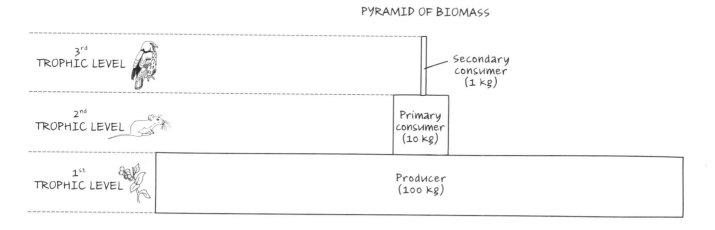

What happens with matter and energy in ecosystems is closely tied to what happens with food because food provides much of the energy and matter organisms need in order to survive and grow. What happens with matter is similar to and connected with what happens with energy (e.g., when animals eat plants they get matter and CPE). However, there are also important differences. For example, there are transfers of matter that don't involve a transfer of chemical potential energy (e.g., animals drinking water and plants releasing oxygen gas), and there are transfers of energy that don't involve matter changing location (e.g., LE is absorbed by plants and HE is transferred to air).

Learning to write is not that different from learning to teach about energy — both are multidimensional processes. Being a top-notch science teacher requires having knowledge about the topic. However, understanding how to teach about energy also requires much more than factual or conceptual knowledge. When doing a Science Investigation or discussing the Teaching Case, each of us brings our own world of experiences and ideas to the table. Together we construct a more robust understanding and explore effective ways of teaching about the topic. This includes how our own personal learning experiences and social interactions affect the choices we make in our own classroom communities. Learning also requires cognitive abilities and strategies to help us make sense of the science, analyze students' thinking, and weigh instructional choices. In both learning about teaching and learning to write, we are most successful when we attend to multiple dimensions — *personal, social, cognitive, and knowledge-building* — and use metacognition to monitor our learning and guide our actions.

LITERACY **KEY CONCEPT**

Metacognitive routines can be tuned to support writers in the personal, social, cognitive, and knowledge-building dimensions of writing. Writing is far from simple. It's a multidimensional process. Writers can improve their writing confidence, skills, and knowledge through writing apprenticeships that support the personal, social, cognitive, and knowledge-building dimensions. And metacognitive routines, such as Think Alouds and Talking to the Text, can be tuned to support any of these dimensions. In this way, metacognition is a powerful tool for developing better writers.

LITERACY **KEY CONCEPT**

Using metacognitive routines in a writing apprenticeship model can help students become better writers of science. Learning to use metacognitive routines requires modeling, practice, and fine-tuning, but the payoffs for writers can be huge. When students learn to use metacognitive routines effectively, they can improve their science writing abilities and attitudes significantly. An effective way of helping students use metacognitive routines is to embrace a classroom writing apprenticeship culture in which teachers and students learn about writing from one another and from their own experiences.

⦿ Supporting writing

Sometimes students get excited about coming to science class because they think science is devoid of writing and the challenges associated with writing. While it's true that science doesn't involve as much writing as a language arts class, writing is still an important part of science classrooms and science as a discipline. Scientists write to capture their observations, to make sense of data collected during experiments, to explore ideas, to learn, and to explain things and persuade others. Science students write for these same reasons, plus more "schoolish" reasons, such as taking exams. Being a proficient writer of a wide variety of science texts supports the acquisition of knowledge, the comprehension of big ideas, and the understanding of scientific practice. Helping students become proficient writers of science texts means supporting them in each of the many dimensions of writing.

Throughout this course, you may have come to understand writing in new ways. It is a lot more complex than most of us give it credit for. The advanced problem-solving and interpretation skills that writing requires must be learned over time and with the exploration of new texts. Proficient writers use strategies in situated ways (i.e., the right strategy at the right time for the right problem) and go beyond simply creating text to *crafting* text. Proficient writers understand themselves as writers, have confidence and stamina, write to communicate and to learn, and are able to write across a range of formats, purposes, and styles.

To become proficient, writers need to understand the role of others in their writing. They need to learn the cognitive skills required for writing texts that have different purposes and formats. Helping writers be metacognitive about their writing process allows writers to self-regulate, which can result in significant progress with writing as well as greater achievement in science.[1] This means students don't have to be "born good writers" to become good writers. Metacognition and metacognitive conversations, such as the ones that occur in writers' groups, teach students they can become more adept and successful writers by taking charge of their own writing process and collaborating with other writers.

Additionally, research shows that when students build a metacognitive understanding of themselves, they are more likely to see themselves as able learners, more motivated to learn, more adept at transferring their expertise from domain to domain, and more likely to take charge of their own learning. In particular, low-achieving students are the least likely to have metacognitive expertise, and helping them develop metacognitive skills, including self-reflection and self-regulation, improves their learning. Research also shows that metacognitive skills are needed in order to learn science, particularly science that is taught through inquiry methods.[2] In short, students who are metacognitive are likely to be not only better writers, but also better learners of science and better learners across the board.

---

[1] Greenleaf, C., et al. (2009). Integrating literacy and science instruction in high school biology: Impact on teacher practice, student engagement, and student achievement. Final Report to the National Science Foundation. Grant #0440379.

[2] White, B., Frederiksen, J., & Collins, A. (2009). The interplay of scientific inquiry and metacognition: More than a marriage of convenience. In D. Hacker, J. Dunlosky, & A. Graesser (Eds.), *Handbook of metacognition in education.* Mahwah, NJ: Lawrence Erlbaum Associates.

Structuring metacognitive routines

To help students develop these metacognitive skills, it helps to implement classroom routines that emphasize metacognition and metacognitive conversations among peers. Metacognitive routines are the process by which an individual's thinking is made visible and analyzed, often by a group of peers.

In this course, you repeatedly used a metacognitive routine that began with a Think Aloud after writing a piece of text and included observing others doing the same. Next you discussed the variety of writing processes used and analyzed them in terms of a specific goal (e.g., to hear and acquire new writing strategies, to learn what makes science texts unique, to discover how to best use images, symbols, and equations in science texts). Then you shared the results of this small-group work with the whole group. Your facilitator likely charted this discussion to encourage you to look for patterns and anomalies in the shared information. Writing and discussing the Literacy Reviews served as an opportunity for you to reflect on and internalize your learning.

An important consideration in planning to use metacognitive routines is what piece of text to base the work on. For example, if you choose a writing assignment that doesn't present writers with any problems, then a metacognitive routine probably will not surface many writing strategies. If surfacing writing strategies is your goal, choose a text that poses a variety of problems for writers and therefore requires them to selectively use writing strategies. If you want to draw writers' attention to the disciplinary ways of writing in science, choose an assignment that requires and supports this format.

The exact structure of metacognitive routines is not critical. They are effective as long as they help learners turn invisible thinking into visible objects, notice variety and discover patterns in how people think, and provide opportunities for reflection.

Metacognitive routines turn thinking into something tangible. They help make the mostly invisible process of thinking into something people can discuss and work with. For example, Talking to the Text helps people write down how they are thinking as they write, and Think Alouds help people verbalize their thinking while writing so others can document it.

Metacognitive routines help people notice variety and discover patterns in how people think. They give people a structure to work with the objects that represent their invisible thinking. For example, Gallery Walks, Whip-Arounds, Human Bar Graphs, and the Four Corners are all structured activities that help individuals see the variety in the writing processes of other people and, in turn, enable them to adapt and modify their own writing process to include the parts they like. Less-structured activities work for this too, such as allowing people to discuss some aspect of their writing process, charting people's ideas, and using different color highlighters to group similar ideas.

Metacognitive routines provide opportunities for reflection. They give people a structure for reflecting on the process of writing and for considering ways they might improve their own writing. These reflections can be written, but they don't have to be.

◉ Supporting writers

A well-structured metacognitive routine can be tuned such that it supports writers in different ways. The same routine can be used to support the personal and cognitive dimensions, simply by changing the focus of the metacognition.

> **LITERACY** **KEY CONCEPT**
>
> **Metacognitive routines can be tuned to support writers in the personal, social, cognitive, and knowledge-building dimensions of writing.**

The following sections describe how metacognitive routines were used in this course to support the writing process, dimension by dimension, and other approaches you might want to consider for supporting students in each dimension.

Dimensions of a Writing Apprenticeship

Personal dimension

The personal dimension is extremely important to writers. Without the ability to know ourselves as writers, it is difficult to improve ourselves as writers. The personal dimension includes a variety of things, such as a writer's metacognitive ability, confidence level, and ability to persist through writing difficult texts — all of which describe a person's identity as a writer. This dimension can come across as "touchy feely" to some people, particularly writers who don't need much support in this dimension of writing.

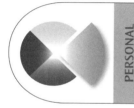

PERSONAL

- Discovering writer identity
- Building writer fluency and stamina
- Developing writer confidence and range
- Practicing and improving metacognition
- Getting into the habit of writing

In this course, we worked with the personal dimension most explicitly in Session 1. There you reflected on your personal writing history. Sharing and discussing your writing history with a partner began to reveal your identity as a writer. While being reflective about your personal writing histories was a metacognitive routine tuned to the personal dimension, it is likely you found it supported other dimensions too. For example, it may have helped create a safe environment for people to talk about writing (part of supporting the social dimension) or revealed some writing strategies people discovered throughout their lives as writers (part of supporting the cognitive dimension).

 PERSONAL

CLASSROOM ACTIVITY 1

Personal Writing Histories

Materials
None.

Individual and small-group procedure
See Session 1, Literacy Investigation.

Whole-group procedure
Share something interesting about a partner's personal writing history. Build off each other's comments or share something completely different. End by reflecting on what these histories reveal about writing (e.g., what's easy about writing, what's hard about writing, what supports writing, etc.).

In addition, throughout the course, you were asked to reflect on your experiences during the Literacy Investigations and consider how they informed your understanding of writing. You were also asked to write for a variety of purposes and formats and authentically use the writing tasks as opportunities to learn. Writing and authentically using a wide variety of texts help to support writer stamina, confidence, and range.

Social dimension

As with the personal dimension, supporting the social dimension is foundational for supporting the cognitive and knowledge-building dimensions. It is difficult to develop our cognitive skills, our knowledge of texts, and disciplinary ways of thinking and writing without having conversations with other writers.

- Creating safety for public sharing
- Exploring the relationship between literacy and power
- Participating in writers' groups
- Investigating writing processes, problems, and solutions
- Noticing and appropriating others' writing strategies

In this course, we supported the social dimension in every session. However, in the second session, we were especially attentive to the social dimension. In Session 2, you wrote and did a Think Aloud about a memorable teaching story (nonscience example), discussed your writing process with others, first in small groups then in the whole group, and then repeated the process for the expanded definition of energy. While the goal of this work was to help us begin to make our writing strategies transparent and begin to recognize how science texts are unique, the process carefully attended to the social dimension. For example, you wrote and discussed the nonscience writing first because we expected it would be an easier, more familiar way of writing. You wrote a small amount of text, so the attention wasn't on you for too long, and in the whole-group discussion, you didn't have to report on your own writing process, but instead on the writing processes of your partner. All of these choices were made with an eye to creating safety, building a community of learners, and establishing a culture of inquiry into writing.

CLASSROOM ACTIVITY 2

SOCIAL

Writing Nonscience Texts Versus Writing Science Texts

Materials
A moderately challenging nonscience writing task and a moderately challenging science writing task. Between the two tasks, writers should need to use several different writing strategies.

Individual and small-group procedure
See Session 2, Literacy Investigation.

Whole-group procedure
After writing the nonscience text, discuss what people did as they wrote. Chart the strategies. After writing the science text, discuss what people did as they wrote. Again, chart the strategies people used. Discuss the similarities and differences between writing nonscience and science texts.

In addition to this activity, the course was designed such that there was an overall focus on the collaborative learning process. For example, a "Group Norms" chart was posted throughout the course, and your facilitator probably helped the group address any concerns about the group's collaborative learning process each morning.

Cognitive dimension

The cognitive dimension is the one that usually comes to mind when we think about supporting writing skills. This is the dimension that includes such things as developing our repertoire of writing strategies and learning the situated use of those strategies. Writers need to learn the situated use of writing strategies through social interaction. They need to see how others solve problems they encounter while writing and use that as a lens to analyze and improve their own use of writing strategies.

COGNITIVE

- Getting the big picture
- Breaking down the text
- Learning writing strategies and when to use them
- Setting writing purposes
- Monitoring and adjusting writing processes

A common, but not very effective way of supporting this dimension of writing is handing writers a list of writing strategies and expecting them to use the strategies appropriately and fluently. Simply being handed a list of "-ing" words (e.g., clarifying, brainstorming, summarizing, outlining) doesn't give writers much traction.

This course explicitly supported the cognitive dimension by using metacognitive routines to generate lists of writing strategies and to discuss the situated use of those strategies. For example, in Session 3, you shared how you think while writing scientific explanations and discussed the variety of problems people encountered and the solutions they implemented. Through this process, you likely learned new writing strategies and new ways to use the ones you already had.

COGNITIVE

CLASSROOM ACTIVITY 3

Strategies for Writing Scientific Explanations

Materials

An authentic writing assignment well matched to a claim-evidence-reasoning format (e.g., an explanation of a science concept or phenomenon).

Note: It is important that the topic is directly related to what students have been learning because writing a scientific explanation requires synthesizing what they know. Make sure students have experienced (or can easily research) two or more pieces of evidence that clearly support the claim.

Individual and small-group procedure

See Session 3, Literacy Investigation.

Whole-group procedure

Share examples from other people's writing that seem important to include in this written explanation. Listen for information about claims, evidence, and reasoning and prompt for any parts that are missing. Then generate a "Tips for Writing Scientific Explanations" chart.

In addition, throughout the course, you continually added to your "Writing Strategies" chart and your "Science Writing Strategies" chart. Also, in Session 4, you were provided reminders of common writing strategies before embarking on the Think Alouds (in a sidebar on your Literacy Investigation pages). Some writers find these Think Aloud reminders especially helpful when they encounter a writing problem and aren't sure what to do about it.

Knowledge-building dimension

This dimension refers to the knowledge writers require to write in a specific way, using particular conventions and formats. For example, to draft a scientific explanation, writers need to know something about the topic, how the information is typically organized (e.g., claim, evidence, and reasoning), and which tone and text-types are expected. Without this familiarity, writers can struggle. The same is true of writing in other disciplines — writing in history and in math requires writers to have different sets of knowledge.

KNOWLEDGE-BUILDING
- Building knowledge of science
- Understanding the purpose of scientific writing
- Understanding the formats used by science writers
- Understanding the expectations readers of science have

The knowledge-building dimension is often overlooked by writers and teachers alike. In grades K–5, some emphasis is placed on learning the characteristics of different genres of writing. For example, students may be taught the differences between informational and narrative text and between persuasive writing and creative writing. However, rarely are students prepared for the complexities of discipline-specific writing such as science arguments, lab reports, explanations, and summaries.

This course places a lot of emphasis on the knowledge-building dimension because this course is specifically about writing in *science*. Learning discipline-specific characteristics of texts and writing processes falls in the knowledge-building dimension. For example, the Literacy Investigation in Session 4 focused on incorporating images, symbols, and equations into science writing and exploring how they support communication about ideas and information — part of the knowledge base writers of science texts require.

KNOWLEDGE-BUILDING

Images, Symbols, and Equations in Science Texts

Materials

Students' first draft of a prior writing assignment that can be strengthened by incorporating images, symbols, and/or equations. Informational writing or an assignment that involves communicating about data or scientific processes can work well.

Individual and small-group procedure

See Session 4, Literacy Investigation.

Whole-group procedure

Look at the use of images, symbols, and equations in a variety of science texts. Discuss which images, symbols, and equations were used in the texts, how they were used, and how they were or were not helpful for understanding the science. Share strategies writers used to decide which images, symbols, and/or equations to include and how to weave them into their writing. Add to the "Science Writing Strategies" chart in your classroom. Discuss what readers need and expect when they come across images, symbols, and equations in science texts and how writers can meet these needs.

In addition, in Session 2, you began to explore the characteristics of writing science texts by contrasting them with writing fiction texts, and in Session 3, you focused on scientific explanations and learned about other formats and text-types used in science. The primary goal in Session 3 was to explore and acquire new strategies for writing scientific explanations (e.g., what counts as evidence, how a claim differs from a summary statement).

In summary, the basic metacognitive routine used in this course consisted of your doing a Think Aloud, discussing some questions in small groups, then hearing the variety in people's writing processes and analyzing patterns in those processes in the whole group. Each session was designed to support one dimension (without excluding other dimensions) by tuning the questions you discussed in small groups and in the whole group. Tuning metacognitive routines such that they support the cognitive and knowledge-building dimensions is essential for helping writers develop disciplinary writing proficiency. The ability to use the same metacognitive routine, just tuned in different ways, reveals the true beauty of metacognitive routines — they are versatile tools. By carefully selecting appropriate writing assignments and discussion prompts, the same basic metacognitive routine can be used to support different dimensions.

In addition to supporting each of the four dimensions of writing and using tuned metacognitive routines to do so, it is important to be strategic about the overall approach you take toward helping writers become fluent users of metacognitive routines and better writers in general. Writing apprenticeships are one good model for doing this.

⊙ Apprenticeships

In essence, an apprenticeship is a context for learning, usually for learning how to do complex tasks with many dimensions, especially those that require lots of problem solving. For example, apprenticeship programs exist for many of the skilled trades, such as carpentry, masonry, and organic farming. Apprenticeship programs typically accept learners of varying abilities and interests — some have a strong desire to learn, while others just end up in the program because they aren't sure what else to do. Most apprenticeships have three basic components. First and foremost is actually doing the work, followed by classroom learning time and discussions with fellow apprentices.

Apprenticeships are generally led, but not dominated, by someone with significant expertise, a "master" in the field. For example, a good carpentry apprenticeship program is led by a master carpenter whose goal is to help his/her apprentices learn about the many dimensions of carpentry and what it means personally, professionally, and socially to be a carpenter. The master carpenter models skills for the apprentice and uses his/her own personal experience as examples. But, more importantly, s/he uses the apprentices' ever-growing body of personal carpentry experiences to instigate discussion. Carpentry apprentices are asked to reflect on what happened at a jobsite, how they handled things, and what they'd do differently next time. In essence, they are being metacognitive about their thinking and experiences.

These discussions help apprentices develop in all the dimensions of carpentry — the personal confidence and stamina, social skills (e.g., learning from and relating to other carpenters and with clients), the carpentry skills (e.g., tool use, blueprint reading), and a carpentry knowledge bank (e.g., safety regulations, the tradeoffs of different materials).

Writing apprenticeships

An apprenticeship in writing isn't all that different from a carpentry apprenticeship. A writing apprenticeship requires a master writer (in this situation a teacher) to guide apprentices, and the majority of writing apprentices' learning comes from actually doing the work of writing, being metacognitive about their writing, and discussing the work of writing and their writing processes with one another.

In this course, you have been part of an apprenticeship in writing, in particular a *science writing apprenticeship,* a context for learning about writing in science and how to teach students to become better writers of science texts. Metacognition and metacognitive conversations have been central to this apprenticeship. The beauty of using metacognition in writing apprenticeships is that being metacognitive opens us up to learn about all the dimensions of writing and gives individuals the freedom to work on the dimensions they are most interested in.

The science writing apprenticeship you experienced in this course was drawn from the work of the Strategic Literacy Initiative (SLI) at WestEd, as well as the work of the National Writing Project (NWP), countless classroom teachers, and research from many other literacy groups. Using metacognition as a tool for learning is a significant contribution from SLI, while NWP provided critical guidance around structuring writers' groups that respond to and learn from each other's writing.

Using metacognitive routines in a writing apprenticeship model can help students become better writers of science.

Rigorous research studies on SLI's work show that its Reading Apprenticeship approach, which includes metacognitive routines similar to those used in our science writing apprenticeship, makes a significant difference in students' reading abilities, as well as in their grade point averages in core academic classes and their performance on state standardized tests in both English language arts and science.[3] In fact, one study of 200 high school freshmen showed that a single school year of Reading Apprenticeship allowed students to improve their reading level by two whole grade levels. They went from an average late 7th grade reading level to an average late 9th grade reading level.[4]

One of SLI's publications, the best-selling book *Reading for Understanding,* available from WestEd, focuses specifically on reading apprenticeships and provides many suggestions for starting, maintaining, and evaluating reading apprenticeships. The following section provides a summary of some of those tips applied to the context of a science writing apprenticeship.

⊙ Planning a science writing apprenticeship

There is no single right way to involve students in a writing apprenticeship. However, SLI's research does provide important insights into structuring successful writing apprenticeships for students. The recommendations are divided into *Ideas for week 1, Ideas for weeks 2–4,* and *Ideas for ongoing work.* The final section, *Evaluating writing apprenticeships,* describes some options for collecting data on the effectiveness of writing apprenticeships and evaluating the data.

Ideas for week 1

Many students aren't really expecting to be taught how to write in science class because it's likely never happened to them before. Therefore, the first week of a science writing apprenticeship is a time of transition and stage-setting. In week 1, try to establish a culture of inquiry about writing in science. Also in week 1, focus on supporting the personal and social dimensions of writing and introduce metacognition.

[3] Greenleaf, C., Schneider, S., & Herman, J. (2005). *An efficacy study of Reading Apprenticeship professional development for high school history and science teaching and learning.* Teacher Quality Research Reading/Writing Grants, Grant # R305M050031. Washington, DC: Institute of Education Sciences, U.S. Department of Education; Summer, M-A., et al. (2010). *The enhanced reading opportunities study final report: The impact of supplemental literacy courses for struggling ninth-grade readers* (NCEE 2010-4021). Washington, DC: National Center for Education Evaluation and Regional Assistance, Institute of Education Sciences, U.S. Department of Education.

[4] Greenleaf, C., Schoenbach, R., Cziko, C., & Mueller, F. (2001). Apprenticing adolescents to academic literacy. *Harvard Educational Review, 71*(1), 79–129.

Good week 1 activities include sharing personal writing histories and beginning a "Science Writing Strategies" chart to support the personal and social dimensions of writing. Also, consider co-developing a set of group norms to post and use, and consider increasing the amount of paired and small-group work so students can interact in a less public, lower-stakes environment as they practice new skills and learn about themselves.

To introduce the concept of metacognition, you might ask students to describe their thinking process as they do something other than write (e.g., create something out of pipe cleaners, style their hair, decide what to wear). Once they know what metacognition is, you can model doing a Think Aloud with a writing activity students typically do outside of class (e.g., texting, sending emails, writing thank-you notes). Then you can model being metacognitive about a science writing task you personally find challenging. While you think aloud, ask students to use Think Aloud bookmarks to identify your thinking process. If you prefer, you can use the Talking to the Text activity.

Ideas for weeks 2–4

As the first month of school progresses, continue to support the personal and social dimensions by maintaining a focus on collaborative inquiry into writing processes. Weeks 2–4 are also a good time to begin working explicitly on the cognitive dimension of writing. Most importantly during this time, focus on helping students practice and learn to use metacognitive routines. Some specific things you might do include:

- Modeling multiple Think Alouds with a variety of writing assignments

- Spending more class time on writing, discussing the writing process for multiple important and difficult types of science writing (e.g., explanations, lab reports, descriptions, informational text), and working in writers' groups to help students refine their writing

- Having students take turns doing Think Alouds after a variety of writing assignments and afterward allowing them to discuss specific questions, such as "Which parts of the writing were hard and why?" "How were you thinking as you wrote?" "What decisions did you have to make? How did you make them?" and "Which writing strategies were used?"

- Beginning and adding to a class writing strategies list

Ideas for ongoing work

As the year progresses, explore the knowledge-building dimension of writing by focusing on the characteristics of science writing (i.e., purposes, structures, and formats). Often, by simply fine-tuning the questions students discuss after writing and thinking aloud or talking to the text, students can describe these characteristics themselves.

Evaluating writing apprenticeships

If you choose to implement a science writing apprenticeship in your classroom, it's important to consider how you will evaluate its effectiveness and collect evidence such that you can make informed decisions about what to modify in future years. It is also important for students to be active participants in this evaluation. Students often benefit from learning what does and doesn't work for them as individuals and seeing their progress with writing. It isn't terribly hard to collect the evidence you and your students will need in order to evaluate the effectiveness of a science writing apprenticeship. The following list describes just a few ways:

- Collect prewriting and postwriting surveys and/or personal writing history assignments. Compare and look for evidence of particular areas of focus. For example, is there evidence of students writing more, using more strategies, writing more broadly, or writing with better engagement, better comprehension, or less frustration?

- Collect Talking to the Text samples at multiple points in the year. Ask students to reflect on their work, discuss with a partner, and write about the changes they notice. You may also want to focus their Talking to the Text work on a particular writing strategy that is challenging (e.g., organizing, clarifying, summarizing) and have students do a Talking to the Text before and after instruction about that particular strategy.

- Have students revise a piece of writing multiple times with some type of intervention between each draft (e.g., a writers' group meeting, a class discussion about writing challenges, learning new relevant content information that should be included, exploring how to incorporate images, symbols, and equations, and so on). Collect these drafts and look for evidence of improvement.

- Listen to conversations students have after writing a text. Have students respond to their peers' Talking to the Texts and discuss their individual writing processes.

- Time how long students stay on-task during discussions about writing in pairs and in small groups. Track whether or not the length of time increases over the year and for which students.

- Count the number of students using writing supports (e.g., highlighters, sticky notes, Talking to the Text) during in-class silent writing.

- Note which students finish first and last and which students revise their writing.

Science Investigation

60 MINUTES

Investigating food webs

a. The food web below is a model for some of the interactions that occur in a boreal forest. Look at the food web and discuss the following questions:

- What do you think the arrows in this food web represent? How might you say what they mean in *words*?

- What can you conclude or say about the boreal forest by looking at *only* the information shown in this food web?

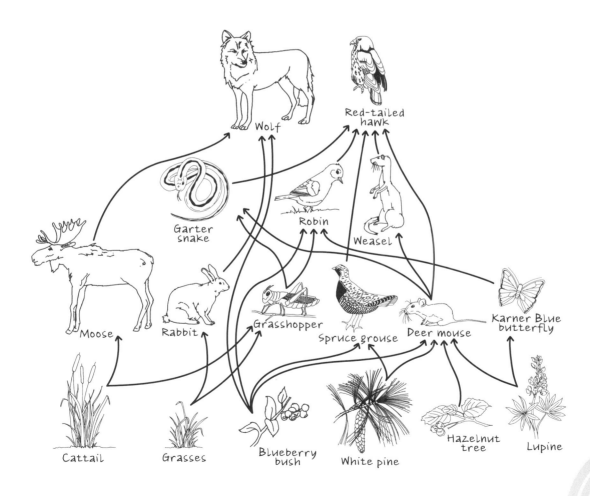

2 # Tracking matter in ecosystems

a. With your group, choose one of the food chains from the boreal food web. Then create a matter web on 11" × 17" paper.

Hint: Think about which kinds of matter are passed up the food chain, which kinds of matter go elsewhere, and where the matter involved in the food chain originally came from. Then make choices about which matter associated with your food chain is "of interest" to you and track it using a matter web.

✳ MAKING MATTER WEBS

Matter webs track what happens with matter in ecosystems, including the kinds and locations of the matter. They can be used to track one kind of matter or many kinds of matter.

In matter webs:

- **Boxes** indicate the *locations* of matter. These could be places, such as soil or organisms.

- **Arrows** indicate *matter moving* from one location to another.

- **Descriptions** are optional and can provide specific details about the *kind of matter* that is moving.

Here is an example for a dog's day:

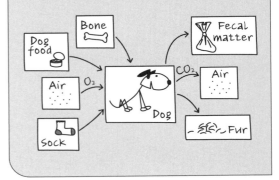

---

b. Discuss the utility of matter webs.

- What does your matter web help you understand about the boreal forest?

- What doesn't it help you understand about this forest?

---

3 # Tracking energy in ecosystems

a. Together, create an energy tree diagram for the same food chain as your matter web, again using 11" × 17" paper.

Hint: First think about how to define the system for which you will construct your energy tree diagram. Then think about which types of energy can be passed up the food chain, which types of energy leave the food chain, and the relative amounts of energy that are likely to be transferred.

 MAKING ENERGY TREE DIAGRAMS

Energy tree diagrams show the types of energy involved in an interaction, along with energy transfers that occur. In energy tree diagrams:

- **Ovals** indicate the *types of energy* (e.g., kinetic energy, heat energy) associated with an interaction.

- **Arrows** indicate the *energy transfers*, either from type to type or from one interaction to another.

- **Descriptions** explain the *event* linked to the energy transfer.

Here is an example for a burning log:

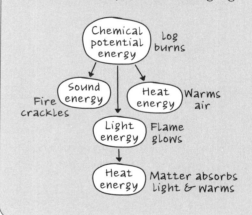

b. Discuss the utility of energy tree diagrams.

- What does your energy tree help you understand about the boreal forest?

- What doesn't it help you understand about this forest?

4 Explaining the 10% rule

a. The Content Notes claim that "only about 10% of the energy associated with any given trophic level is passed up to the nest trophic level." Work together to draft a scientific explanation for why this so-called 10% rule is true.

Hint: Your matter webs and energy tree diagrams are a good source of evidence. What you know about the conservation of energy and energy transfers is a good source of reasoning.

5 Checking your understanding

a. Work together to decide whether each statement is true or false. Use evidence from your hands-on work and information from the Content Notes.

T   F

☐ ☐ The arrows in food webs show all the energy transfers in an ecosystem.

☐ ☐ Food webs include only organisms and arrows. It is wrong to include the Sun.

☐ ☐ Plant food is sunlight, fertilizer, and water.

☐ ☐ Matter and energy cycle within ecosystems.

☐ ☐ The 1st trophic level in a food chain has more energy than all other trophic levels combined.

b. Rewrite any ambiguous or false statements to make them correct.

Classroom Connection

40 MINUTES

20 MINUTES **1** Reviewing key concepts

a. Individually, read the Science Review. Feel free to pick and choose the sections that are most valuable to you.

As you read, take notes and think about these questions:

- What is interesting or new to you?

- Which examples and images do you find especially helpful?

- What are you still wrestling with?

b. Individually, take a few minutes to think and write about your own big takeaways from today.

2 **Exploring the ideas of this session**

    a. As a group, discuss the Science Review. Use the questions on the previous page as a guide.

3 **Considering classroom implications**

    a. Based on your experiences today, discuss implications for *what* and *how* you teach your students.

Literacy Investigation

 1 **Reviewing the Literacy Notes**

a. Individually, reread the Key Concepts box on the first page of your Literacy Notes. Then take 2 minutes to think and write about the following questions.

- Which of the four dimensions do you personally need the *least* support in? Are there dimensions in which you feel that you need to grow as a writer?

- Do you think the same is true for your students, or do they excel and struggle in different dimensions?

b. Individually, take 2 minutes to think and write about the following questions.

- How confident do you feel about being metacognitive yourself and teaching students to be metacognitive?

- Are there things about metacognition you are still wrestling with?

c. Individually, take 2 minutes to think and write about the following questions.

- What do you like and not like about the writing apprenticeship model?

- What do you like and not like about writers' groups?

- Do you think your students will feel the same? How or how not?

② Discussing the Literacy Notes

a. In your small group, take turns sharing your thoughts and ideas about the preceding questions.

a. Start by deciding whether you will work alone or with a partner to make your plan for how to incorporate supporting students' science writing.

b. Next, determine 2–5 overarching goals you have for your students that are specific to their science writing abilities and attitudes. Try to write these goals in language you could share with students.

c. For each goal, develop a plan for the year that moves students toward the goal in a purposefully sequenced way by:

- Introducing students to the idea

- Helping students build the skill

- Giving students practice using the skill

- Encouraging students to apply the skill in new contexts and advanced ways

d. Review your plan and make sure you are satisfied with how each goal is developed and how the plan came together among the goals. Make any adjustments you feel are needed now that you see the whole.

e. If time permits, consider how you and your students will monitor their progress with science writing. Which examples and other data will you collect? What will you evaluate? How will you gauge students' progress toward the goals?

f. Finally, record your goals and your plan on a poster to share with your colleagues.

Session Review

SCIENCE REVIEW

Understanding the relationships between energy and matter is essential to making sense of the many complex interactions that occur in ecosystems. Simultaneously, understanding these complex interactions reveals important things about energy, including how sometimes it is associated with matter and how other times it is not.

SCIENCE **KEY CONCEPT**

All living organisms require food to survive, grow, and reproduce. Even producers require food — they just make their own food internally. Food is *organic* matter in a form that provides organisms a source of matter and energy. Producers synthesize this organic matter internally from *inorganic* matter they take in from their environment (e.g., carbon dioxide and water). Light energy enables this synthesis to occur. Consumers cannot do this. They must eat other organisms to obtain their food.

SCIENCE **KEY CONCEPT**

Matter cycles within and among Earth's ecosystems. Energy transfers through them on a one-way route. Matter is a physical substance that is used and reused as it cycles within the ecosystem of Earth. For example, an organism's body is passed on to its consumer, and oxygen and carbon dioxide are passed between organisms and the air. By contrast, energy takes a one-way route. There is an input of energy to a food chain (incoming LE is transferred to CPE during photosynthesis) and an output of energy from the food chain to another system (biological processes transfer this CPE into other types of energy, for example, HE, SE, or KE). Once CPE transfers to these types of energy and the energy is no longer available to help meet the CPE needs of organisms, it has left the system and is no longer part of the food chain.

SCIENCE **KEY CONCEPT**

The amount of energy in a food chain is *inversely* related to the trophic level. Higher trophic levels have less energy than lower ones. Plants form the base of ecological pyramids, the first trophic level. The amount of CPE in this base is the total amount of energy available for all the higher trophic levels. This amount of energy is *not* parsed out equally among all the trophic levels. Instead, each trophic level has only about 10% of the energy the preceding trophic level had. This means higher trophic levels have only a very small percentage of the energy originally put in by producers.

⊙ Food in ecosystems

Food provides organisms the matter needed to build tissue and the energy required for this work and the work of thinking, digesting, breathing, and moving. Different organisms consume different foods because they are able to digest different things. If an organism's digestive processes can break the chemical bonds in the matter *and* the process results in a net transfer of energy to the organism's cells, then that matter is considered food for that particular organism.

SCIENCE **KEY CONCEPT**

All living organisms require food to survive, grow, and reproduce. Even producers require food — they just make their own food internally.

Different organisms may consume different foods, but all organisms, even plants, need food. Plants are special because they are able to use the glucose they make during photosynthesis as food. While it is incorrect to say plants don't need food, this idea hints at the big difference between plants and animals. Plants and other producers don't need external food sources. Plants do not use fertilizer, sunlight, light energy, or anything they obtain directly from their environment as food.

IDEAS ABOUT *Plants' Food*

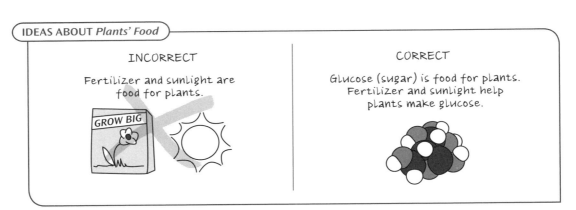

INCORRECT

Fertilizer and sunlight are food for plants.

GROW BIG

CORRECT

Glucose (sugar) is food for plants. Fertilizer and sunlight help plants make glucose.

It's easy to assume that if plants need nutrients and sunlight to make food, then nutrients and sunlight *are* food. One helpful way to think about this is that food provides a significant amount of both matter *and* energy to an organism. Nutrients are not food because although they are made of matter, they are very low-energy molecules. Sunlight is not food because although it is high in energy, it is not made of matter.

A related common, yet incorrect idea is that plants get the matter they use to synthesize glucose from water. Not true! In fact 93% of the mass of the glucose actually comes from carbon dioxide the plants absorb from the air.

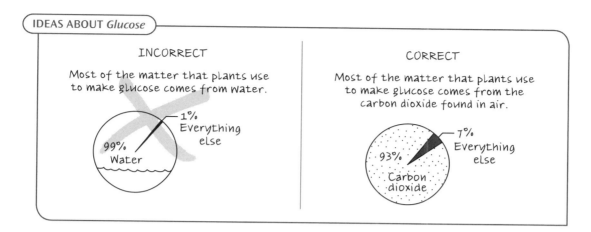

IDEAS ABOUT *Glucose*

INCORRECT

Most of the matter that plants use to make glucose comes from water.

99% Water — 1% Everything else

CORRECT

Most of the matter that plants use to make glucose comes from the carbon dioxide found in air.

93% Carbon dioxide — 7% Everything else

The logic behind this incorrect idea may be rooted in our everyday experience with air. We think of air as very light, perhaps even massless, when in fact air is made of matter and has mass just like every other physical substance. Since a cup of water is much heavier than a cup of air, it's logical to think water provides most of the matter for glucose. However, the chemical formulas that describe the synthesis of glucose in plants show that this isn't true. (The Content Notes for this session have a more detailed description of the formulas.)

Food chains and food webs

It is important to realize what food chains and food webs do and do not show about ecosystems. Food chains and food webs are models that show what organisms consume. Although food webs show more of the interdependence that exists in nature than food chains do, even food webs do not show all the things every organism eats. If food webs showed all the eating that occurred in an ecosystem, you wouldn't be able to make heads or tails of all the arrows.

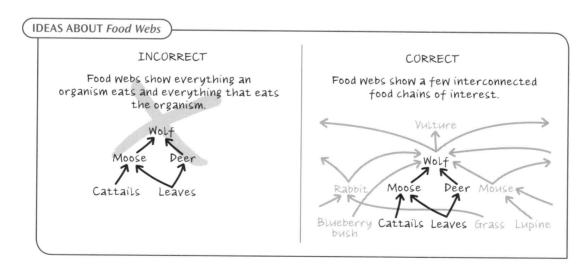

IDEAS ABOUT *Food Webs*

INCORRECT

Food webs show everything an organism eats and everything that eats the organism.

Wolf
Moose   Deer
Cattails   Leaves

CORRECT

Food webs show a few interconnected food chains of interest.

Vulture
Wolf
Rabbit   Moose   Deer   Mouse
Blueberry bush   Cattails   Leaves   Grass   Lupine

Since food webs do a much better job of showing the many paths food takes in ecosystems, there is some logic in thinking they show everything that's being eaten. However, food webs are just models for ecosystems and, like all models, do not represent everything about an ecosystem perfectly. When drawing a food web, the writer has to decide which organisms are "of interest" and therefore important to show.

In addition to showing only select organisms, food webs do not show any of the nonfood matter that organisms consume. In other words, food webs do not show that organisms consume water and air, nor do they show that organisms consume indigestible matter that does not provide a significant source of matter and energy and thus is not food. For example, dogs and cats often eat grass, but grass does not provide a significant source of matter and energy. Thus grass is not shown as a food source for dogs and cats in a food chain. Our pets eat grass for other reasons, for example, to help them remove a hairball or other unwanted substance, such as a lost sock, from their bellies.

Also, by convention, food webs do not show what plants use as food (i.e., glucose). Additionally, since food webs show only food, it is incorrect to include the Sun in food webs because the Sun itself is not food for anything. Instead, the Sun is an *energy source* for photosynthesis.

Arrows in food webs

During the Science Investigation, you were asked to talk about what the arrows in food webs mean and what food webs alone can tell you about an ecosystem. A sample correct answer follows.

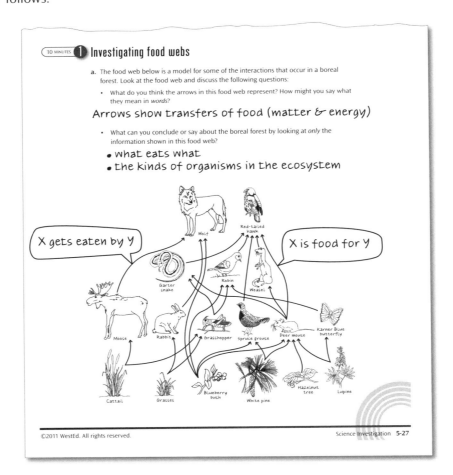

Science Investigation 5-27

Arrows in food webs represent one organism being eaten by another — they represent a transfer of food, which is a significant source of *both* energy *and* matter for an organism.

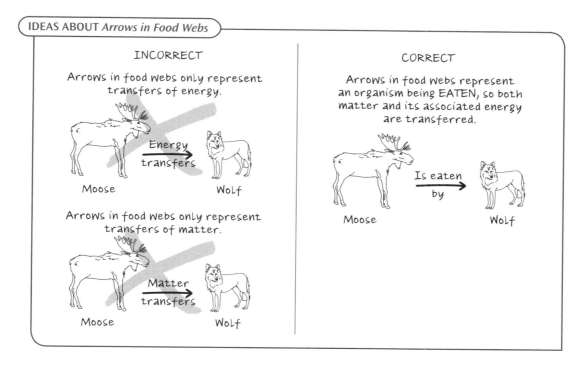

IDEAS ABOUT *Arrows in Food Webs*

INCORRECT

Arrows in food webs only represent transfers of energy.

Moose — Energy transfers → Wolf

Arrows in food webs only represent transfers of matter.

Moose — Matter transfers → Wolf

CORRECT

Arrows in food webs represent an organism being EATEN, so both matter and its associated energy are transferred.

Moose — Is eaten by → Wolf

It is logical to think about arrows as "energy transfers" or as "matter transfers," as that is part of their story. But it is important to be precise about what the arrows in food webs mean or incorrect ideas can arise about what happens with energy and matter in ecosystems.

By incorrectly thinking that the arrows in food webs represent the "energy transfers" that occur in ecosystems, people miss the fact that there are many nonfood-related energy transfers that occur in ecosystems (e.g., LE is transferred to CPE in plants, KE is transferred to HE as the wolf moves). And by incorrectly thinking that the arrows in food webs represent the "matter transfers" that occur in ecosystems, people miss the fact that there are many nonfood-related matter transfers that occur in ecosystems (e.g., the moose exhales carbon dioxide into the air, the wolf consumes soil stuck to the moose's body).

⦿ Energy and matter in ecosystems

The nonfood-related transfers of matter and the nonfood-related transfers of energy that occur in ecosystems cannot be tracked using food chains and food webs, but they can be tracked with other representations, such as matter webs and energy tree diagrams. And by doing so, it becomes apparent that what happens with matter in ecosystems is not the same as what happens with energy in ecosystems.

Matter cycles within and among Earth's ecosystems. Energy transfers through them on a one-way route.

Matter in ecosystems

Much like food webs show the movement of food in ecosystems, matter webs show the movement of matter in ecosystems. Matter webs illustrate a more complete picture of what happens with matter in ecosystems. They can be used to track many kinds of matter, including food, nutrients, oxygen, carbon, and heavy metals.

During the Science Investigation, you made a matter web for a food chain in the boreal forest. As the writer, you made choices about which matter was "of interest" and therefore was worth tracking in your diagram. A sample correct answer follows.

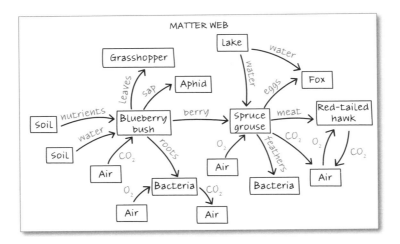

Matter webs can illustrate the age-old adage "nothing in nature is wasted." Every bit of an organism's body, the air it breathes in and out, and the waste it produces during its lifetime is all transferred somewhere — either directly to another living organism or to a nonliving part of the environment (e.g., the air, water, the ground) where it is often used by another organism at some later point in time.

In addition to showing *conservation of matter,* matter webs are used for other purposes, such as tracking carbon, phosphorous, nitrogen, and calcium. Carbon is the most common element to track using a matter web because carbon is the backbone of organic molecules in an ecosystem.

The following diagram is an illustrated matter web showing the paths carbon might take as it cycles through ecosystems (a.k.a. the carbon cycle). The black arrows show processes that cause carbon to move into the atmosphere as CO_2. The gray arrows indicate processes that keep carbon out of or remove it from the atmosphere.

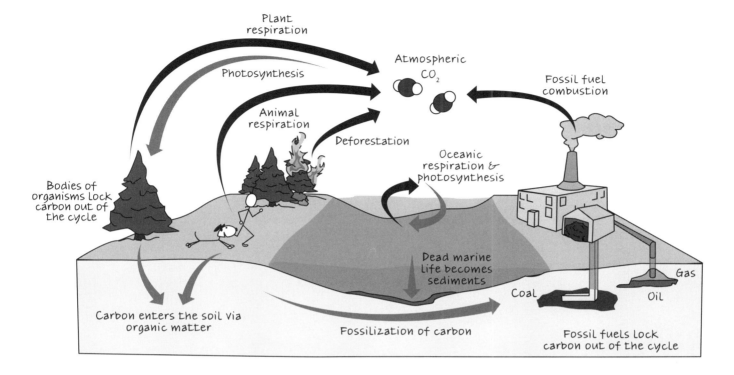

While this diagram clearly shows carbon cycling, the scale of this cycle is less clear. It is often said that "carbon cycles in ecosystems," but you can imagine that carbon is not trapped within any single ecosystem. There are several ways carbon moves from one ecosystem to another. Fires release carbon into the air, which wind can carry to another ecosystem. Plants pull carbon from air that might have once been part of another ecosystem. Some organisms (e.g., birds and insects) travel between ecosystems, taking their matter with them. Streams, rivers, and oceans transport matter from one ecosystem to another.

Therefore, it is more precise to say that matter cycles *within and among* ecosystems or to define Earth as one big ecosystem and say carbon cycles within the larger ecosystem of Earth. How you choose to define the system determines whether you talk about carbon cycling within an ecosystem or among ecosystems. But the point is that carbon, like all matter, cycles within the large ecosystem of Earth.

The cycles of matter within and among ecosystems are complex and have many paths. In the end, the matter of a blueberry bush may become part of many other organisms — the air, the ocean, the soil — and someday it could even again be part of a blueberry bush.

Energy in ecosystems

While matter is always being passed around and ultimately conserved within the larger ecosystem of Earth, energy takes a one-way trip through ecosystems. The Sun provides an input of energy to a food web. Producers transfer this incoming LE into CPE associated with the chemical bonds of glucose during photosynthesis. Then the metabolic processes of producers and their consumers transfer this CPE into other types of energy. Once this energy transfers into HE, it is lost from the food web and becomes an output of energy to another system, as shown in the following linked box and arrow diagram.

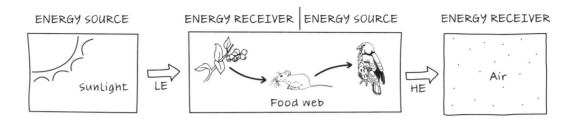

During the Science Investigation, you made an energy tree diagram to show the many branching energy transfers for a boreal forest food chain. A sample correct answer follows. The stars (☆☆) indicate energy dead ends, places where energy leaves the food chain.

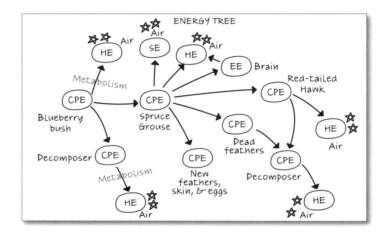

This energy tree diagram shows CPE being transferred to KE, HE, SE, and EE as organisms move, keep themselves warm, make sound, and send impulses to their nerves. As these and subsequent energy transfers occur, the CPE eventually transfers to HE and leaves the food web. The energy once associated with organisms' bodies and waste is now HE associated with air and other nonliving parts of the environment (e.g., water and rock).

Once these (and other) biological processes transfer CPE into other types of energy, the energy is no longer available to be transferred on to the next consumer in the ecosystem. Only the CPE associated with an organism's body (and consumable waste products) can be transferred up the food chain. This is energy's one-way trip through ecosystems.

IDEAS ABOUT *Energy in Food Chains*

INCORRECT

Energy is used up by food chains.

Energy cycles within food chains.

CORRECT

Food chains have an input of energy from the Sun and outputs of energy to other systems.

External systems

If there were a limited supply of energy available for ecosystems, life on Earth would be in big trouble, since energy doesn't cycle. However, the Sun provides an ample amount of light energy to Earth, so ecosystems are continually supplied with the needed input of energy. The following Venn Diagram helps visually represent some of the similarities and differences in what happens with energy and matter in ecosystems.

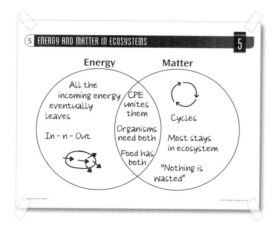

5 ENERGY AND MATTER IN ECOSYSTEMS   5

Energy

All the incoming energy eventually leaves

In - n - Out

CPE unites them

Organisms need both

Food has both

Matter

Cycles

Most stays in ecosystem

"Nothing is wasted"

◉ Energy and trophic level

All organisms require a certain amount of CPE from their food to keep them alive. They need more to grow or reproduce. Photosynthetic producers have a plentiful supply of energy from the Sun. Between 0.1% and 8% of the light energy that reaches producers is transferred into CPE, depending on the light intensity and wavelength, the availability of molecules such as water, nitrogen, and carbon dioxide, the reflectivity of the plant leaves, and the temperature.

The only limitation on the amount of CPE available to a plant is how fast the plant is able to complete photosynthesis and other metabolic processes.

This is not true for consumers. Consumers only have as much CPE available to them as they can obtain from their food. When herbivores eat plants, about 90% of the plants' CPE is either wasted (passes through the herbivores' bodies without being digested) or used in metabolism, movement, thinking, and other daily activities. Herbivores retain only about 10% of the energy from the producers they eat.

SCIENCE ⟩ **KEY CONCEPT**

The amount of energy in a food chain is _inversely_ related to the trophic level. Higher trophic levels have less energy than lower ones.

The "remaining" energy, a mere 10% of what was associated with producers, is all that is available to the secondary consumers who eat these herbivores. The available energy gets worse for the tertiary consumers. They too acquire only about 10% of the energy associated with their food. And so it goes. Thus, since only about 10% of the previous trophic level's energy is passed up the food web, the amount of available energy drops off rapidly. The 90% that is not retained is transferred to HE, SE, EE, KE, and CPE in waste or indigestible matter and therefore is not shown on a pyramid of energy.

Ecological pyramids of energy are used to show what happens with energy at each trophic level. The following pyramid shows the "classic" shape of a pyramid of energy. Each level is about one-tenth the size of the previous level to represent the amount of CPE in each trophic level. The theoretical numbers of joules on the pyramid show the magnitude of the drop in energy. At each trophic level in the pyramid, about 90% of the energy is transferred to air and other abiotic matter as organisms breathe, move, digest, and think. This energy is not destroyed — it is conserved within the entire universe, but it is "lost" by this particular system of organisms.

PYRAMID OF ENERGY

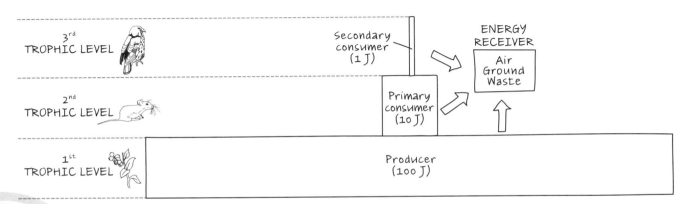

During the Science Investigation, you discussed several true/false questions. The last of these questions directly addressed the relationship among trophic levels in terms of energy. Sample correct and corrected responses follow.

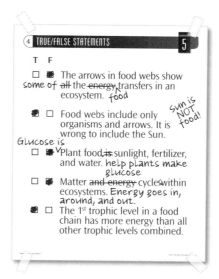

⊙ Tradeoffs of ecosystem models

Food chains, food webs, matter webs, energy tree diagrams, and ecological pyramids are all models that represent interactions and events that occur in ecosystems. So how do you decide which model to use and when to use it? There is no single right answer. There are only tradeoffs. Often a combination of models is a good way to represent and understand what happens with energy and matter in ecosystems. The following paragraphs describe some of these tradeoffs.

Food chains and food webs

Food chains are the most common model for studying ecosystems in schools, and food webs are a close second. The simplicity of food chains means they cannot paint a very complete picture of an ecosystem, but they are easy to understand. However, food chains can incorrectly suggest that each organism is eaten only by one consumer *and* that a single consumer eats only one kind of organism. In nature this is rarely true, as the survival of populations would be severely jeopardized if they relied on only one food source and that food source became extinct. The norm for consumers is that they eat many kinds of organisms, thus protecting their populations. Food webs represent this diversity of food sources more accurately than food chains. However, food webs can be visually overwhelming and the plethora of arrows can make the fate of a single organism hard to track.

A drawback of both food chains and food webs is that they show very little of what actually happens with matter and energy in ecosystems. Most food chains and food webs track only what a few organisms of interest eat. Most often they leave out scavengers (e.g., vultures), detritivores (e.g., worms), and decomposers (e.g., fungi) altogether. They also leave out other transfers of matter and energy that are not associated with food, such as carbon cycling and heat energy transfers.

Ecological pyramids

Ecological pyramids do something that food chains and food webs do not — they show proportional relationships between trophic levels in ecosystems. Ecological pyramids can visually represent how much energy or how much biomass is at each trophic level in a food chain, food web, or ecosystem. From an ecological standpoint, this is sometimes more important than knowing what different consumers eat. One limitation of ecological pyramids is that sometimes it's easy to forget they are not just displaying "what eats what" in a new stacked format. Instead, the size of each level in a pyramid represents the relative amount of either energy or biomass associated with an individual trophic level in comparison with other trophic levels. Another limitation is that, like food chains and food webs, ecological pyramids do not show most of what happens with energy in ecosystems (i.e., they don't track nonfood-related transfers of energy or energy inputs and outputs).

Matter webs and energy tree diagrams

Matter webs and energy tree diagrams are slightly less common ways of representing ecosystems. They can represent details about what happens with matter and energy in ecosystems that none of the preceding food-based representations can. Matter webs let you keep track of the tiniest bits of matter and show the details of how matter cycles. Matter webs are especially useful for studying the carbon cycle, climate change, decomposition, and photosynthesis. Energy tree diagrams are especially useful to help account for why only about 10% of the energy associated with any given trophic level is transferred up to the next trophic level. The branching nature of energy tree diagrams helps make these energy losses visible.

While the level of detail in matter webs and energy tree diagrams is extremely useful, it is also a limitation. It can be very hard to get a general picture of the relationships between organisms in an ecosystem from these representations — there is simply too much other stuff in them to see the big picture.

LEARNING OBJECTIVES

Food in Ecosystems

5.1 All living organisms, including plants and other producers, require food to survive, grow, and reproduce.

5.2 Food is organic matter that provides an organism with a significant source of matter and energy.

5.3 Producers are plants, algae, and bacteria that synthesize their food internally from inorganic matter (largely CO_2 from the air). In photosynthesis, LE is transferred to CPE in sugars.

5.4 Consumers are animals, fungi, and bacteria that cannot synthesize their own food from inorganic matter. They must eat other organisms.

5.5 Food chains and food webs show what organisms eat. The arrows start at the food and point toward the organism doing the eating.

5.6 The first organism in a food chain is always a producer. Consumers make up all higher levels of food chains.

Matter and Energy in Ecosystems

5.7 Matter cycles in Earth's ecosystems. Matter is a physical substance that is not destroyed, just converted to new substances during the interactions that occur in ecosystems.

5.8 Energy flows through Earth's ecosystems. Energy does not cycle. During the interactions that occur in ecosystems, energy is transferred to types that are not useful.

5.9 Higher trophic levels have less energy than lower ones. Each trophic level has only approximately 10% of the energy of the preceding level. Ecological pyramids of energy show this.

MISCONCEPTIONS

5.A It is incorrect to think living things need only matter or only energy or that food provides only one of these.

5.B It is incorrect to think plants do not need food.

5.C It is incorrect to think that sunlight, water, soil, and fertilizer are foods for plants or that plants make food from light alone or from soil, nutrients, and water alone.

5.D It is incorrect to think the matter that plants use to make sugar predominantly comes from the soil or from water.

5.E It is incorrect to think the Sun belongs in food chains, as it is not food for anything. The Sun provides the energy producers need to make food, not the matter they need to make food.

5.F It is incorrect to think consumers eat only one kind of organism (e.g., hawks eat only rabbits) or are always bigger than what they eat.

5.G It is incorrect to think that the amount of food available for organisms is based on how much they need.

5.H It is incorrect to think energy is "used up" in an ecosystem.

LOOKING AT STUDENT WORK™ GUIDE

Introduction

Students' words and drawings offer an incredible window into their ways of thinking about science. Their work is also a mirror for teachers. It reflects important information that helps us teach.

By piecing together evidence and clues from our students' work, we can figure out what is confusing to some, gaps that others have in their learning, what to teach when, and how best to help students (who have differing abilities and ideas) move toward a solid understanding of the science. In short, productively examining your own students' work with colleagues is a gift, one that inspired this **Looking at Student Work™** approach to professional development. Enjoy!

What should I expect?

Looking at Student Work offers a structured process for collaborating with colleagues to examine student work from each other's classrooms. It consists of 10 hours of professional development divided into five 2-hour sessions that focus on the specifics of your curriculum, your instruction, and relevant science assessments. The materials are designed to help you:

- Examine your own students' science ideas

- Recognize evidence of understanding and proficiency

- Analyze instructional tasks and assessments

- Make instructional choices grounded in evidence

Because the process highlights what is happening in the moment with your students and your colleagues' students as they learn about specific science concepts, the sessions are likely to be most useful if they coincide with your teaching about the related science topic.

Looking at Student Work takes place in study groups, such as professional learning communities, in which teachers facilitate their own discussions supported by this guide. You may be a group of two or a group with many teachers from around your district or region. If you are a larger group, some time will be spent working in pairs or groups of three, and some time will be set aside to talk as a whole group. In order to facilitate the process, you and your colleagues will need to take on the roles of *Reader*, *Timekeeper*, and *Recorder*. These roles can be rotated from session to session, and prior to each meeting it is helpful to decide who will do what.

How should we choose roles?

When deciding roles, one option is to rotate roles among participants in your study group. Another option is to choose a single Reader for the five sessions and share the other roles. For groups of two, try combining the Timekeeper and Recorder roles. Another option is to omit the Recorder role and have each person take notes. Feel free to make modifications to fit the needs and style of your group.

Reader 💬

This person's job is…(you guessed it)…to read. More specifically, the Reader takes the lead role in helping the group meet its goals for the session. This involves reading parts of the procedure out loud so everyone is clear about *what* to do, *why,* and *how.* The Reader's "script" helps set the stage, describe the flow of events, move the group along, and keep everyone on the same page (so to speak). The Reader also "reads" the room and, as appropriate, can choose to ask follow-up questions to clarify an idea, focus the conversation, or broaden the discussion. The Reader helps the group keep to the recommended agenda and/or make changes to get the most out of the time together. However, it is *not* the Reader's role to be the expert, to provide "answers," or to summarize the group's thinking.

A shaded box with a talk bubble (💬) gives the Reader instructions. An open bubble (◯) marks the beginning of a spoken section and suggests what the Reader should say. A square (▪) marks the end of a spoken section.

Timekeeper 🕒

This person's job is to periodically remind the group of the time and help folks stay on task. The Timekeeper moves the group along by writing the "stop time" on the board, announcing when there are a few minutes remaining, and telling people when it's time to stop an activity and regroup.

A shaded box with a clock (🕒) gives the Timekeeper instructions for communicating about the amount of time allotted for a given activity.

Sidebars prompt the Timekeeper to announce when participants should stop one activity and move on to another.

Recorder ✎

This person's job is to write on a chart (or whiteboard) to keep a public record of the group's ideas at various points during a discussion. This record helps everyone stay focused, revisit ideas, and build on what others say. For example, when the group is brainstorming, the Recorder could write down the ideas generated. When the group is summarizing, the Recorder could write a bulleted list as people share.

A shaded box with a marker pen (✎) suggests when the Recorder should make a public record. A sample mini chart suggests what to write and/or draw.

How can we work most productively?

In general, collaborative study groups are most successful when they operate with clear goals and shared expectations. Their discussions are especially rich when participants see their work as an act of inquiry. An inquiry stance establishes openness for questions, an appreciation for diverse ideas, and expectations for evidence-based conversations. Following are some suggestions for working productively in your group.

Decide on group norms. Because everyone will bring in student work as part of this process, it is especially important to develop an environment that feels welcoming and respectful. Respect for each other can be shown by honoring your beginning and ending times, coming prepared, and staying focused on the learning. A sense of welcome can be shown by acknowledging it's okay to "try on" new ideas, be wrong, change your mind, and revise your thinking. Guidance is provided in the first session for helping your group figure out what norms make sense for you.

Rotate small groups. You will spend a lot of working time in pairs or groups of three. From one session to the next, you will want to vary groups to allow people to work with a range of colleagues. Not only will you learn different things from different people, but also changing groups signals that everyone's contributions are valuable and each person's perspective can contribute to the learning of the whole group.

Talk from evidence. Looking at Student Work is a process of inquiry. This means you will want to talk from evidence, for example, when you examine students' work, analyze instructional tasks and assessments, and inquire into your own teaching. You can help each other stay focused on evidence by asking questions such as:

- Where do you see that in the student work?

- What led you to that idea?

- What evidence supports your interpretation?

Encourage a variety of viewpoints. Sometimes the goal of a group is to reach consensus or agreement on ideas. For example, this is important when identifying what is correct or incorrect in terms of science content. However, the intent is different when analyzing student work and exploring instruction. Here your goal is *not* to seek agreement, but rather to share interpretations and consider tradeoffs. This means the most productive work comes from stretching your thinking, encouraging participation from everyone, and listening openly to different perspectives. These are good marks of success!

What materials are provided?

Looking at Student Work is meant to be read *and* used as a sort of "journal." It is organized into five sequential sessions (A–E) and should be used as a place to record ideas and track your thinking. Please write in it!! You can always print another clean copy from the accompanying CD. In this guide, you will find:

Sessions A–E. Each session includes the session *goals,* a suggested *agenda,* a scripted *procedure* describing the sequence of events, and *guiding questions* for the discussion with space to write.

Learning Objectives & Misconceptions. Appendix A provides a list of science *learning objectives* and a summary of classic *misconceptions* related to the science in this course. These are useful when analyzing student tasks, evaluating student work, and identifying intended learning outcomes.

Task Bank. Appendix B offers a treasure trove of optional *assessments* and thought-provoking *activities* related to the science topic for this course and specifically designed for middle school students.

Student Work. Two sample sets of student work — one that can be used in Session A to get your group started and another for use as a backup — are provided on the CD accompanying this book.

What should I know about sharing student work?

During these sessions you will bring in 9–12 samples of student work at least once, along with an assessment task from your own curriculum for Session E. The purpose of sharing artifacts from your classroom is to gain insight into how students are thinking about the science, to analyze a variety of assessment tasks, and to weigh the tradeoffs of instructional choices.

When it is your turn to bring in student work, you have the option of using an assignment from the Task Bank (see Appendix B) or one from your own curriculum that focuses on science concepts related to this course and reveals how your students' are thinking about the science.

Exactly when you bring in student work from your own classroom depends on several things, including how many people are in this study group, when you are teaching the related science, and what is convenient for both you and others in your group. Generally, at the end of Session A, groups discuss the options and decide on a schedule for who will bring in student work for Sessions B, C, and D. If more than one teacher chooses the same session, it is extremely helpful for these teachers to use the same task. To help coordinate, a schedule is provided at the end of this introduction.

Selecting student work

After you have identified a fitting task and your students have completed the assignment, look through their work and choose 9–12 samples. This is interesting and can be fun to do with a buddy.

When selecting samples of student work, it is important to remember the purpose is to provide classroom artifacts that allow for a rich discussion about children's ways of thinking about the science. Rich discussions come from rich student work, so your choices will help you and others in your study group make the most of this opportunity.

Preparing to share student work

After you decide on the samples of student work you want to share with the group, you will need to black out actual student names to protect their identities. To make it easier to discuss the work, please give each student an alias (e.g., Lucy becomes Lily).

Next copy a set of the student work for each teacher in your study group. You will also need to copy the blank task you used so teachers can complete the task for themselves during the session.

During the session you will be asked to provide some context for your students' work — a brief 1- to 2-minute introduction is all that's needed. Thinking and writing about the questions on the following page is a helpful way to organize your thinking and prepare for sharing this context. When you introduce your students' work during the session, avoid sharing information about individual students or your own insights into their work.

👍 SELECT STUDENT WORK THAT…

- Relates to the science topics addressed in this course
- Reveals how students are thinking about the science, including misconceptions
- Shows a variety of interesting, surprising, and/or logical ways of thinking
- Represents a range of student responses (high, medium, and low)

👎 AVOID STUDENT WORK THAT…

- Showcases only your "best and brightest" students
- Includes exceptionally poor, incomplete, off-task, or off-the-wall unusual responses
- Is extremely difficult to read
- Promotes stereotypes or prejudice
- Contains information that allows individual students to be identified

1 Which task did students complete? Why was this task selected?

STUDENT WORK CHECKLIST

- ☐ Select 9–12 pieces of appropriate student work.
- ☐ Black out student names and replace them with aliases.
- ☐ Copy the selected student work for each teacher in your group.
- ☐ Copy the blank task for each teacher in your group.
- ☐ Prepare to introduce your student work and, optionally, copy this page for each teacher in your group.

2 What instructions did students receive about the task?

3 What did students do before completing the task?

4 What were the intended outcomes for students? What was the task designed to help them learn or demonstrate?

SCHEDULE FOR SHARING STUDENT WORK

SESSION A

Date: _____ Location: _____

Presenting Teacher(s)	Description of task or assignment for students
1. _____	
2. _____	
3. _____	

SESSION B

Date: _____ Location: _____

Presenting Teacher(s)	Description of task or assignment for students
1. _____	
2. _____	
3. _____	

SESSION C

Date: _____ Location: _____

Presenting Teacher(s)	Description of task or assignment for students
1. _____	
2. _____	
3. _____	

SESSION D

Date: _____ Location: _____

Presenting Teacher(s)	Description of task or assignment for students
1. _____	
2. _____	
3. _____	

SESSION E

Date: _____ Location: _____

Presenting Teacher(s)	Description of task or assignment for students
Everyone!	A task from your own classroom related to the science in this course. It can be one you have used before or one you might use if it better fit your needs.

MENTAL MODELS

⦿ Materials

- ☐ A full set of student work samples for each person

  Note: Sample student work can be printed from the CD that accompanies this book (use Sample Set A). Alternatively, your group may choose to use student work from your own classes. See the Looking at Student Work™ Introduction for more information about selecting and sharing your students' work.

- ☐ A blank copy of today's task for each person

  Note: If you are using the sample student work from the CD, the blank task to copy will be Task Ⓐ in Appendix B.

- ☐ A copy of standards (e.g., national, state, district) for each person if your group chooses to use something other than the list of learning objectives provided in Appendix A

- ☐ Easel paper
- ☐ 2–3 dark blue, green, purple, or black markers
- ☐ Bright red, pink, or orange marker

SESSION AGENDA	
GETTING STARTED	**20** MINUTES
❶ Choose roles	10 MIN.
❷ Get an overview of the session	5 MIN.
❸ Decide on our group norms	5 MIN.
TODAY'S TASK	**30** MINUTES
❹ Work today's task	5 MIN.
❺ Share responses	10 MIN.
❻ Analyze the task	15 MIN.
ANALYZING STUDENT WORK	**50** MINUTES
❼ Read and sort student work	30 MIN.
❽ Compare and discuss findings	15 MIN.
❾ Identify misconceptions	5 MIN.
WRAP UP	**20** MINUTES
❿ Prepare to bring in student work	15 MIN.
⓫ Reflect on today's discussion	5 MIN.
TOTAL TIME	**2** HOURS

Mental Models

GETTING STARTED   20 MINUTES

---

10 MINUTES **1** ## Choose roles

WHOLE GROUP **10 MINUTES**

If you are a new group or haven't met recently, take a few minutes to introduce yourselves.

If you have not yet chosen roles — *Reader, Timekeeper,* and *Recorder* — take a few minutes to read the Looking at Student Work™ Introduction, then select roles for this session.

To ensure an efficient session, the Reader, Timekeeper, and Recorder should do their work simultaneously in each step. For example, as the Reader begins speaking instructions, the Recorder should begin charting and the Timekeeper should note the stop time.

5 MINUTES **2** ## Get an overview of the session

WHOLE GROUP **5 MINUTES**

READER

This first session is designed to help us:

- Interpret student work based on evidence found in that work

- Identify patterns in the way students think about the science

- Evaluate student work on the basis of specific learning outcomes

- Identify what one particular task reveals about students' science understandings

To reach these goals, we'll start by establishing some norms for our group. Then we'll work through an assessment and talk about the science a student would need to know to successfully complete the task. Next we'll dig into a set of 9 to 12 pieces of student work. This will give us a chance to identify the mental models behind students' thinking. In our discussions, we'll aim to talk about students' work in terms of the evidence it presents. ■

RECORDER

Post an agenda for today's session (as needed).

TODAY's AGENDA

Getting Started	20 min
Today's Task	30 min
Analyzing Student Work	50 min
Wrap Up	20 min

---

3 ## Decide on our group norms

WHOLE GROUP | 5 MINUTES

READER

Let's take 5 minutes to talk about the group norms we'd like to have. Group norms describe our expectations, or "ground rules," for participation. They help us create a welcoming environment in which everyone feels comfortable participating.

Here are some ideas to get us started:

- Listen respectfully and be open to differences.
- Analyze the work, but avoid judging people.
- Don't let our expectations cloud our vision.
- Stay focused on the evidence.
- Look for what we see as interesting and surprising.
- What norms would we like for our group? ■

RECORDER

Make a public chart of your group's norms. Revise as needed so it represents everyone's ideas.

Post the completed chart in a visible place and make sure to bring it to future meetings.

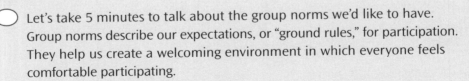

OUR GROUP NORMS
FOR LOOKING AT STUDENT WORK

▶

▶

▶

TIMEKEEPER

After 5 minutes, call time.

 **Work today's task**

5 MINUTES **4**

WHOLE GROUP 1 MINUTE

READER

 Before we look at the student work, it is helpful to become familiar with the task students did. To do this, we'll take several minutes and **individually** complete the task by writing our own responses.

Then we'll work in **small groups** to share responses, check the correctness of our thinking, and hear different ways people solved the task. Lastly, we'll figure out the science knowledge a student would need to have to successfully complete the assignment.

Go ahead and start writing your response. As you work, take note of how you approach the task. ◾

Note: If you are using the provided student work (found on the CD that accompanies this book), distribute a blank copy of the corresponding task from the Task Bank. Alternatively, distribute a blank copy of the task that matches the student work brought in by a teacher today.

INDIVIDUALLY 4 MINUTES

a. Complete today's task. As a reminder, write your own adult-level response (not what a student would write) and think about:

- What I notice about how I approached the task…

TIMEKEEPER

After 5 minutes, call time.

5 Share responses

WHOLE GROUP   1 MINUTE

READER

💬 Please form a **small group** (preferably with a total of three people) and begin to share your responses with each other.

You will have about 10 minutes for this discussion. When our Timekeeper calls time, please move on to the next step — analyzing the task. ∎

TIMEKEEPER

Write the stop time on the board (9 minutes from now).

SMALL GROUPS   9 MINUTES

a. Take turns sharing your written answers and describing how you solved the task. For example:

- Did you think of another similar situation?

- Did you draw a picture or diagram?

- Did you remember some specific facts or information?

b. Verify the correctness of your response(s). As needed, look at other references (e.g., Content Notes, Session Reviews) to confirm your answers.

TIMEKEEPER

After 9 minutes, call time and ask people to move on to the next step.

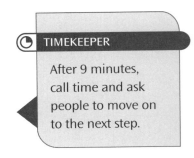

6 **Analyze the task**

> **SMALL GROUPS** ┃ **15** MINUTES
>
> 🕐 **TIMEKEEPER**
>
> Write the stop time on the board (15 minutes from now). Remind people when there is 1 minute remaining.

a. Discuss the task in terms of the science it covers and take notes.

  • If students correctly completed this same task, what would we know about the science they understand?

b. Together read the list of learning objectives (see Appendix A), discuss which science concepts are best aligned with this task, and take notes. Alternatively, you can use your own district standards, national standards, or another appropriate resource.

  • These learning objectives are a good fit with the task...

🕐 **TIMEKEEPER**

After 15 minutes, call time and ask people to reconvene as a whole group.

---

30 MINUTES **7 Read and sort student work**

WHOLE GROUP   5 MINUTES

READER

When we look at the student work today, we'll focus on identifying common, yet incorrect ways they are thinking about the science. Typically, more than one student shares the same mental model or way of thinking. However, each student may express this idea differently. In later sessions, we will consider what instructional next steps might be most fitting for students based on their ideas.

Each time we look at student work, the teacher or teachers who brought in the work will give us a short introduction to help us understand what students did and the context for their work. It is most helpful to hear about:

- Which task you chose and why

- The instructions you gave students

- What students did before completing the task

- What you hoped they would learn or demonstrate by doing the task ■

If teacher(s) brought in student work, then read the following section. If not, and the group is using the provided samples of student work printed from the CD, then skip to the next spoken section.

Each teacher presenting work today should take a minute to talk through these points and/or hand out your written description of these points. ■

Read this *only* if the group is using the provided samples of student work printed from the CD.

Today's task, Energy for Hawks, was a check of how students were thinking about energy in food webs. Before doing this task, the 6th graders did experiments to determine how the amount of light affected plant growth and read about plant needs and where plants get energy to make glucose. They also explored food webs for various ecosystems and discussed why organisms eat food. To complete Energy for Hawks, students worked individually and did not have their notebooks, but the class definitions of food, energy, and matter were posted. The teacher hoped students would mark things that provided energy to the hawk and describe whether they provided it directly or indirectly. ■

TIMEKEEPER

Help teachers stick to brief presentations (1–2 minutes per teacher).

● READER

 To start, take 5 minutes or so to **individually** read through the samples of student work before you talk with your group. Begin by reading and sorting the student work into piles according to groups of students who have similar ways of thinking about the science. Then discuss with your **small group** what you are noticing. Lastly, you will look at the list of misconceptions in Appendix A to see if any apply to these students. You will have 25 minutes for this entire step. ∎

Note: Distribute the student work that has been printed and copied from the CD that accompanies this book (one full set per person). Alternatively, ask the presenting teacher(s) to distribute copies of her/his students' work. If more than one person brought in work, have various small groups focus on different class sets.

● TIMEKEEPER

Write the stop time on the board (24 minutes from now).

INDIVIDUALLY   5 MINUTES

a. First, read through the samples of student work **individually** and take notes.

- What I notice about how each student is thinking about the science…

● TIMEKEEPER

 After 5 minutes, call time and ask people to move to their small groups.

b. Discuss what you are noticing about these students' science ideas and their underlying mental models. Then sort their work into piles according to students who share similar ways of thinking.

Use these questions to guide your discussion and take notes:

- Which ideas do most students seem to understand?

- What are some points of confusion?

- How can we sort the work so students with similar ways of thinking are grouped together?

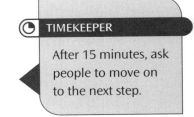

TIMEKEEPER

After 15 minutes, ask people to move on to the next step.

c. Read the lists of common misconceptions (found in Appendix A), talk about which, if any, fit the way these students are thinking, and take notes.

  • We found these misconceptions or errors in the student work…

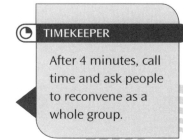

TIMEKEEPER

After 4 minutes, call time and ask people to reconvene as a whole group.

8 Compare and discuss findings

● READER

💬 There are many things to notice when looking at student work. It will be interesting to see the different patterns and common errors or misconceptions various groups identified. As a reminder, there is no single correct way to sort the work. By pointing out the specific evidence we used, such as a student's choice of words or aspects of a drawing, we can help each other understand what led us to interpret the student work in a particular way.

We'll start our discussion by having each small group briefly tell us about one of their piles of sorted student work.

In 2 minutes or less, please tell us about:

- One *category* (or pile of student work)

- The *names* of the students you included in this category

- Some *evidence* that suggests these students share a similar mental model or way of thinking

In general, you want to talk about interesting things you noticed and different choices you made and why. ■

✎ RECORDER

Make a chart capturing how the groups categorized students' responses.

Also document evidence the groups noticed in students' work.

Remember, it is *not* necessary to write every word or every detail shared.

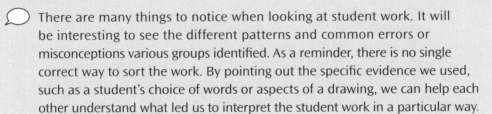

DIFFERENT WAYS STUDENTS THOUGHT ABOUT THE SCIENCE...

▶

▶

▶

◷ TIMEKEEPER

Write the stop time on the board (15 minutes from now) and announce when time is up.

9 Identify misconceptions

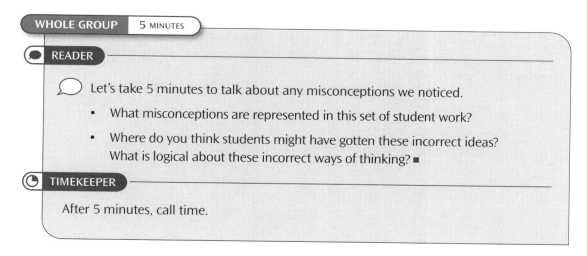

WHOLE GROUP 5 MINUTES

READER

Let's take 5 minutes to talk about any misconceptions we noticed.

- What misconceptions are represented in this set of student work?

- Where do you think students might have gotten these incorrect ideas? What is logical about these incorrect ways of thinking? ∎

TIMEKEEPER

After 5 minutes, call time.

Use this space to take notes about main points from the discussion.

TIMEKEEPER

After 5 minutes, call time.

(15 MINUTES) **10** Prepare to bring in student work

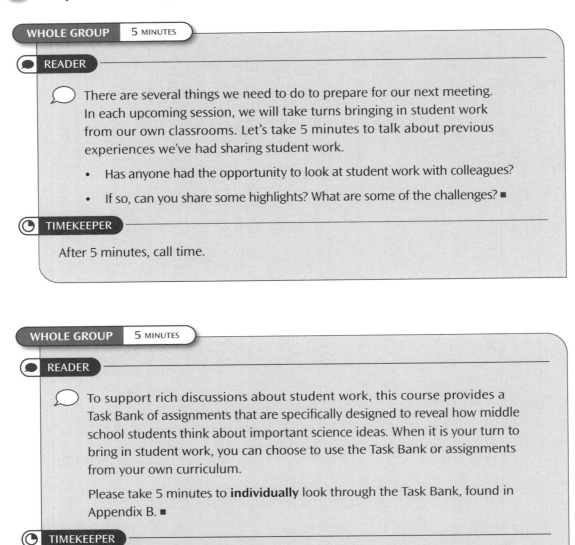

WHOLE GROUP   5 MINUTES

💬 **READER**

There are several things we need to do to prepare for our next meeting. In each upcoming session, we will take turns bringing in student work from our own classrooms. Let's take 5 minutes to talk about previous experiences we've had sharing student work.

- Has anyone had the opportunity to look at student work with colleagues?

- If so, can you share some highlights? What are some of the challenges? ▪

🕐 **TIMEKEEPER**

After 5 minutes, call time.

WHOLE GROUP   5 MINUTES

💬 **READER**

To support rich discussions about student work, this course provides a Task Bank of assignments that are specifically designed to reveal how middle school students think about important science ideas. When it is your turn to bring in student work, you can choose to use the Task Bank or assignments from your own curriculum.

Please take 5 minutes to **individually** look through the Task Bank, found in Appendix B. ▪

🕐 **TIMEKEEPER**

After 5 minutes, call time.

READER

Please sign up to bring in student work for the next few sessions. It's helpful to review the Introduction for more information about selecting and sharing your students' work. Keep in mind that if more than one teacher chooses to bring in work for a session, it's helpful for these teachers to use the same task. Is there anything we need to discuss to help us figure out who will bring in work and when? ∎

Read this *only* if your group is rotating roles between sessions.

Before we leave today, we also need to decide who will take on the role of Reader, Timekeeper, and Recorder next time. What do you suggest? ∎

TIMEKEEPER

After 5 minutes, call time.

---

5 MINUTES **11** **Reflect on today's discussion**

WHOLE GROUP 1 MINUTE

READER

Every session ends with 5 minutes to **individually** think about our discussion. Give yourself the gift of this reflective time.

As a reminder, our next meeting is on _____ [date/time], at _____ [location]. Our Reader will be _____ [name], our Recorder will be _____ [name], and our Timekeeper will be _____ [name]. Remember, if you have one of these roles, it is helpful to read the session ahead of time so you know the big picture. See you then! ∎

Note: You should also make note of any other details relevant to the next meeting.

Take a few minutes to think about the following questions and jot down some notes.

- What were my big takeaways from today?

- What did I learn about:

  …how children think about the science?

  …how they demonstrate their understanding of the science?

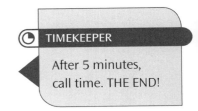

TIMEKEEPER

After 5 minutes, call time. THE END!

LEARNING GAPS

◉ Materials

- ☐ A full set of 9–12 pieces of student work for each person

  Note: If no one is able to bring in student work samples for this session, a spare set can be printed from the CD that accompanies this book. If more than one person provides samples of student work, it's best to use the same task. See the Looking at Student Work™ Introduction for more information about selecting and sharing your students' work.

- ☐ A blank copy of today's task for each person
- ☐ A copy of standards (e.g., national, state, district) for each person if your group chooses to use something other than the list of learning objectives provided in Appendix A
- ☐ Easel paper
- ☐ 2–3 dark blue, green, purple, or black markers
- ☐ Bright red, pink, or orange marker

SESSION AGENDA	
GETTING STARTED	**20** MINUTES
❶ Confirm roles	3 MIN.
❷ Get an overview of the session	2 MIN.
❸ Discuss hopes, fears, and norms	15 MIN.
TODAY'S TASK	**25** MINUTES
❹ Get an introduction to today's task	5 MIN.
❺ Work the task	5 MIN.
❻ Analyze the task	15 MIN.
ANALYZING STUDENT WORK	**65** MINUTES
❼ Read and sort student work	21 MIN.
❽ Identify learning gaps	39 MIN.
❾ Reflect on learning gaps	5 MIN.
WRAP UP	**10** MINUTES
❿ Take care of housekeeping items	4 MIN.
⓫ Reflect on today's discussion	6 MIN.
TOTAL TIME	*2 HOURS*

Learning Gaps

GETTING STARTED

20 MINUTES

---

3 MINUTES **1** ## Confirm roles

WHOLE GROUP **3 MINUTES**

Reintroduce yourselves, as needed. Let the group know if you are the *Reader, Timekeeper,* or *Recorder.* If you haven't chosen roles, quickly decide who will take on each role. To ensure an efficient session, the Reader, Timekeeper, and Recorder should do their work simultaneously in each step. For example, as the Reader begins speaking instructions, the Recorder should begin charting and the Timekeeper should note the stop time.

2 MINUTES **2** ## Get an overview of the session

WHOLE GROUP **2 MINUTES**

 READER

This Learning Gaps session is designed to help us:

- Evaluate student work on the basis of specific learning objectives
- Identify various ways students might show a correct and complete understanding of a specific science concept
- Recognize what students are missing that may contribute to errors or limitations in their thinking
- Identify learning gaps between students' actual performance and a correct and complete understanding

Today we'll look at student work from our own classrooms as an opportunity to experience a new task and see how students think about the science. After describing what students understand, we'll identify learning gaps they need to bridge to reach a complete, accurate understanding of a specific key concept. ∎

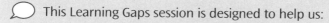 **RECORDER**

Post an agenda for today's session (as needed).

> **TODAY's AGENDA**
>
> Getting Started   20 min
> Today's Task   25 min
> Analyzing Student Work   65 min
> Wrap Up   10 min

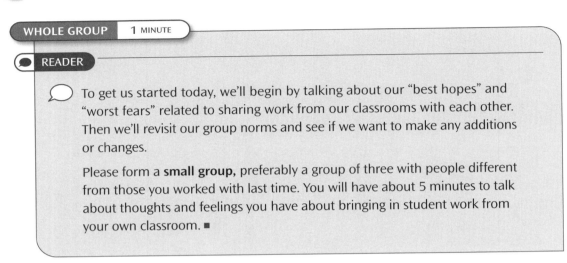

WHOLE GROUP | 1 MINUTE

READER

To get us started today, we'll begin by talking about our "best hopes" and "worst fears" related to sharing work from our classrooms with each other. Then we'll revisit our group norms and see if we want to make any additions or changes.

Please form a **small group,** preferably a group of three with people different from those you worked with last time. You will have about 5 minutes to talk about thoughts and feelings you have about bringing in student work from your own classroom. ▪

SMALL GROUPS | 5 MINUTES

a. Discuss your thoughts and feelings about sharing our own students' work. Make sure each person in the group has a chance to talk.

As fitting, use these questions to guide your conversation:

- What are you looking forward to as we share student work?

- What, if anything, are you feeling worried about?

- What would make you feel most comfortable when sharing your own students' work?

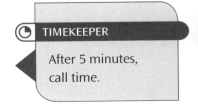

TIMEKEEPER

After 5 minutes, call time.

READER

 In order to make sure we have respectful and productive conversations about student work, let's briefly review our group norms. Take a minute to read them on your own.

What would you like to talk more about or change, especially in light of your conversations about "best hopes" and "worst fears" around sharing student work? Is there anything you would like to add to or change about our Group Norms chart?

Remember, our goal is to create an environment for collaborative learning that feels welcoming and comfortable. ■

RECORDER

Post the chart with the norms for your group.

Be prepared to modify the chart based on group members' wishes and the discussion about bringing in student work from their own classrooms.

OUR GROUP NORMS
FOR LOOKING AT STUDENT WORK

▸

▸

▸

TIMEKEEPER

Write the stop time on the board (9 minutes from now) and announce when time is up.

5 MINUTES **4** Get an introduction to today's task

WHOLE GROUP 5 MINUTES

READER

Today, the teacher (or teachers) who brought in student work will give us an introduction by telling us what they had students do and very briefly sharing some background information to help us understand the context for their work.

As a reminder, it is most helpful to hear about:

- Which task you chose and why
- The instructions you gave students
- What students did before completing the task
- What you hoped they would learn or demonstrate by doing the task

Each presenting teacher should take 1–2 minutes to talk through these points and/or hand out what you've written. ∎

Note: As needed, distribute a blank copy of the task.

TIMEKEEPER

Help teachers stick to brief presentations (1–2 minutes per teacher).

5 **Work the task**

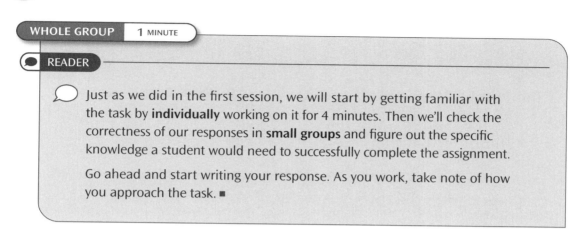

WHOLE GROUP   **1** MINUTE

READER

💬 Just as we did in the first session, we will start by getting familiar with the task by **individually** working on it for 4 minutes. Then we'll check the correctness of our responses in **small groups** and figure out the specific knowledge a student would need to successfully complete the assignment.

Go ahead and start writing your response. As you work, take note of how you approach the task. ■

INDIVIDUALLY   **4** MINUTES

a. Complete the task the presenting teacher(s) used with students. As a reminder, write an adult-level response (not what a student would write) and think about:

  • What I notice about how I approached the task...

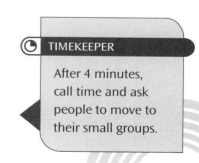

🕐 **TIMEKEEPER**

After 4 minutes, call time and ask people to move to their small groups.

SMALL GROUPS   **15** MINUTES

TIMEKEEPER

Write the stop time on the board (15 minutes from now). Remind everyone when there is 1 minute remaining.

a. Take turns sharing your written answers and verifying the correctness of your response(s). As needed, look at other references (e.g., Content Notes, Session Reviews) to confirm your answers.

b. Discuss the task in terms of the science it covers and take notes.

- If students correctly completed this same task, what would we know about the science they understand?

c. Identify which learning objectives are best aligned with this task. Remember to consult the list of learning objectives (see Appendix A) or any other resource your group has decided to use (e.g., state standards).

- These learning objectives are a good fit with the task…

TIMEKEEPER

After 15 minutes, call time and ask people to reconvene as a whole group.

21 MINUTES **7** **Read and sort student work**

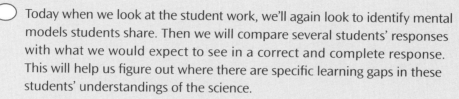

WHOLE GROUP   **1** MINUTE

🔘 **READER**

💬 Today when we look at the student work, we'll again look to identify mental models students share. Then we will compare several students' responses with what we would expect to see in a correct and complete response. This will help us figure out where there are specific learning gaps in these students' understandings of the science.

First, we'll take 5 minutes or so to **individually** read through the samples of work and notice how students are thinking about the science. Then, as **small groups,** we'll share what we're noticing, sort the work into piles of students who think in similar ways, and look at the list of misconceptions in Appendix A to see if any apply to these students. We will have 20 minutes for this entire step. ∎

Note: Ask the presenting teacher (or teachers) to distribute copies of student work. If more than one teacher brought in work, have various small groups focus on different class sets rather than having everyone look at everything.

🕐 **TIMEKEEPER**

Write the stop time on the board (20 minutes from now).

INDIVIDUALLY   **5** MINUTES

   a. First, read through the samples of student work **individually** and take notes.

     • What I notice about how each student is thinking about the science…

🕐 **TIMEKEEPER**

After 5 minutes, call time and ask people to move to their small groups.

---

b. Discuss what you are noticing about these students' science ideas and their underlying mental models. Then sort their work into piles according to students who share similar ways of thinking.

Use these questions to guide your discussion and take notes:

- Which ideas do most students seem to understand?

- What are some points of confusion?

- How can we sort the work so students with similar ways of thinking are grouped together?

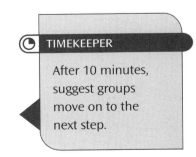

TIMEKEEPER

After 10 minutes, suggest groups move on to the next step.

c. Read the list of common misconceptions (found in Appendix A) and talk about which, if any, fit the way these students are thinking.

- We found these misconceptions or errors in the student work...

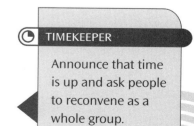

TIMEKEEPER

Announce that time is up and ask people to reconvene as a whole group.

8 Identify learning gaps

READER

As a next step, we will work to figure out the learning gaps that stand in the way of individual students reaching proficiency in their understanding. A learning gap describes something a student can't yet do or doesn't yet know, but if the student could do it or did know it, his/her response on the task would be correct and complete. In other words, it is the space between a learning objective and what a student knows and can do.

We'll discuss *one* student's learning gaps as a **whole group.** Then, in **small groups,** we'll look at several other students. We'll end by sharing some examples and discussing what we are noticing about learning gaps.

To get started, we first need to select one of the learning objectives or science concepts that was especially central to this task. ■

Now, to talk about specific learning gaps, we need to choose *one* student to focus on. Will someone suggest a student who may not have a complete understanding of this learning objective?

With this student in mind, let's use these questions to guide our discussion:

- What is *incorrect* or *missing* from this student's response to the task?
- What *evidence* makes us think so?
- What would this student need to write, draw, and/or explain to provide convincing evidence s/he solidly understands this learning objective? ■

RECORDER

Make a chart capturing the group's ideas.

Remember, it is *not* necessary to write every word or every detail shared.

STUDENT:_____ TASK: ___

KEY LEARNING OBJECTIVE:

LEARNING GAP:
What is incorrect or missing from this student's response?

▶

TIMEKEEPER

Write the stop time on the board (15 minutes from now). Remind everyone when there is 1 minute remaining.

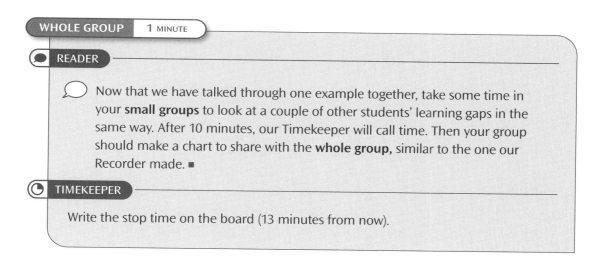

WHOLE GROUP **1** MINUTE

READER

Now that we have talked through one example together, take some time in your **small groups** to look at a couple of other students' learning gaps in the same way. After 10 minutes, our Timekeeper will call time. Then your group should make a chart to share with the **whole group,** similar to the one our Recorder made. ■

TIMEKEEPER

Write the stop time on the board (13 minutes from now).

SMALL GROUPS **13** MINUTES

a. Look for students who may have different mental models and therefore different learning gaps. Choose one or two students to talk about.

Use these questions to guide your discussion and take notes:

• What *incorrect* or *missing* from this student's response to the task?

• What *evidence* makes us think so?

• What would this student need to write, draw, and/or explain to provide convincing evidence s/he has a solid understanding of the chosen learning objective?

TIMEKEEPER

After 10 minutes, suggest each group make its chart.

b. Make a chart to share with the whole group.

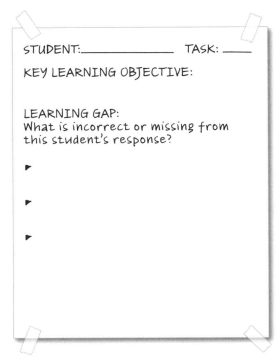

STUDENT:_____ TASK: _____

KEY LEARNING OBJECTIVE:

LEARNING GAP:
What is incorrect or missing from
this student's response?

▶

▶

▶

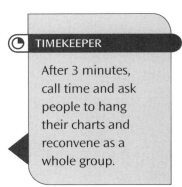

TIMEKEEPER

After 3 minutes,
call time and ask
people to hang
their charts and
reconvene as a
whole group.

WHOLE GROUP | **10** MINUTES

READER

 Let's take 10 minutes to look across groups to see the various learning gaps we've identified. Each group can take 1–2 minutes to share interesting things you noticed and what clued you in to this particular student's learning gap.

It is especially helpful if you can be specific about the following questions:

- What does this student need in order to better understand?
- What evidence helped you figure this out?

Feel free to ask each other questions to clarify what you hear. ∎

TIMEKEEPER

Write the stop time on the board (10 minutes from now). Help groups stick to brief presentations by announcing the time (1–2 minutes per group), as needed. Announce when time is up.

Use this space to take notes about main points from the discussion.

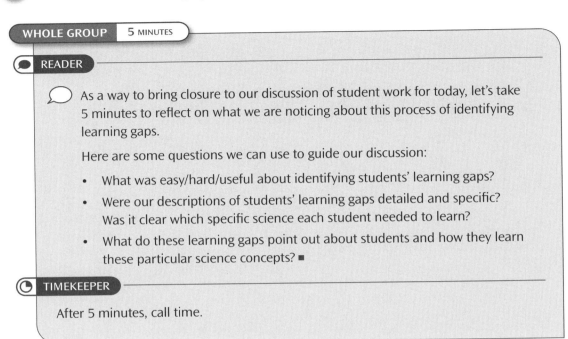

(5 MINUTES) **9** **Reflect on learning gaps**

WHOLE GROUP | 5 MINUTES

READER

As a way to bring closure to our discussion of student work for today, let's take 5 minutes to reflect on what we are noticing about this process of identifying learning gaps.

Here are some questions we can use to guide our discussion:

- What was easy/hard/useful about identifying students' learning gaps?

- Were our descriptions of students' learning gaps detailed and specific? Was it clear which specific science each student needed to learn?

- What do these learning gaps point out about students and how they learn these particular science concepts? ∎

TIMEKEEPER

After 5 minutes, call time.

Use this space to take notes about the main points of the discussion.

(4 MINUTES) **10** # Take care of housekeeping items

WHOLE GROUP   4 MINUTES

READER

💬 Let's confirm who will bring in student work for the next session. It's helpful to review the Introduction for more information about selecting and sharing your students' work. ▪

Note: If more than one teacher is bringing in work, ask these teachers to confer so they use the *same* task or assignment with their students.

💬 If you brought in student work samples today, do you have any helpful hints for teachers who are sharing next time? ▪

Read this *only* if your group is rotating roles between sessions.

💬 Before we leave today, we also need to decide who will take on the role of Reader, Timekeeper, and Recorder next time. What do you suggest? ▪

Note: Help the group address any logistical issues or other concerns that come up.

(6 MINUTES) **11** # Reflect on today's discussion

WHOLE GROUP   1 MINUTE

READER

💬 Every session ends with 5 minutes to **individually** think about our discussion. Give yourself the gift of this reflective time.

As a reminder, our next meeting is on _____ [date/time], at _____ [location]. Our Reader will be _____ [name], our Recorder will be _____ [name], and our Timekeeper will be _____ [name]. Remember, if you have one of these roles, it is helpful to read the session ahead of time so you know the big picture. See you then! ▪

Note: You should also make note of any other details relevant to the next meeting.

a. Take a few minutes to think about the following questions and jot down some notes.

- What were my big takeaways from today?

- What did I learn about:

   …how children think about the science?

   …learning gaps related to this science?

TIMEKEEPER

After 5 minutes,
call time. THE END!

NEXT STEPS

◉ Materials

- ☐ A full set of 9–12 pieces of student work for each person

  Note: If more than one person provides samples of student work, it's best to use the same task. See the Looking at Student Work™ Introduction for more information about selecting and sharing your students' work. If no one is able to bring in student work samples for this session, a spare set can be printed from the CD that accompanies these materials.

- ☐ A blank copy of today's task for each person
- ☐ A copy of standards (e.g., national, state, district) for each person if your group chooses to use something other than the list of learning objectives provided in Appendix A
- ☐ Easel paper
- ☐ 2–3 dark blue, green, purple, or black markers
- ☐ Bright red, pink, or orange marker

SESSION AGENDA	
GETTING STARTED	**5** MINUTES
❶ Confirm roles	3 MIN.
❷ Get an overview of the session	2 MIN.
TODAY'S TASK	**25** MINUTES
❸ Get an introduction to today's task	5 MIN.
❹ Work the task	5 MIN.
❺ Analyze the task	15 MIN.
ANALYZING STUDENT WORK	**70** MINUTES
❻ Read and analyze the student work	26 MIN.
❼ Plan and evaluate instructional next steps	44 MIN.
WRAP UP	**20** MINUTES
❽ Reflect on our collaborative learning	10 MIN.
❾ Take care of housekeeping items	4 MIN.
❿ Reflect on today's discussion	6 MIN.
TOTAL TIME	*2 HOURS*

Next Steps

GETTING STARTED   5 MINUTES

3 MINUTES **1 Confirm roles**

> **WHOLE GROUP** 3 MINUTES

Greet each other and announce if you are the *Reader, Timekeeper,* or *Recorder* for today. If you haven't chosen roles, quickly decide who will take on each role. To ensure an efficient session, the Reader, Timekeeper, and Recorder should do their work simultaneously in each step. For example, as the Reader begins speaking instructions, the Recorder should begin charting and the Timekeeper should note the stop time.

2 MINUTES **2 Get an overview of the session**

> **WHOLE GROUP** 1 MINUTE
>
> **● READER**

This Next Steps session is designed to help us:

- Recognize what students are missing that may contribute to errors or limitations in their thinking
- Identify learning gaps between students' actual performance and a correct and complete understanding
- Make decisions about instructional next steps for an individual student based on her/his ideas and understandings
- Weigh the tradeoffs of various instructional next steps

Today we will look at a new task and different student work from some of our own classrooms. This will give us the opportunity to revisit the idea of learning gaps and allow us to brainstorm instructional next steps to help move an individual student toward a more accurate and thorough understanding of a given learning objective. Because every instructional choice comes with a set of benefits and limitations, we will think together about the tradeoffs of various options.

At the end of today's session, we'll reflect on how we are working together as a collaborative learning group and what might strengthen our process. ■

RECORDER

Post an agenda for today's session (as needed).

If you haven't already done so, post the chart with the norms for your group.

TODAY's AGENDA

Getting Started	5 min
Today's Task	25 min
Analyzing Student Work	70 min
Wrap Up	20 min

OUR GROUP NORMS
FOR LOOKING AT STUDENT WORK

▸

▸

▸

5 MINUTES **3** ## Get an introduction to today's task

WHOLE GROUP **5 MINUTES**

● READER

 Today, the teacher (or teachers) who brought in student work will give us an introduction by telling us what they had students do and very briefly sharing some background information to help us understand the context for their work.

As a reminder, it is most helpful to hear about:

- Which task you chose and why
- The instructions you gave students
- What students did before completing the task
- What you hoped they would learn or demonstrate by doing the task

Each presenting teacher should take 1–2 minutes to talk through these points and/or hand out what you've written. ■

Note: As needed, distribute a blank copy of the task.

● TIMEKEEPER

Help teachers stick to brief presentations (1–2 minutes per teacher).

WHOLE GROUP · 1 MINUTE

● READER

💬 Just as we did in previous sessions, we will start by getting familiar with the task by **individually** working on it for several minutes. Then we'll check the correctness of our responses in **small groups** and figure out the specific knowledge a student would need to successfully complete the assignment.

Go ahead and start writing your response. As you work, take note of how you approach the task. ■

Note: If teachers have not already formed new small groups, ask them to do so, preferably as threesomes with people different from previous sessions.

INDIVIDUALLY · 4 MINUTES

a. Complete the task the presenting teacher(s) used with students. As a reminder, write an adult-level response (not what a student would write) and think about:

- What I notice about how I approached the task…

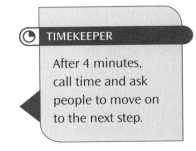

🕐 TIMEKEEPER

After 4 minutes, call time and ask people to move on to the next step.

5 # Analyze the task

> **SMALL GROUPS** | **15** MINUTES
>
> 🕐 **TIMEKEEPER**
>
> Write the stop time on the board (15 minutes from now). Remind everyone when there is 1 minute remaining.

a. Take turns sharing your written answers and verifying the correctness of your response(s). As needed, look at other references (e.g., Content Notes, Session Reviews) to confirm your answers.

b. Discuss the task in terms of the science it covers and take notes.

- If students correctly completed this same task, what would we know about the science they understand?

c. Identify which learning objectives are best aligned with this task. Remember to consult the list of learning objectives (see Appendix A) or any other resource your group has decided to use (e.g., state standards).

- These learning objectives are a good fit with the task…

> 🕐 **TIMEKEEPER**
>
> After 15 minutes, call time and ask people to reconvene as a whole group.

26 MINUTES **6** Read and analyze the student work

WHOLE GROUP 1 MINUTE

READER

Today we'll look at the student work with an eye to how these students are thinking about the science and identify specific learning gaps individuals may have in their understanding. Then we will look at one student's work, brainstorm possible instructional next steps, and evaluate several options.

First, we'll take 5 minutes or so to **individually** read through the samples of work and notice how students are thinking about the science. Then, as **small groups,** we'll share what we're noticing, discuss students' correct and incorrect ideas, and talk about the learning gaps. We will have 25 minutes for this entire step. ■

Note: Ask the presenting teacher (or teachers) to distribute copies of student work. If more than one teacher brought in work, have various small groups focus on different class sets rather than having everyone look at everything.

TIMEKEEPER

Write the stop time on the board (25 minutes from now).

INDIVIDUALLY 5 MINUTES

a. First, read through the samples of student work **individually** and take notes.

   • What I notice about how each student is thinking about the science…

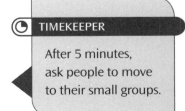

TIMEKEEPER

After 5 minutes, ask people to move to their small groups.

b. Choose a few pieces of student work that are especially interesting. Discuss what you are noticing about these students' correct and incorrect science ideas. Remember to look at the list of common misconceptions (found in Appendix A).

Use these questions to guide your discussion and take notes:

• What are some things these students seem to understand?

• What are some misconceptions or points of confusion?

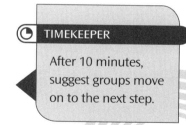

TIMEKEEPER

After 10 minutes, suggest groups move on to the next step.

c. Talk about the learning gaps you are noticing. As a reminder, a learning gap describes something a student can't yet do or doesn't yet know, but if the student could do or did know it, his/her response on the task would be correct and complete.

Use these questions to guide your discussion and take notes:

- Which learning objective or science concept is especially central to this task?

- What is incorrect or missing from this student's response to the task (related to the learning outcome)?

- What would this student need to write, draw, and/or explain to provide convincing evidence that s/he has a solid understanding of the chosen key science concept?

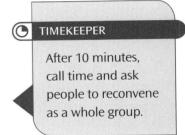

TIMEKEEPER

After 10 minutes, call time and ask people to reconvene as a whole group.

44 MINUTES ⑦ Plan and evaluate instructional next steps

WHOLE GROUP | 5 MINUTES

💬 READER

One way to set the stage for thinking about the instructional next steps that could help a student become proficient in understanding a given science concept is to identify the student's learning gaps. Let's start our discussion of next steps by focusing on *one* student's learning gap. Can someone nominate a student whose work is interesting and who shows a clear learning gap?

What seems to be the most significant learning gap for this student? ▪

Do the words on our chart feel like a specific and detailed description of this student's learning gap? If not, is there something we could add to clarify? ▪

✎ RECORDER

Make a chart to record the group's description of *one* student's learning gap.

Remember, it is *not* necessary to write every word or every detail shared.

ANALYZING _____'S WORK

Learning Gap	Possible Next Steps
This student needs to better understand...	

🕐 TIMEKEEPER

After 5 minutes, call time.

Use this space to take notes about main points from the discussion.

WHOLE GROUP · **1** MINUTE

 READER

Next we'll think about how to help this one student move toward a more accurate and thorough understanding of the learning objective. In your **small groups,** take 5 minutes to brainstorm possible next steps. During this brainstorming stage, all ideas are valid and should be received without judgment. However, it is extremely helpful to be as detailed and specific as possible when describing your ideas to each other. For example, rather than saying, "I would have the student do a hands-on assignment," you will want to describe *exactly* what you would have the student do, observe, or compare. After you come up with ideas, we'll weigh the tradeoffs of some. ▪

SMALL GROUPS · **5** MINUTES

a. Brainstorm some possible next steps. Go crazy. Have fun!

Use these questions to prompt each other to clarify or elaborate on an idea:

• What would this look like in your classroom?

• What exactly would you say/do?

• What would the student do?

 TIMEKEEPER

After 5 minutes, call time and ask people to reconvene as a whole group.

● READER

💬 Let's discuss some of our ideas about next steps in more detail.

- What is one good idea you heard someone else in your group share as a possible next step? Does anyone have a clarifying question about this idea?
- What is a different idea someone heard? Any clarifying questions?
- How about a third idea? Any clarifying questions? ■

Note: It is important to take the time to hear a full description of each idea presented. The goal is to help the group paint a picture so people can clearly understand what the teacher and student would do. It is not necessary to share every idea; rather, ask teachers to focus on a few they think are especially interesting.

✎ RECORDER

As teachers describe possible next steps, add these options to the chart.

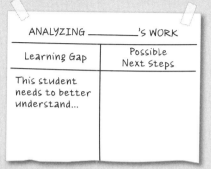

ANALYZING _____'S WORK

Learning Gap	Possible Next Steps
This student needs to better understand...	

🕐 TIMEKEEPER

Write the stop time on the board (7 minutes from now) and announce when time is up.

Use this space to take notes about main points from the discussion.

READER

Now let's think together about the benefits and limitations of these various next steps. As a reminder, every instructional choice we make comes with a set of tradeoffs. Can someone nominate *one* of these options to evaluate?

Here are some questions to guide our discussion:

- How well matched is the instructional idea to the student's learning gap?
- Does the next step build on the student's own science ideas?
- How responsive is it to the student's level of understanding?
- Does the next step address what's most challenging for this student? ▪

RECORDER

Make a chart of the tradeoffs identified by the group.

Although it is important to record each person's idea, it is *not* necessary to write every word or every detail shared.

Tradeoffs of Option ____	
Benefits	Limitations

TIMEKEEPER

Write the stop time on the board (10 minutes from now) and announce when time is up.

Use this space to take notes about main points from the discussion.

● READER

> 💬 In the remaining time, we'll work in our **small groups** to plan and evaluate instructional next steps for another student using this same process. ■

🕐 TIMEKEEPER

Write the stop time on the board (15 minutes from now). Remind everyone when there is 1 minute remaining.

SMALL GROUPS   **15** MINUTES

a. Choose another student whose work you found interesting. Describe the student's learning gap, then brainstorm possible next steps, and end by weighing the tradeoffs of one or more of those options. Use the following tables to take notes.

Analyzing _____'s Work

Learning Gap	Possible Next Steps
This student needs to better understand…	Option A
	Option B
	Option C

Tradeoffs of Option _____

Benefits	Limitations

TIMEKEEPER

After 15 minutes, call time and ask people to reconvene as a whole group.

10 MINUTES
8 Reflect on our collaborative learning

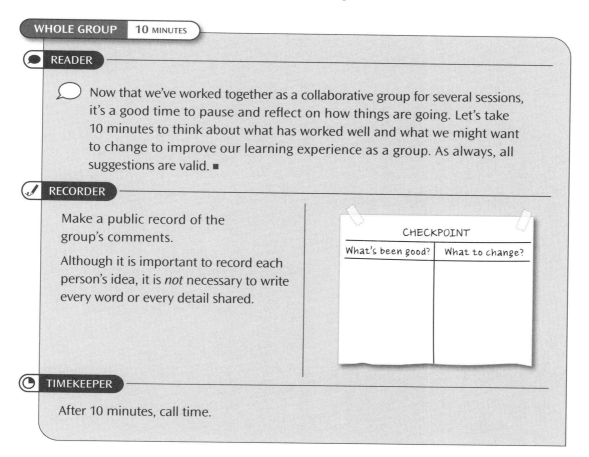

WHOLE GROUP | 10 MINUTES

READER

Now that we've worked together as a collaborative group for several sessions, it's a good time to pause and reflect on how things are going. Let's take 10 minutes to think about what has worked well and what we might want to change to improve our learning experience as a group. As always, all suggestions are valid. ■

RECORDER

Make a public record of the group's comments.

Although it is important to record each person's idea, it is *not* necessary to write every word or every detail shared.

CHECKPOINT	
What's been good?	What to change?

TIMEKEEPER

After 10 minutes, call time.

Use this space to take notes about main points from the discussion.

4 MINUTES **9** Take care of housekeeping items

WHOLE GROUP **4 MINUTES**

💬 **READER**

> Let's confirm who will bring in student work for the next session. It's helpful to review the Introduction for more information about selecting and sharing your students' work. ■

Note: If more than one teacher is bringing in work, ask these teachers to confer so they use the *same* task or assignment with their students.

Read this *only* if your group is rotating roles between sessions.

> Before we leave today, we also need to decide who will take on the role of Reader, Timekeeper, and Recorder next time. What do you suggest? ■

Note: Help the group address any logistical issues or other concerns that come up.

---

6 MINUTES **10** Reflect on today's discussion

WHOLE GROUP **1 MINUTE**

💬 **READER**

> Every session ends with 5 minutes to **individually** think about our discussion. Give yourself the gift of this reflective time.
>
> As a reminder, our next meeting is on _____ [date/time], at _____ [location]. Our Reader will be _____ [name], our Recorder will be _____ [name], and our Timekeeper will be _____ [name]. Remember, if you have one of these roles, it is helpful to read the session ahead of time so you know the big picture. See you then! ■

Note: You should also make note of any other details relevant to the next meeting.

INDIVIDUALLY | 5 MINUTES

a. Take a few minutes to think about the following questions and jot down some notes.

- What were my big takeaways from today?
- What did I learn about:

    …how children think about the science?

    …learning gaps related to this science?

    …instructional next steps related to this science?

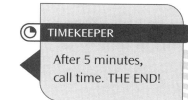

TIMEKEEPER

After 5 minutes, call time. THE END!

ANALYZING TASKS

⊙ Materials

☐ A full set of 9–12 pieces of student work for each person

Note: If more than one person provides samples of student work, it's best to use the same task. See the Looking at Student Work™ Introduction for more information about selecting and sharing your students' work. If no one is able to bring in student work samples for this session, a spare set can be printed from the CD that accompanies this book.

☐ A blank copy of today's task for each person

☐ A copy of standards (e.g., national, state, district) for each person if your group chooses to use something other than the list of learning objectives provided in Appendix A

☐ Easel paper

☐ 2–3 dark blue, green, purple, or black markers

☐ Bright red, pink, or orange marker

SESSION AGENDA	
GETTING STARTED	**5** MINUTES
❶ Confirm roles	3 MIN.
❷ Get an overview of the session	2 MIN.
TODAY'S TASK	**25** MINUTES
❸ Get an introduction to today's task	5 MIN.
❹ Work the task	5 MIN.
❺ Analyze the task	15 MIN.
ANALYZING STUDENT WORK	**80** MINUTES
❻ Read and sort student work	26 MIN.
❼ Evaluate the task	14 MIN.
❽ Match learning objectives with the task	20 MIN.
❾ Identify characteristics of good tasks	20 MIN.
WRAP UP	**10** MINUTES
❿ Take care of housekeeping items	4 MIN.
⓫ Reflect on today's discussion	6 MIN.
TOTAL TIME	*2 HOURS*

Analyzing Tasks

GETTING STARTED   5 MINUTES

3 MINUTES **1** ## Confirm roles

> **WHOLE GROUP** | 3 MINUTES

Greet each other and announce if you are the *Reader, Timekeeper,* or *Recorder* for today. If you haven't chosen roles, quickly decide who will take on each role. To ensure an efficient session, the Reader, Timekeeper, and Recorder should do their work simultaneously in each step. For example, as the Reader begins speaking instructions, the Recorder should begin charting and the Timekeeper should note the stop time.

2 MINUTES **2** ## Get an overview of the session

> **WHOLE GROUP** | 1 minute
>
> **READER**
>
> This Analyzing Tasks session is designed to help us:
>
> - Evaluate tasks for their potential to elicit and capture students' science ideas
> - Evaluate tasks for their potential to reveal a range of students' abilities beyond "right" and "wrong" answers
> - Evaluate the match between a task and intended learning outcomes
> - Identify the characteristics of "good" tasks for student learning and/or assessment
>
> In this session, we will shift our focus from analyzing students' science ideas to analyzing tasks. This includes figuring out if a task is a good match with what we want students to learn. It also means determining the extent to which an instructional assignment or assessment is able to elicit a student's science ideas and show more about the student's understanding, rather than whether the student can produce a right or wrong answer.
>
> After carefully analyzing today's task, we'll reflect on a variety of different tasks we have seen and used and generate a list describing the characteristics of good tasks so we readily know a good task when we see one. ■

RECORDER

Post an agenda for today's session (as needed).

If you haven't already done so, post the chart with the norms for your group.

TODAY'S AGENDA

Getting Started	5 min
Today's Task	25 min
Analyzing Student Work	80 min
Wrap Up	10 min

OUR GROUP NORMS
FOR LOOKING AT STUDENT WORK

►

►

►

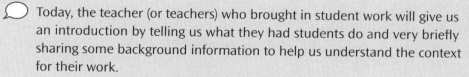

5 MINUTES ③ Get an introduction to today's task

WHOLE GROUP   5 MINUTE

● READER

💬 Today, the teacher (or teachers) who brought in student work will give us an introduction by telling us what they had students do and very briefly sharing some background information to help us understand the context for their work.

As a reminder, it is most helpful to hear about:

- Which task you chose and why

- The instructions you gave students

- What students did before completing the task

- What you hoped they would learn or demonstrate by doing the task

For this session, it is especially helpful to hear specifics about your intended learning objectives — what you hoped your students would learn or demonstrate by doing this task.

Each presenting teacher should take 1–2 minutes to talk through these points and/or hand out what you've written. ■

Note: As needed, distribute a blank copy of the task.

🕐 TIMEKEEPER

Help teachers stick to brief presentations (1–2 minutes per teacher).

5 MINUTES **4** ## Work the task

WHOLE GROUP 1 MINUTE

READER

💬 Just as we did in previous sessions, we will start by getting familiar with the task by **individually** working on it for several minutes. Then we'll check the correctness of our responses in **small groups** and figure out the specific knowledge a student would need to successfully complete the assignment.

Go ahead and start writing your response. As you work, take note of how you approach the task. ■

Note: If teachers have not already formed new small groups, ask them to do so, preferably as threesomes with people different from previous sessions.

INDIVIDUALLY 4 MINUTES

a. Complete the task the presenting teacher(s) used with students. As a reminder, write an adult-level response (not what a student would write) and think about:

• What I notice about how I approached the task…

 TIMEKEEPER

After 4 minutes, call time and ask people to move to their small groups.

15 MINUTES **5** Analyze the task

SMALL GROUPS 15 MINUTES

🕐 TIMEKEEPER

Write the stop time on the board (15 minutes from now).

a. Take turns sharing your written answers and verifying the correctness of your response(s). As needed, look at other references (e.g., Content Notes, Session Reviews) to confirm your answers.

b. Discuss the task in terms of the science it covers and take notes.

- If students correctly completed this same task, what would we know about the science they understand?

c. Identify which learning objectives are best aligned with this task. Remember to consult the list of learning objectives (see Appendix A) or any other resource your group has decided to use (e.g., state standards).

- These learning objectives are a good fit with the task…

🕐 TIMEKEEPER

After 15 minutes, call time and ask people to reconvene as a whole group.

26 MINUTES **6** **Read and sort student work**

WHOLE GROUP   1 MINUTE

READER

Today we'll analyze the student work and the task according to several different lenses. First, you will look at the different ways students are thinking about the science and identify their mental models and common errors. Then you will sort their work into three piles — *proficient, making strides,* and *beginning.* By looking at the work in this way, we can better evaluate the task itself.

First, we'll take 5 minutes or so to **individually** read through the samples of work and notice how students are thinking about the science. Then, in **small groups,** we'll share what we're noticing and sort the work into three piles according to students' relative understanding of one specific learning objective. We will have 25 minutes for this entire step. ■

Note: Ask the presenting teacher (or teachers) to distribute copies of student work. If more than one teacher brought in work, have various small groups focus on different class sets rather than having everyone look at everything.

TIMEKEEPER

Write the stop time on the board (25 minutes from now).

INDIVIDUALLY   5 MINUTES

a. First, read through the samples of student work individually and take notes.

   • What I notice about how these students are thinking about the science…

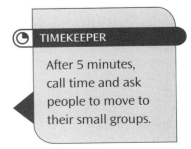

TIMEKEEPER

After 5 minutes, call time and ask people to move to their small groups.

b. Discuss any patterns you are noticing in these students' work. Remember to look at the list of common misconceptions (found in Appendix A).

Use these questions to guide your discussion and take notes:

- What commonalities or shared mental models are we noticing in this work?

- What are some misconceptions or points of confusion?

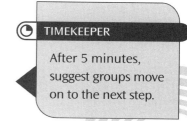

TIMEKEEPER

After 5 minutes, suggest groups move on to the next step.

c. Now discuss and sort each student's work into one of three piles according to the student's relative understanding of one learning objective.

Use these questions to guide your discussion and take notes:

- What is *one* learning objective that is directly addressed by this task?

- Is this student work an example of *proficient, making strides,* or *beginning* understanding of the learning objective? What makes us think so?

Proficient	There is clear evidence the student has a correct and complete understanding of the *one* learning objective. Proficient does *not* mean perfect. A student with a correct understanding of this learning objective may be simultaneously confused about another objective or have poor spelling.
Making Strides	There is some evidence the student has a correct understanding of the *one* learning objective. There may be minor errors and/or omissions.
Beginning	There is little or no evidence the student has a correct understanding of the *one* learning objective. There may be major errors and/or omissions, along with information unrelated to the task.

 TIMEKEEPER

After 15 minutes, call time and ask people to reconvene as a whole group.

7 Evaluate the task

WHOLE GROUP   7 MINUTES

READER

> Now let's shift our focus to evaluating this particular task. More specifically, what did the students' work show us about the strengths and limitations of this task? How well did it elicit students' science ideas? How well did the task show us a range of students' abilities? What did it *not* reveal about students?
>
> In our discussion, we can take on these topics one at a time. As always, it is helpful to support the claims we make about the task with evidence of things we noticed when evaluating the student work.
>
> Here are a couple of questions to get us started:
>
> - To what extent did this task allow students to express different science ideas? What's our evidence?
>
> - What did this task *not* show about students' science ideas? ∎

TIMEKEEPER

Write the stop time on the board (7 minutes from now) and announce when time is up.

Use this space to take notes about main points from the discussion.

READER

A good task does more than show us right and wrong answers. When we sorted the student work by ability level — *proficient, making strides, beginning* — we likely learned some things about the task. In particular:

- What did we notice about the range of student responses?

- What did it look like when students had a partial understanding? Were there multiple shades of gray in their understanding?

- What does this tell us about the strengths and limitations of this task? ∎

TIMEKEEPER

Write the stop time on the board (7 minutes from now) and announce when time is up.

Use this space to take notes about main points from the discussion.

TIMEKEEPER

After 7 minutes, suggest the group move on to the next step.

8 Match learning objectives with the task

WHOLE GROUP 5 MINUTES

 READER

> Perhaps the most important question we can ask ourselves when choosing instructional activities or assessments is "Does the science in this task match what I want my students to learn?"

Let's look together at how closely today's task was aligned to what the presenting teacher (or teachers) wanted students to know.

Will today's presenter(s) remind us of your specific learning objectives? Try to state them clearly and concisely because our Recorder needs to make a chart so we can better evaluate the task. ■

RECORDER

Make a chart of the stated student learning objectives.

For this part, it is important to keep the language precise and detailed, rather than summarizing.

TASK: ____

LEARNING OBJECTIVES:
What I hoped my students would learn or demonstrate by doing the task...

►

►

READER

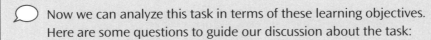 Now we can analyze this task in terms of these learning objectives. Here are some questions to guide our discussion about the task:

- When we looked at the student work, what science did it show these students were understanding?

- Which aspects of this task matched the intended learning objectives?

- Where did it fall short? ■

TIMEKEEPER

Write the stop time on the board (15 minutes from now). Remind everyone when there is 1 minute remaining.

Use this space to take notes about main points from the discussion.

TIMEKEEPER

After 15 minutes, call time.

20 MINUTES ❾ Identify characteristics of good tasks

WHOLE GROUP 1 MINUTE

READER

> You have probably noticed ways in which the items in the Task Bank are different from many other assignments or assessments. They are certainly a contrast from traditional multiple choice, short answer, and true/false questions. Yet some of the Task Bank items have a format similar to these traditional test questions. So how exactly are they different?
>
> We are going to finish our discussion today by thinking — first in our **small groups,** then as a **whole group** — about what makes a "good" task good. It's true that no assignment or assessment is perfect. However, by describing the characteristics of good tasks, we can be better consumers of existing tasks and/or can modify tasks to make them better. ▪

TIMEKEEPER

Write the stop time on the board (9 minutes from now).

SMALL GROUPS 9 MINUTES

a. Talk about what makes a "good" task good. One way to start is to think about some of your favorite tasks. Then use the following questions to guide your discussion.

- How are the Task Bank items similar to and different from others you have used?

- Which types of tasks are particularly good at revealing students' ideas?

- Which types of tasks are particularly good at showing a range of understandings?

- Which types of tasks are particularly good at helping different students learn important science concepts?

- What are other characteristics of good classroom tasks?

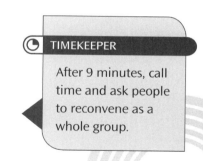

TIMEKEEPER

After 9 minutes, call time and ask people to reconvene as a whole group.

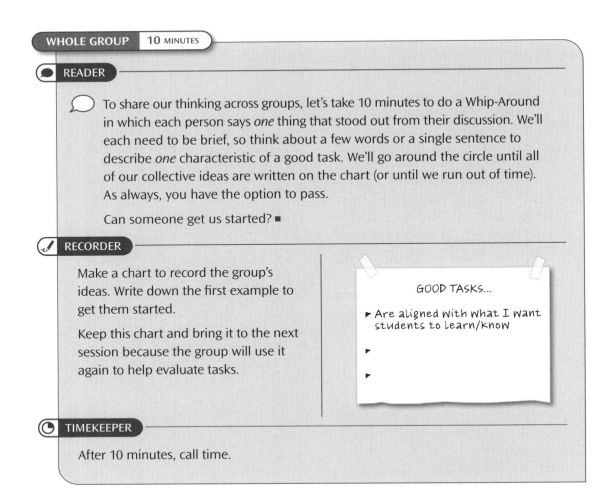

WHOLE GROUP | **10** MINUTES

READER

💬 To share our thinking across groups, let's take 10 minutes to do a Whip-Around in which each person says *one* thing that stood out from their discussion. We'll each need to be brief, so think about a few words or a single sentence to describe *one* characteristic of a good task. We'll go around the circle until all of our collective ideas are written on the chart (or until we run out of time). As always, you have the option to pass.

Can someone get us started? ∎

RECORDER

Make a chart to record the group's ideas. Write down the first example to get them started.

Keep this chart and bring it to the next session because the group will use it again to help evaluate tasks.

GOOD TASKS...

► Are aligned with what I want students to learn/know

►

►

TIMEKEEPER

After 10 minutes, call time.

Use this space to take notes about main points from the discussion.

4 MINUTES ⑩ Take care of housekeeping items

WHOLE GROUP | 4 MINUTES

💬 **READER**

🗨 The focus of our last meeting will be on analyzing and modifying tasks, so everyone needs to bring in a task from his/her own classroom related to what you want your students to learn about the science we've been studying. The task can be one you have used before or one you might use if it better fit your needs. For example, you might have a couple of multiple choice items that are an excellent match to the science you want students to learn, but they are limited in their ability to elicit a range of responses. Alternatively, you might have a wonderful task that isn't about the right science concepts. ∎

Read this *only* if your group is rotating roles between sessions.

🗨 Before we leave today, we also need to decide who will take on the role of Reader, Timekeeper, and Recorder next time. What do you suggest? ∎

Note: Help the group address any logistical issues or other concerns that come up.

6 MINUTES ⑪ Reflect on today's discussion

WHOLE GROUP | 1 MINUTE

💬 **READER**

🗨 Every session ends with 5 minutes to **individually** think about our discussion. Give yourself the gift of this reflective time.

As a reminder, our next meeting is on _____ [date/time], at _____ [location]. Our Reader will be _____ [name], our Recorder will be _____ [name], and our Timekeeper will be _____ [name]. Remember, if you have one of these roles, it is helpful to read the session ahead of time so you know the big picture. See you then! ∎

Note: You should also make note of any other details relevant to the next meeting.

a. Take a few minutes to think about the following questions and jot down some notes.

- What were my big takeaways from today?

- What did I learn about:

...how to elicit and capture students' science ideas?

...matching learning objectives with instructional activities and assessments?

...criteria that are helpful for identifying good tasks?

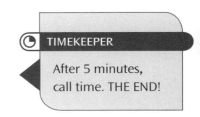

TIMEKEEPER

After 5 minutes, call time. THE END!

MODIFYING TASKS

SESSION

E

◉ Materials

- ☐ A copy of *one* task from each teacher for each person
  Note: No student work is needed.

- ☐ A copy of standards (e.g., national, state, district) for each person if your group chooses to use something other than the list of learning objectives provided in Appendix A

- ☐ A Completion Certificate for each person
  Note: The file is found on the CD that accompanies this book.

- ☐ Easel paper

- ☐ 2–3 dark blue, green, purple, or black markers

- ☐ Bright red, pink, or orange marker

SESSION AGENDA	
GETTING STARTED	**5** MINUTES
❶ Confirm roles	2 MIN.
❷ Get an overview of the session	3 MIN.
MODIFYING THE 1ST TASK	**29** MINUTES
❸ Get to know the 1st task	9 MIN.
❹ Evaluate the 1st task	15 MIN.
❺ Modify the 1st task	5 MIN.
MODIFYING THE 2ND TASK	**28** MINUTES
❻ Get to know the 2nd task	8 MIN.
❼ Evaluate the 2nd task	15 MIN.
❽ Modify the 2nd task	5 MIN.
MODIFYING THE 3RD TASK	**28** MINUTES
❾ Get to know the 3rd task	8 MIN.
❿ Evaluate the 3rd task	15 MIN.
⓫ Modify the 3rd task	5 MIN.
LIMITATIONS OF TASKS	**15** MINUTES
⓬ Identify shortcomings	15 MIN.
WRAP UP	**15** MINUTES
⓭ Reflect on today's discussion	6 MIN.
⓮ Celebrate accomplishments and bring closure	9 MIN.
TOTAL TIME	*2 HOURS*

.

Modifying Tasks

GETTING STARTED   5 MINUTES

 2 MINUTES **1 Confirm roles**

WHOLE GROUP   2 MINUTES

Greet each other and announce if you are the *Reader, Timekeeper,* or *Recorder* for today. If you haven't chosen roles, quickly decide who will take on each role. To ensure an efficient session, the Reader, Timekeeper, and Recorder should do their work simultaneously in each step. For example, as the Reader begins speaking instructions, the Recorder should begin charting and the Timekeeper should note the stop time.

3 MINUTES **2 Get an overview of the session**

 WHOLE GROUP   2 MINUTES

 READER

This Modifying Tasks session is designed to help us:

- Evaluate the strengths and limitations of various tasks

- Identify the shortcomings of tasks we typically use

- Choose assignments and assessments that have characteristics of good tasks

- Modify tasks so they are better aligned with our intended outcomes and the characteristics of good tasks

This last session brings together much of what we have done in the previous meetings and applies it to each of our own classrooms. However, rather than looking at samples of student work, we will work in small groups to evaluate the instructional activities and assessments we each brought in. Then we will take turns helping each other modify the tasks to better meet each of our needs and match the specific science learning objectives we have for our students.

Today we have the choice of forming new small groups to work with people we have spent less time with or we can work as grade-level groups or school teams to better collaborate and modify the tasks we might use. Decide which works best for you and go ahead and form small groups for today. ■

RECORDER

Post an agenda for today's session (as needed).

If you haven't already done so, post the chart with the norms for your group.

Also post the "Good Tasks" chart from the previous session.

TODAY's AGENDA

Getting Started	5 min
Modifying the 1st Task	29 min
Modifying the 2nd Task	28 min
Modifying the 3rd Task	28 min
Limitations of Tasks	15 min
Wrap Up	15 min

OUR GROUP NORMS
FOR LOOKING AT STUDENT WORK

▸

▸

▸

GOOD TASKS...

▸ Are aligned with what I want students to learn/know

▸

▸

9 MINUTES ❸ Get to know the 1st task

WHOLE GROUP   **1 MINUTE**

READER

> We'll primarily work in **small groups** today to collaboratively evaluate and modify the task each person brought in. You'll get oriented to a task, work the task, discuss the strengths and limitations of the task, and suggest a few ways of modifying the task to address some of its limitations. Then you will repeat the same process with the next tasks. ▪

Read this *only* if the group is working two tasks instead of three.

> The times listed in your guide are based on evaluating and modifying three tasks. Since we are working in pairs and only have two tasks to evaluate and modify, we have about 14 extra minutes for each task. Feel free to use the extra 14 minutes for each task at a time when it best suits the work at hand, but keep the total time dedicated to each task about 40 minutes. ▪

TIMEKEEPER

Write the stop time on the board (29 minutes from now if you are working three tasks or 43 minutes from now if you are working two tasks).

SMALL GROUPS   **2 MINUTES**

a. Decide whose task you will focus on first. Have this presenting teacher briefly introduce the task by sharing:

- Which task the teacher chose and why

- What the teacher hopes students will learn or demonstrate by doing the task

b. Write an adult-level response to this task.

SMALL GROUPS   3 MINUTES

c. Verify the correctness of your response(s). As needed, look at other references (e.g., Content Notes, Session Reviews) to confirm your answers.

---

15 MINUTES **4** **Evaluate the 1ˢᵗ task**

SMALL GROUPS   15 MINUTES

a. Discuss which science concepts are best aligned with this task. As needed, refer to the list of learning objectives (found in Appendix A) or any other resource your group decided to use (e.g., state standards).

- Which specific learning objectives or science concepts does the task get at?

- Which aspects of this task match the teacher's intended learning objectives?

- Where does it fall short?

b. Discuss the potential strengths/limitations of this task. Refer to your group's chart showing characteristics of good tasks (or use the sample chart below).

Use these questions to guide your discussion and take notes:

- To what extent does the task (as it is currently written) allow students to express different science ideas?

- What might this task *not* show about students' science ideas?

- To what extent does the task reveal only "right" and "wrong" answers versus a range of responses?

- How might a student show partial understanding when doing this task?

GOOD TASKS...

- ▶ Are well aligned with what I want students to learn/know
- ▶ Go beyond facts or simple recall
- ▶ Can be solved in a number of ways
- ▶ Give students a chance to explain their science thinking
- ▶ Might ask them to communicate in several modes (words & drawings)
- ▶ Are accessible and interesting
- ▶ Encourage students to think
- ▶ Require students to decide what knowledge to apply when
- ▶ Invite students to share their own ideas and ways of figuring things out

TIMEKEEPER

Remind groups when 5 minutes remain for the 1st task.

5 **Modify the 1ˢᵗ task**

a. Identify one or two things you would like to change about this task. Discuss why these changes would be useful. If you have time, revise the task to better meet your needs.

 TIMEKEEPER

Announce when time is up for the 1ˢᵗ task and ask groups to move on to the 2ⁿᵈ task.

8 MINUTES **6** Get to know the 2ⁿᵈ task

SMALL GROUPS | 2 MINUTES

a. Decide whose task you will focus on this time. Have this presenting teacher briefly introduce the task by sharing:

- Which task the teacher chose and why

- What the teacher hopes students will learn or demonstrate by doing the task

INDIVIDUALLY | 3 MINUTES

b. Write an adult-level response to this task.

SMALL GROUPS | 3 MINUTES

c. Verify the correctness of your response(s). As needed, look at other references (e.g., Content Notes, Session Reviews) to confirm your answers.

SMALL GROUPS 15 MINUTES

a. Discuss which science concepts are best aligned with this task. As needed, refer to the list of learning objectives (found in Appendix A) or any other resource your group decided to use (e.g., state standards).

- Which specific learning objectives or science concepts does the task get at?

- Which aspects of this task match the teacher's intended learning objectives?

- Where does it fall short?

b. Discuss the potential strengths/limitations of this task. Refer to the chart showing characteristics of good tasks.

Use these questions to guide your discussion and take notes:

- To what extent does the task (as it is currently written) allow students to express different science ideas?

- What might this task *not* show about students' science ideas?

- To what extent does the task reveal only "right" and "wrong" answers versus a range of responses?

- How might a student show partial understanding when doing this task?

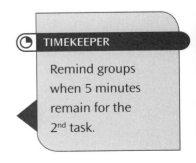

TIMEKEEPER

Remind groups when 5 minutes remain for the 2nd task.

SMALL GROUPS   5 MINUTES

a. Identify one or two things you would like to change about this task. Discuss why these changes would be useful. If you have time, revise the task to better meet your needs.

TIMEKEEPER

Announce when time is up for the 2ⁿᵈ task and ask groups to move on to the 3ʳᵈ task.

8 MINUTES **9** Get to know the 3ʳᵈ task

SMALL GROUPS   2 MINUTES

Note: **Skip steps 9–11 if the group is working on two tasks instead of three.**

a. Have this presenting teacher briefly introduce the task by sharing:

- Which task the teacher chose and why

- What the teacher hopes students will learn or demonstrate by doing the task

INDIVIDUALLY   3 MINUTES

b. Write an adult-level response to this task.

SMALL GROUPS   3 MINUTES

c. Verify the correctness of your response(s). As needed, look at other references (e.g., Content Notes, Session Reviews) to confirm your answers.

SMALL GROUPS | **15** MINUTES

a. Discuss which science concepts are best aligned with this task. As needed, refer to the list of learning objectives (found in Appendix A) or any other resource your group decided to use (e.g., state standards).

- Which specific learning objectives or science concepts does the task get at?

- Which aspects of this task match the teacher's intended learning objectives?

- Where does it fall short?

b. Discuss the potential strengths/limitations of this task. Refer to the chart showing characteristics of good tasks.

Use these questions to guide your discussion and take notes:

- To what extent does the task (as it is currently written) allow students to express different science ideas?

- What might this task *not* show about students' science ideas?

- To what extent does the task reveal only "right" and "wrong" answers versus a range of responses?

- How might a student show partial understanding when doing this task?

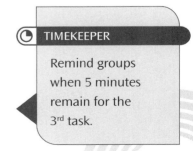

TIMEKEEPER

Remind groups when 5 minutes remain for the 3ʳᵈ task.

SMALL GROUPS 5 MINUTES

a. Identify one or two things you would like to change about this task. Discuss why these changes would be useful. If you have time, revise the task to better meet your needs.

TIMEKEEPER

Announce when time is up and ask people to reconvene as a whole group.

15 MINUTES **12** Identify shortcomings

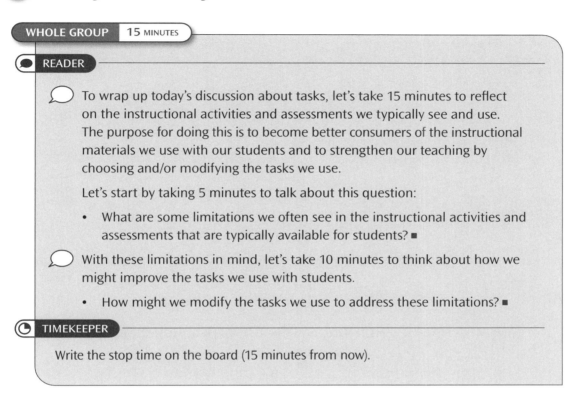

WHOLE GROUP   15 MINUTES

READER

To wrap up today's discussion about tasks, let's take 15 minutes to reflect on the instructional activities and assessments we typically see and use. The purpose for doing this is to become better consumers of the instructional materials we use with our students and to strengthen our teaching by choosing and/or modifying the tasks we use.

Let's start by taking 5 minutes to talk about this question:

- What are some limitations we often see in the instructional activities and assessments that are typically available for students? ▪

With these limitations in mind, let's take 10 minutes to think about how we might improve the tasks we use with students.

- How might we modify the tasks we use to address these limitations? ▪

TIMEKEEPER

Write the stop time on the board (15 minutes from now).

Use this space to take notes about main points from the discussion.

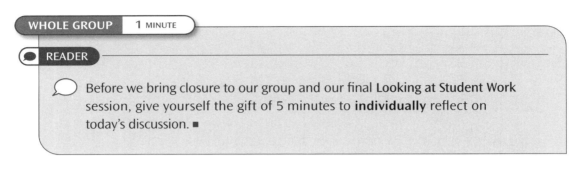

6 MINUTES **13** Reflect on today's discussion

WHOLE GROUP 1 MINUTE

READER

Before we bring closure to our group and our final **Looking at Student Work** session, give yourself the gift of 5 minutes to **individually** reflect on today's discussion. ∎

INDIVIDUALLY 5 MINUTES

a. Take a few minutes to think about the following questions and jot down some notes.

- What were my big takeaways from today?

- What did I learn about the tasks I use?

- What did I learn about modifying instructional activities and assessments?

- What are some of my overall takeaways from the **Looking at Student Work** series?

14 Celebrate accomplishments and bring closure

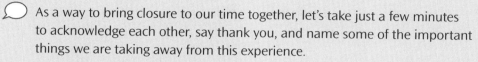

WHOLE GROUP 9 MINUTES

READER

As a way to bring closure to our time together, let's take just a few minutes to acknowledge each other, say thank you, and name some of the important things we are taking away from this experience.

We can go around the room and each person can say 1–2 sentences, for example:

- Something you want to thank the group for
- Something you are taking away from this experience ▪

Note: Distribute the Completion Certificates. Address remaining logistical issues, such as course credit, what's next for this group, other evaluation needs, and other thank-yous (e.g., administrators and/or support staff).

TIMEKEEPER

After 9 minutes, call time. THE END!

APPENDIX A
LEARNING OBJECTIVES & MISCONCEPTIONS

This collection of learning objectives and misconceptions about energy is taken from the Making Sense of SCIENCE™: Energy for Teachers of Grades 6–8 course. The learning objectives and misconceptions were compiled from national standards, research about misconceptions, frameworks of common high-quality student curricula, and documents published by the American Association for the Advancement of Science and other leading science education organizations.

It is very likely your state, district, school, or student curriculum also describes what middle school students should know about this topic. It is fine to use any of these resources instead of the list of learning objectives provided here. Choose whichever resource is most fitting for your group. Keep in mind some documents describe only "big ideas" students should know and don't provide specific learning objectives, which you will need when evaluating the demands of student tasks during the Looking at Student Work™ sessions. Therefore, it may be helpful to use this list in conjunction with another resource specific to your context.

LEARNING OBJECTIVES

Energy and Energy Transfers

1.1 Energy is a measure of how much change can happen in a system (e.g., change in motion or change in conditions such as shape, temperature, or composition).

1.2 Energy is not a substance or an object, nor is it a force or power.

1.3 Energy is involved in every interaction.

1.4 Energy is a quantity that is conserved despite the many changes that occur in the world. It is often measured in joules, calories, and kilocalories.

1.5 The amount of energy associated with an object can change during an interaction.

1.6 When the amount of energy associated with one object goes down, the amount of energy associated with another object must go up.

1.7 The type of energy associated with an object can change during an interaction.

Types of Energy and Systems

1.8 Various types of energy result from objects moving or from the position of one object in relation to the position of another object.

1.9 In different parts of systems, energy is called by different names — kinetic energy, heat energy, chemical potential energy, and so on.

1.10 A system is defined by the objects of interest and forces of interest present in a timeframe of interest.

1.11 Thinking about energy as having different types helps us understand what is occurring in systems.

MISCONCEPTIONS

1.A It is incorrect to think of energy as something physical, made of matter or as some yet-to-be-discovered type of magical essence that is pulled out of one object and moved to another object during energy transfers. In fact, only the name and location of the energy really changes, and no physical substance moves object to object.

1.B It is incorrect to think energy is a force, similar to gravity or magnetic force, or to think of it as a nonscientific force (e.g., a magical force).

1.C It is incorrect to think the renewable and nonrenewable fuels used to power cars, homes, and businesses are energy. While humans use these natural resources in a variety of interactions that result in the presence of many types of energy, the fuels themselves are not energy.

1.D It is incorrect to think energy is involved only when objects are moving or things are changing. In fact, energy can also be involved when there is no visible change (e.g., holding a ball stationary in the air).

1.E It is incorrect to think energy transfers are perfectly linear, that one event triggers only one event. In fact, one event can trigger many simultaneous events and in turn involve many energy transfers.

Potential Energy

2.1 Potential energy results from the relative position of objects, be they large or small (e.g., planets, atoms, and the smallest particles of matter).

2.2 Chemical potential energy (CPE) results from the relative positions, or structural arrangements, of particles of matter (e.g., atoms and molecules).

2.3 Elastic potential energy (EPE) depends on an object's position relative to its own natural position (e.g., an expanded or compressed position).

2.4 Gravitational potential energy (GPE) depends on an object's position relative to another mass, such as Earth. The amount of GPE is related to the object's mass, the acceleration due to gravity, and the object's distance from the other object (or height above Earth).

2.5 The amount of GPE can be calculated with formulas, such as $GPE = mgh$ or $W = \Delta E = Fd$, where $F = ma$.

2.6 If there is potential energy in a system, there is the potential for change. More potential energy means more change can happen.

2.7 Potential energy is not matter or a substance stored in objects.

2.8 Nearly all matter, when subjected to the right conditions, can release energy. For example, food releases energy in a digestive system.

2.9 Potential energy is a property of a system measured in calories, joules, or other units.

2.10 Potential energy does not just appear in a system. It transfers from other types of energy.

2.A It is incorrect to think the energetic feeling we get after eating certain foods means the food provided lots of energy. How a food makes us feel has little to do with the number of Calories of energy it has.

2.B It is incorrect to think Calories are a type of matter contained in food.

2.C It is incorrect to think Calories are "bad" for us. While too many Calories cause weight gain and being overweight does affect our health, all living things require a certain amount of energy to survive.

2.D It is incorrect to think that only food or only fuels can release energy, when anything with chemical bonds can release energy under the right conditions.

2.E It is incorrect to think that only the energy in food can be quantified with calories or that the energy in food must be quantified with calories.

LEARNING OBJECTIVES

Conduction and Convection

3.1 Conduction is the spontaneous *transfer of heat energy* from a hotter object to a colder object. Conduction stops when the average kinetic energies of the particles in objects are the same.

3.2 Convection is a *movement of matter* driven by differences in density. As the matter moves, the heat energy it carries moves with it.

3.3 Conduction and convection can occur together (e.g., hot air rises by convection and then its heat energy can transfer to nearby colder air by conduction).

Heat Energy and Temperature

3.4 An object's heat energy is the sum of the kinetic energy each particle in the object has as a result of its random, unorganized motion.

3.5 Temperature is an indication of the average kinetic energy of the particles in a substance.

3.6 It is possible for two objects at the same temperature to have different amounts of heat energy. It is also possible for two objects with the same amount of heat energy to be at different temperatures.

3.7 Sunlight has light energy, not heat energy, associated with it. When objects absorb light, their temperatures increase (i.e., LE is transferred to HE).

3.8 Heat energy and temperature both increase when an object is warmed because its particles move more. This increase in motion means the object has a higher temperature *and* has more heat energy.

MISCONCEPTIONS

3.A It is incorrect to think of conduction as "cold" transfer. A cold temperature (a low average molecular motion) is not a physical "thing" that can transfer or flow between objects, nor is it the opposite of heat energy.

3.B It is incorrect to think that when objects are in direct contact, the hotter object gives all its heat energy to the colder object and then takes back however much heat energy it "needs." Conduction is a one-way street that stops when temperatures are equal.

3.C It is incorrect to think that conduction equalizes the amount of heat energy each object has (that's only true if the objects are exactly the same mass and composition and in the same phase).

3.D It is incorrect to think insulators provide objects with heat energy. Instead, insulators reduce the conduction of heat energy away from warm objects.

3.E It is incorrect to think heat energy and temperature are the same things.

3.F It is incorrect to think adding a cold object to a container of warm liquid lowers the total heat energy of the container. Instead, there is more mass in the container, thus there is more total heat energy, even if the overall temperature is lower.

3.G It is incorrect to think temperature is a physical "thing" that can be transferred during conduction.

LEARNING OBJECTIVES

Conservation of Energy

4.1   Energy is not created or destroyed.

4.2   The same amount of energy exists today as existed in years past as will exist in the future.

4.3   Energy is conserved overall — it's the law — but energy is not always conserved within a single system.

4.4   Systems can gain and lose energy, depending on the forces and objects defined in the system.

4.5   If one system gains energy, another system loses energy. If one system loses energy, another system gains energy.

Kinetic Energy and Potential Energy

4.6   Kinetic energy (KE) depends on an object's mass (m) and its velocity (v). The amount of KE can be calculated using the formula $KE = \frac{1}{2}mv^2$.

4.7   A change in velocity has a much greater influence on KE than a change in mass. Twice the mass results in twice the KE, but twice the velocity results in four times the KE.

4.8   Gravitational potential energy (GPE) depends on an object's mass (m), the rate of acceleration due to gravity (g), and its height (h) or distance from another mass. The amount of GPE can be calculated using the formula $GPE = mgh$.

4.9   A change in energy (ΔE) in a system equals the work (W) done. Work is a measure of the energy transferred by a force (F) acting over a distance (d).

4.10 Transfers of energy between GPE and KE are never perfectly efficient. Some energy is always converted to heat energy during the process.

MISCONCEPTIONS

4.A   It is incorrect to think the law of conservation of energy is obeyed only in theory and not in real-world scenarios.

4.B   It is incorrect to think energy is created when an object moves and destroyed when it stops moving.

4.C   It is incorrect to think forces create or destroy energy.

4.D   It is incorrect to think energy is created in an interaction that generates heat energy or light energy (such as nuclear reactions).

4.E   It is incorrect to think energy is destroyed in an interaction just because some types of the energy are difficult (or impossible!) to measure.

4.F   It is incorrect to think energy is destroyed when calculations for the initial and final energies are not equal.

4.G   It is incorrect to think energy is always conserved within every single system.

4.H   It is incorrect to think a system (or object) cannot lose or gain energy.

4.I   It is incorrect to think if a system loses energy then energy was destroyed and if a system gains energy then energy was created.

4.J   It is incorrect to think energy transfers are 100% efficient.

4.K   It is incorrect to think a large moving object always has more kinetic energy than a small moving object.

4.L   It is incorrect to think all forms of energy can be readily transferred to usable forms. For example, it is incorrect to think dispersed HE can be readily converted to KE, resulting in the motion of objects.

LEARNING OBJECTIVES

Food in Ecosystems

5.1 All living organisms, including plants and other producers, require food to survive, grow, and reproduce.

5.2 Food is organic matter that provides an organism with a significant source of matter and energy.

5.3 Producers are plants, algae, and bacteria that synthesize their food internally from inorganic matter (largely CO_2 from the air). In photosynthesis, LE is transferred to CPE in sugars.

5.4 Consumers are animals, fungi, and bacteria that cannot synthesize their own food from inorganic matter. They must eat other organisms.

5.5 Food chains and food webs show what organisms eat. The arrows start at the food and point toward the organism doing the eating.

5.6 The first organism in a food chain is always a producer. Consumers make up all higher levels of food chains.

Matter and Energy in Ecosystems

5.7 Matter cycles in Earth's ecosystems. Matter is a physical substance that is not destroyed, just converted to new substances during the interactions that occur in ecosystems.

5.8 Energy flows through Earth's ecosystems. Energy does not cycle. During the interactions that occur in ecosystems, energy is transferred to types that are not useful.

5.9 Higher trophic levels have less energy than lower ones. Each trophic level has only approximately 10% of the energy of the preceding level. Ecological pyramids of energy show this.

MISCONCEPTIONS

5.A It is incorrect to think living things need only matter or only energy or that food provides only one of these.

5.B It is incorrect to think plants do not need food.

5.C It is incorrect to think that sunlight, water, soil, and fertilizer are foods for plants or that plants make food from light alone or from soil, nutrients, and water alone.

5.D It is incorrect to think the matter that plants use to make sugar predominantly comes from the soil or from water.

5.E It is incorrect to think the Sun belongs in food chains, as it is not food for anything. The Sun provides the energy producers need to make food, not the matter they need to make food.

5.F It is incorrect to think consumers eat only one kind of organism (e.g., hawks eat only rabbits) or are always bigger than what they eat.

5.G It is incorrect to think that the amount of food available for organisms is based on how much they need.

5.H It is incorrect to think energy is "used up" in an ecosystem.

APPENDIX B
TASK BANK

This Task Bank is a collection of individual science assignments intended for middle school students. The tasks are designed to give you insight into students' ways of thinking, including common, yet incorrect ideas they may have about science. Some tasks are best suited for use as either an introductory activity or a preassessment to identify students' initial ideas and/or questions prior to formal instruction. Other tasks serve well as instructional activities — they ask students to figure something out, look at things in a different way, make sense of a phenomenon, or apply their knowledge to a new context. Still other tasks are useful as part of an end-of-unit assessment because they tell you about students' understandings and progress in learning. These tasks can be printed from the CD that accompanies this book.

While the tasks may be useful assignments, this Task Bank is not intended for use as a curriculum. Your students would not learn all they needed to know about the related science unit by simply completing these tasks. However, you may find that selected tasks work well as a supplement to your own curriculum to help you better understand your students' ideas and inform your instruction.

Name: _____

ENERGY FOR HAWKS

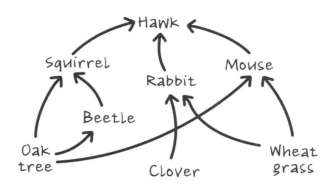

1 Put a ✓ next to things that provide energy to hawks.

_____ sun   _____ squirrel   _____ wheat grass

_____ beetle   _____ water   _____ air

_____ rabbit   _____ clover   _____ oak tree

2 Describe the "rule" or reasoning you used to decide which things provide energy to hawks. Use the back of this page if you need more room to write or draw.

_____

_____

_____

_____

_____

ENERGY TREE: YOU ON WHEELS

Draw an energy tree diagram to represent what happens with energy during an interaction that involves you on something with wheels.

Making an Energy Tree

Energy tree diagrams show the types of energy and energy transfers involved in interactions.

In energy tree diagrams:

- **Ovals** indicate the *type of energy*, such as kinetic energy or heat energy. There is a list of types of energy on the next page.

- **Arrows** indicate the *transfer of energy* from one type to another type.

- **Descriptions** explain the *event* linked to the energy transfer.

Here is an example for a person kicking a ball:

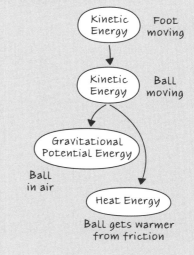

OVER

ENERGY OF MOTION

Energy due to the motion of matter

Kinetic Energy (KE)

Kinetic energy is a result of an *individual* object's motion (e.g., a hockey puck sliding on ice, a car speeding along a road, and a particle moving through space). Objects with more mass and those moving at higher velocities have more KE.

Heat Energy (HE)

Heat energy is a result of the random motion of all the atoms and molecules that make up an object. Objects with more mass and at higher temperatures have more HE. The kind of matter and its phase (e.g., solid, liquid, gas) affect the amount of HE.

Light Energy (LE)

Light energy is a result of the coordinated motion of photons that are emitted when electrons, protons, and other charged particles accelerate. High-frequency colors (e.g., blue) transmit more LE.

Sound Energy (SE)

Sound energy is a result of atoms and molecules moving in concert to form temporary regions of compression and expansion in a medium (e.g., air or water). Louder sounds and higher-pitched sounds transmit more SE.

Electrical Energy (EE)

Electrical energy is a result of charged particles moving through a conductor (e.g., current from electrons moving through a wire). The more current that flows and the longer the period of time it flows, the more EE is present.

ENERGY OF POSITION

Energy due to the relative positions of matter

Gravitational Potential Energy (GPE)

Gravitational potential energy is a result of an object's position relative to another mass — typically, but not always, Earth. More massive objects and objects that are farther apart have more GPE.

Elastic Potential Energy (EPE)

Elastic potential energy is a result of an object (e.g., rubber band) being compressed or expanded, such that the relative positions of its own atoms change. The more an object is squished or stretched while still being able to regain its previous form, the more EPE.

Chemical Potential Energy (CPE)

Chemical potential energy is a result of the structural arrangement of atoms and molecules. When bonds are broken and new bonds form, atoms rearrange. This rearrangement changes the relative positions of atoms and in turn changes the amount of CPE present.

Nuclear Potential Energy (NPE)

Nuclear potential energy is a result of the relative positions and kinds of subatomic particles in the nuclei of atoms (e.g., protons and neutrons). When the nuclei are either split or fused, the subatomic particles are rearranged. As a result, the amount of NPE changes and often so does the mass.

Electrostatic Potential Energy (ESPE)

Electrostatic potential energy is a result of the relative spacing of stationary charged particles. Objects and particles with greater charges and those that are closer together have more ESPE.

Name:

ENERGY TREE: YOU AND A ROCK

Draw an energy tree diagram to represent what happens with energy during an interaction that involves you and a rock.

Making an Energy Tree

Energy tree diagrams show the types of energy and energy transfers involved in interactions.

In energy tree diagrams:

- **Ovals** indicate the *type of energy*, such as kinetic energy or heat energy. There is a list of types of energy on the next page.

- **Arrows** indicate the *transfer of energy* from one type to another type.

- **Descriptions** explain the *event* linked to the energy transfer.

Here is an example for stopping a moving car:

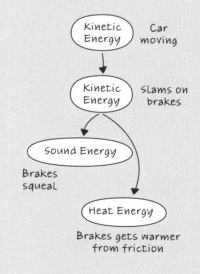

OVER

ENERGY OF MOTION

Energy due to the motion of matter

Kinetic Energy (KE)

Kinetic energy is a result of an *individual* object's motion (e.g., a hockey puck sliding on ice, a car speeding along a road, and a particle moving through space). Objects with more mass and those moving at higher velocities have more KE.

Heat Energy (HE)

Heat energy is a result of the random motion of all the atoms and molecules that make up an object. Objects with more mass and at higher temperatures have more HE. The kind of matter and its phase (e.g., solid, liquid, gas) affect the amount of HE.

Light Energy (LE)

Light energy is a result of the coordinated motion of photons that are emitted when electrons, protons, and other charged particles accelerate. High-frequency colors (e.g., blue) transmit more LE.

Sound Energy (SE)

Sound energy is a result of atoms and molecules moving in concert to form temporary regions of compression and expansion in a medium (e.g., air or water). Louder sounds and higher-pitched sounds transmit more SE.

Electrical Energy (EE)

Electrical energy is a result of charged particles moving through a conductor (e.g., current from electrons moving through a wire). The more current that flows and the longer the period of time it flows, the more EE is present.

ENERGY OF POSITION

Energy due to the relative positions of matter

Gravitational Potential Energy (GPE)

Gravitational potential energy is a result of an object's position relative to another mass — typically, but not always, Earth. More massive objects and objects that are farther apart have more GPE.

Elastic Potential Energy (EPE)

Elastic potential energy is a result of an object (e.g., rubber band) being compressed or expanded, such that the relative positions of its own atoms change. The more an object is squished or stretched while still being able to regain its previous form, the more EPE.

Chemical Potential Energy (CPE)

Chemical potential energy is a result of the structural arrangement of atoms and molecules. When bonds are broken and new bonds form, atoms rearrange. This rearrangement changes the relative positions of atoms and in turn changes the amount of CPE present.

Nuclear Potential Energy (NPE)

Nuclear potential energy is a result of the relative positions and kinds of subatomic particles in the nuclei of atoms (e.g., protons and neutrons). When the nuclei are either split or fused, the subatomic particles are rearranged. As a result, the amount of NPE changes and often so does the mass.

Electrostatic Potential Energy (ESPE)

Electrostatic potential energy is a result of the relative spacing of stationary charged particles. Objects and particles with greater charges and those that are closer together have more ESPE.

BOX AND ARROW: YOU ON WHEELS

Draw a box and arrow diagram to represent what happens with energy during an interaction that involves you on something with wheels.

Making a Box and Arrow

Box and arrow diagrams identify energy sources and energy receivers in interactions. They are useful for tracking energy changes in a system.

In box and arrow diagrams:

- **Boxes** indicate the *energy source* and *energy receiver*.

- **Arrows** indicate the *direction* energy transfers. They go from the energy source to the energy receiver.

- **Descriptions** explain the *event* linked to the energy transfer.

Here is an example for a person kicking a ball:

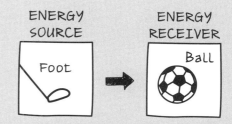

Energy from the moving foot is transferred to the ball.

Name:

FRAYER MODEL: ENERGY

Complete the Frayer Model for the word **ENERGY** (see the sample on the next page).

4 Write a clear, concise definition   **3** List things that describe it

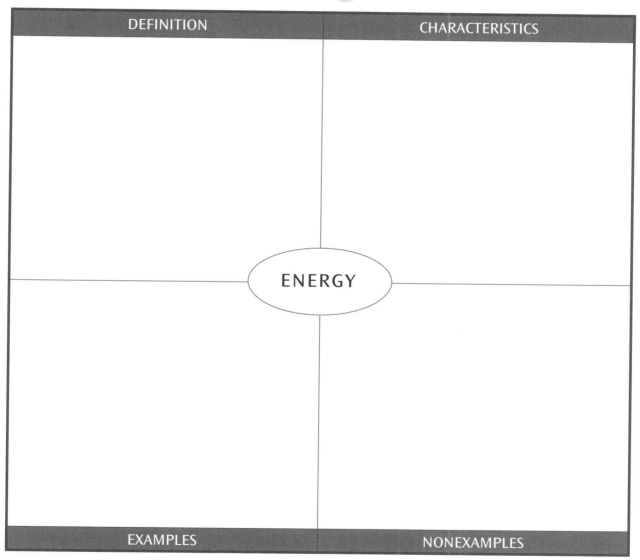

DEFINITION	CHARACTERISTICS

ENERGY

| EXAMPLES | NONEXAMPLES |

1 List examples or things that are similar   **2** List opposites or things that are different

OVER

DEFINITION	CHARACTERISTICS
A random collection of items you can usually see or hold	- you can hold it or see it (sometimes) - objects or items - has mass and volume - can be big or small - clutter - some people have more than others

STUFF

EXAMPLES	NONEXAMPLES
- things found in a backpack - shoes - junk drawer items - anything random - leftovers	- thoughts - ideas - freedom - friendship - feelings

Name:

DOES IT STORE ENERGY?

1 Read statements Ⓐ, Ⓑ, Ⓒ, and Ⓓ below. Decide if each statement is true or false.

True	False		
☐	☐	Ⓐ	A slice of pizza stores energy.
☐	☐	Ⓑ	A hat on a person's head stores energy.
☐	☐	Ⓒ	A rubber band stores energy.
☐	☐	Ⓓ	A plane flying through the air stores energy.

2 Pick one statement _____ and explain your answer. Use words and drawings.

_____

_____

_____

_____

_____

_____

_____

OVER

3 Pick another statement _____ and explain your answer. Use words and drawings.

_____

_____

_____

_____

_____

_____

_____

FRAYER MODEL: POTENTIAL ENERGY

Complete the Frayer Model for the term **POTENTIAL ENERGY** (see the sample on the next page).

4 Write a clear, concise definition   **3** List things that describe it

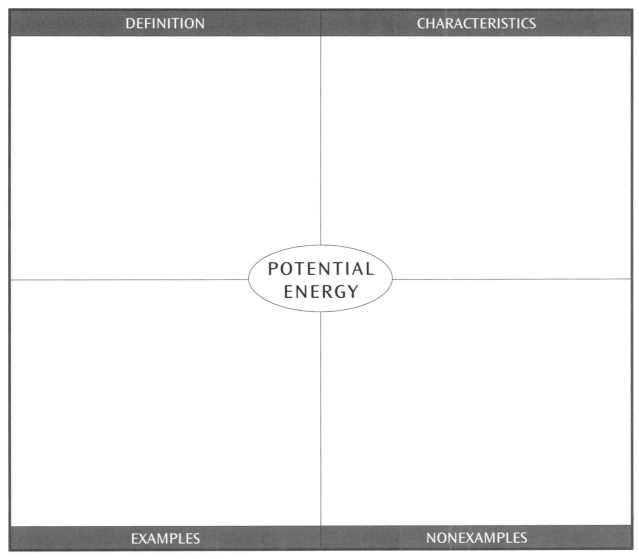

DEFINITION	CHARACTERISTICS

POTENTIAL ENERGY

EXAMPLES	NONEXAMPLES

1 List examples or things that are similar   **2** List opposites or things that are different

OVER

DEFINITION	CHARACTERISTICS
A random collection of items you can usually see or hold	- you can hold it or see it (sometimes) - objects or items - has mass and volume - can be big or small - clutter - some people have more than others

STUFF

EXAMPLES	NONEXAMPLES
- things found in a backpack - shoes - junk drawer items - anything random - leftovers	- thoughts - ideas - freedom - friendship - feelings

CALORIE PUZZLER

Look at the data below showing the potential energy associated with different objects.

OBJECT	POTENTIAL ENERGY
Peanut with a mass of 1 gram	1380 calories
Marshmallow with a mass of 1 gram	190 calories
Paper napkin with a mass of 1 gram	1000 calories
Soccer ball held 10 meters above the ground	10 calories
Rubber band stretched 10 centimeters	0.24 calories

1 Write three *claims* about potential energy based on this data.

CLAIM ①
_____
_____
_____

CLAIM ②
_____
_____
_____

CLAIM ③
_____
_____
_____

OVER

OBJECT	POTENTIAL ENERGY
Peanut with a mass of 1 gram	1380 calories
Marshmallow with a mass of 1 gram	190 calories
Paper napkin with a mass of 1 gram	1000 calories
Soccer ball held 10 meters above the ground	10 calories
Rubber band stretched 10 centimeters	0.24 calories

2 Choose one of your claims. ———
What **evidence** supports this claim? It's okay to use data from the table, along with other evidence you know about.

_____

_____

_____

_____

_____

_____

_____

3 What is similar about the potential energy of a peanut and the potential energy of a stretched rubber band? What is different?

_____

_____

_____

_____

_____

_____

TASK
(H) Making Sense of SCIENCE™

CALORIE CONVERSATIONS

Peanuts are good for you because they have more calories than marshmallows. Everybody needs calories to live.

Victor says...

Yeah, but I have way more energy after I eat marshmallows. It's the sugar calories that are bad for you.

Manny says...

Too many calories are bad for you. There is no such thing as good calories and bad calories.

ELLa says...

1 Which student do you most agree with? Explain what you agree and disagree about. Use the back if you need more space to write or draw.

_____

_____

_____

_____

_____

_____

_____

_____

_____

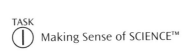

Name: _____

MORE PLEASE!

1 Describe at least *two* different ways you could increase
the amount of energy associated with the cup of hot cocoa.
Explain how each way increases the total energy.

_____

_____

_____

_____

_____

_____

_____

_____

_____

_____

_____

_____

_____

Name:

MIND MAP: ENERGY & TEMPERATURE TASK K

1 What are some ways these words are related?

- hot
- ice
- heat
- temperature

- sun
- water
- energy

Draw a mind map to show your thinking about how these words are related to each other. You may use as many additional words as you like.

Making a Mind Map

A mind map is a drawing that represents your thinking about a set of related terms.

Mind maps have:

- **Ovals** with a single term written inside each one
- **One-way arrows** to show relationships between terms
- **Linking verbs** to describe how the terms are related

Here is an example made from these terms:

- rain
- water
- mountains
- clouds

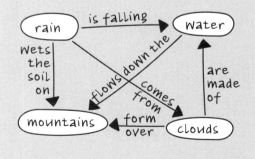

Name:

HOT & COLD WATER

Three students did an experiment. They put a cup of cold water in a pan of hot water. Each student had a different way to explain what happened.

Cold water
Hot water

The cold water gets warmer and the hot water gets colder until they get to a middle temperature. This happens because cold is transferred into the hot water. See my graph.

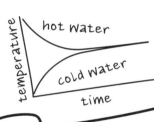

Jorge thinks...

Energy goes from the hot water in the pan to the cold water in the cup because they are touching. This stops when the temperatures are equal.

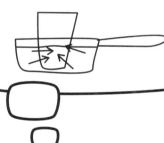

Chris thinks...

All the energy from the hot goes into the cold cup and then the pan takes back what it needs so they are even, like this.

same temperature and same energy

Maya thinks...

1 Which student do you most agree with? Explain what you agree and disagree with. Use the back if you need more space to write or draw.

_____

_____

_____

_____

_____

Name: _____

GETTING WARMER

Read statements Ⓐ, Ⓑ, and Ⓒ below.

Ⓐ   Close the refrigerator door. You are letting the cold out.

Ⓑ   Hotter objects always have more heat energy than colder objects.

Ⓒ   When you hold a cold spoon, energy is conducted from the spoon to your hand and from your hand to the spoon.

1 Pick one statement you think is wrong. Explain why you think statement _____ is wrong.

_____

_____

_____

_____

_____

2 Rewrite statement _____ so it is correct.

_____

_____

_____

_____

BOUNCE, BOUNCE, BOUNCE

Drop a ball and watch it bounce. Then drop the ball again and measure how high it goes for each of 5 bounces.

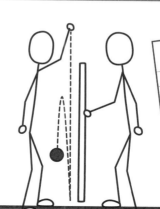

Materials
- meter stick
- bouncy ball (such as a ping pong ball, tennis ball, or rubber ball)

 Record your data and make a graph.

BOUNCE #	HEIGHT (cm)
1	
2	
3	
4	
5	

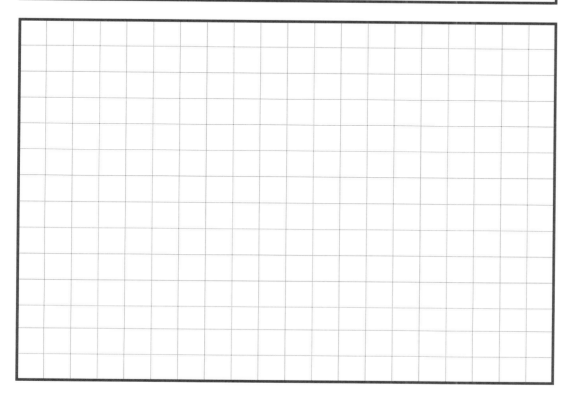

OVER

2 Describe the bouncing ball in terms of energy. Include a drawing.

_____

_____

_____

_____

_____

_____

_____

3 Why do you think the height of the bounces changed?

_____

_____

_____

_____

_____

_____

PENDULUM PUZZLER

Start a pendulum swinging. Make observations about the height of the pendulum after each swing.

Materials

- pencil
- string
- heavy weight (such as a large washer)

SEE 1 What do you see happening each time the pendulum swings?

_____

_____

_____

_____

_____

_____

THINK 2 Why do you think the height of the pendulum swing changes?

_____

_____

_____

_____

_____

_____

_____

OVER

PUZZLE 3 The *law of conservation of energy* says that energy cannot be created or destroyed. Is it puzzling that the pendulum does not swing back up to its original height? Why or why not?

_____

_____

_____

_____

_____

_____

_____

_____

_____

_____

Name:

PAPER SHOOTER

BEFORE	LAUNCH	DURING FLIGHT
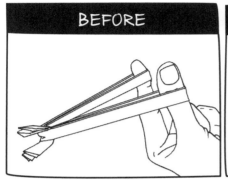	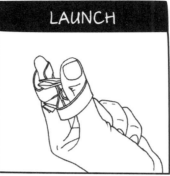	

1 Explain what happens with energy when you use a rubber band to shoot a piece of paper. Use the words *potential energy, kinetic energy,* and *transfer* or *change* in your answer.

_____

_____

_____

_____

_____

_____

_____

_____

_____

_____

Name:

FACT OR FICTION?

Energy can't be created or destroyed, so you always have the same amount in the ecosystem.

Mitch says...

The Law isn't really true because you always get energy from the Sun until it dies.

José says...

Sure you can gain energy from the Sun and lose little bits here and there, so it's a good idea, but the law doesn't work for ecosystems.

Ming says...

1 Which student do you most agree with? Explain what you agree and disagree with.
Use the back if you need more space to write or draw.

_____

_____

_____

_____

_____

_____

_____

_____

Name: _____

HAWKS AND RABBITS

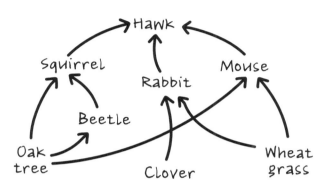

1 This food web shows what each organism consumes. For example, rabbits eat clover. How many hawks would you expect to find compared with rabbits? (Circle ONE.)

Ⓐ I would expect more hawks than rabbits.

Ⓑ I would expect more rabbits than hawks.

Ⓒ I would expect equal numbers of rabbits and hawks.

2 Describe your thinking. Explain how **_energy_** is related to your choice. Use the back of this page if you need more room to write or draw.

_____

_____

_____

_____

_____

_____

_____

PLANTS NEED...

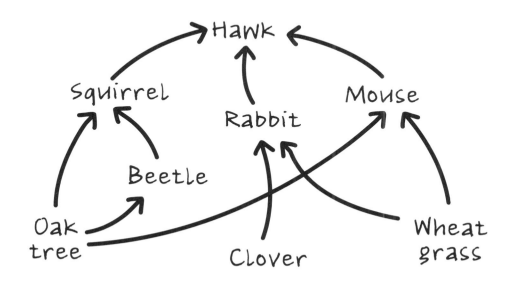

1 Oak trees, clover, and wheat grass form the base of this food web. What do these plants need in order to live and grow?

_____

_____

_____

_____

_____

_____

_____

OVER

2 Where do you think plants get the *matter* they need in order to grow?

_____

_____

_____

_____

_____

_____

_____

3 Where do plants get the *energy* they need in order to grow?

_____

_____

_____

_____

_____

_____

_____

Name:

ENERGY IS...

Energy is a hard thing to define. Read the correct and incorrect descriptions below.

CORRECT	INCORRECT
Energy is a quantity that describes how much change can happen. You can calculate how much energy things have. Energy can't be created or destroyed, but it can be transferred to different places.	Energy is an invisible thing, like air, that moves around inside everything. It is what makes living things alive. If things are dead or not moving, they don't have any energy associated with them.

1 What do you like about the correct description? What would you add to make it a more complete definition? Use the back if you need more room to write or draw.

_____

_____

_____

_____

_____

_____

2 What do you like about the incorrect description? Why is it incorrect?

_____

_____

_____

_____

_____

_____

Name:

MIND MAP: FOOD

1 What are some ways these words are related?

- food
- water
- kinetic energy
- potential energy

- sun
- animal
- matter

Draw a mind map to show your thinking about how these words are related to each other. You may use as many additional words as you like.

Making a Mind Map

A mind map is a drawing that represents your thinking about a set of related terms.

Mind maps have:

- **Ovals** with a single term written inside each one

- **One-way arrows** to show relationships between terms

- **Linking verbs** to describe how the terms are related

Here is an example made from these terms:

- rain
- water
- mountains
- clouds

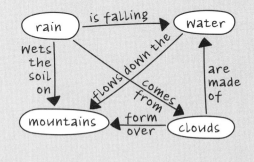

WestEd.org

WestEd is a San Francisco–based nonpartisan, nonprofit, mission-focused organization. WestEd develops research-based programs, intervention strategies, and other resources, including publications and services for teacher education. In educational research, educational evaluation, policy support, and technical assistance, WestEd works to find the best answers to enduring challenges and emerging questions in education and human development. Among WestEd's specialties are education assessment and accountability; professional development; early childhood and youth development; program evaluation; community building; and policy analysis.

National Science Teachers Association

The National Science Teachers Association (NSTA), founded in 1944, is the largest organization in the world committed to promoting excellence and innovation in science teaching and learning for all. NSTA's current membership of 60,000 includes science teachers, science supervisors, administrators, scientists, business and industry representatives, and others involved in and committed to science education.

About the Authors

Kirsten R. Daehler began her work in science education as a high school chemistry and physics teacher and department chair, delighting in her work with adolescents and her fellow science teachers. Upon joining WestEd in 1994, Kirsten served as the lead teacher developer and content expert for the National Board for Professional Teaching Standards. Currently, Kirsten directs the Understanding Science for Teaching project. Her goal is to transform the way teachers learn about science and the complex art of teaching. Kirsten holds a BA in chemistry from Wellesley College and an MA in secondary education from San Francisco State University.

Jennifer Folsom holds a BA in biology and has studied many other branches of science, environmental education, English, and anthropology. She began her career in science education in high school, conducting research in a pharmacology lab and teaching K–5 students at a neighborhood environmental education center. Since then, she has worked with numerous school districts, nonprofits, and universities to conceptualize and produce innovative science curricula for students and teachers in collaboration with scientists, teachers, and science education professors. Currently, Jennifer combines her writing skills, teaching insights, and science knowledge to develop Making Sense of SCIENCE courses with the Understanding Science for Teaching project at WestEd.

Mayumi Shinohara is currently at Vanderbilt University as a doctoral student, where she is cultivating her inner egghead with Rich Lehrer and Leona Schauble. Her research focuses on children's mathematical and scientific reasoning in and out of school, particularly social and material mechanisms for developing thinking (e.g., participation structures, argumentation, inscription, and models). Originally trained in physics, Mayumi co-directed Understanding Science for Teaching for 15 years, focusing on children's thinking in science and practice-based professional development. Mayumi holds a BS in physics from the University of Illinois, Champaign-Urbana, and an MS in physics from Brandeis University.

Also Available from WestEd

Discussion Builders Posters and Teaching Guides K–1, 2–3, & 4–8

By Carne Clarke and Alma Ramírez

" I like Discussion Builders because they help us get to the point. "

~Third grader

By talking to learn, students also learn how to think. The sentence stems on these colorful posters provide students with a scaffold for voicing their ideas and questions, valuing others' contributions, and incorporating increasingly sophisticated thinking strategies. Using Discussion Builders, students learn through active participation in classroom discussions. Accompanying quick-guides for teachers explain how to get students talking — and thinking — more conceptually, in any subject.

Proven powerful for English language learners and students of all achievement levels, Discussion Builders scaffold progressively more complex reasoning across the grades and increasingly complex use of academic language. In grades K–1, the focus is on helping students present, expand, and reflect on important ideas. In grades 2–3, Discussion Builders prompt students to use these skills at more sophisticated levels. The grades 4–8 poster helps strengthen complex reasoning, including students' abilities to consider counterexamples and conjectures and to justify options.

Discussion Builders Poster & Teaching Guide: K–1
$14.95 • 24 × 36 • MATH-05-01

Discussion Builders Poster & Teaching Guide: 2–3
$14.95 • 24 × 36 • MATH-05-02

Discussion Builders Poster & Teaching Guide: 4–8
$14.95 • 24 × 36 • MATH-05-03

Set *Save 15% off the individual price by ordering the set*
$38.00 • MATH-05-04

Also Available from WestEd

Reading
Apprenticeship
at WestEd IMPROVING ACADEMIC LITERACY

Reading Apprenticeship® Professional Development

Reading Apprenticeship supports students to become motivated, strategic, and critical readers, thinkers, and writers in the content areas. This proven approach:

- Helps teachers of grades 6–12 develop a repertoire of classroom routines for building students' literacy skills

- Transfers increasing responsibility to students through routines for text-based social interaction

- Builds students' motivation, stamina, and repertoire of strategies for understanding and engaging with challenging academic texts

Reading Apprenticeship has been implemented effectively in classrooms across the United States, serving students who struggle as well as students in advanced classes. It qualifies as Tier 1 Response to Intervention in Pennsylvania.

Demonstrated Impact

A large-scale experimental study funded by the National Science Foundation demonstrated positive and statistically significant impact on student reading comprehension and science scores when teachers were trained in Reading Apprenticeship methods.

Teacher Institutes in Reading Apprenticeship

Teacher Institutes in Reading Apprenticeship are designed primarily for cross-disciplinary teams of middle and high school teachers and instructional leaders. Depending on your needs, on-site teacher institutes are offered over two to seven days at your site.

Leadership Institute

The Leadership Institute in Reading Apprenticeship is a training-of-trainers experience that prepares school or district teams to lead professional development in Reading Apprenticeship in their local communities.

The literacy portion of this **Making Sense of SCIENCE™** course was developed in collaboration with the Strategic Literacy Initiative, developers of Reading Apprenticeship at WestEd.

For more information » **WestEd.org/ra**

or call the WestEd Publications Center » **888.293.7833**

Also Available from WestEd

Reading
Apprenticeship
at WestEd IMPROVING
ACADEMIC LITERACY

Reading Apprenticeship® 9th Grade Academic Literacy Course

Curriculum & Professional Development

The Reading Apprenticeship Academic Literacy Course is designed to accelerate 9th grade students' reading achievement, engagement, and fluency. This yearlong course is appropriate for a wide range of students, from struggling readers to students reading at or above grade level.

Reading Apprenticeship Academic Literacy builds students' motivation and increases their strategic and critical reading capabilities, enabling them to construct meaning from academic texts. Students engage with challenging, high-interest texts; analyze the way words and sentences are constructed; and use writing as a tool for learning. The course is organized around three thematic units:

Unit 1: **Reading Self and Society**

Unit 2: **Reading History**

Unit 3: **Reading Science**

Who Should Participate

This institute prepares educators to teach the yearlong 9th grade Reading Apprenticeship Academic Literacy Course. Past participants have been specialists in English, reading, English language development, humanities, mathematics, science, and social sciences.

Demonstrated Impact

Findings from a large-scale experimental study funded by the U.S. Department of Education demonstrated a positive and statistically significant impact on student reading comprehension scores. Reading comprehension scores for students represented a 33 percent improvement over and above what students would have achieved if they had not attended the course. Additionally, WestEd collected standardized reading comprehension test data for 580 participating students. In six months, the students made statistically significant gains in reading scores.

For more information » WestEd.org/ra

or call the WestEd Publications Center » 888.293.7833

WestEd End User License Agreement for Making Sense of SCIENCE™

We have chosen to make these materials easily available and reproducible for the benefit of teachers and their students. In exchange, we ask you to honor the hard work that goes into developing them. Before reproducing, please read the following End User License Agreement, then sign and return to WestEd a copy of the End User Registration found on the CD.

Please read this End User License Agreement ("Agreement") carefully. By printing, copying, or using any of the files or content on the enclosed CD ("Materials"), You or the entity You represent (collectively, "You") agree that this Agreement is enforceable like any written contract signed by You. If You do not agree to the foregoing, WestEd does not authorize You to print, copy, or use the Materials.

1. *Limited License.* Subject to the terms and conditions of this Agreement, WestEd ("WestEd") hereby grants to You a non-exclusive, non-transferable, and royalty-free limited license to print, copy, and use the Materials for the sole purpose of teacher professional development and/or course implementation at Your school, district, community college, university, or educational entity.

2. *License Restrictions.* Except as expressly set forth in this Agreement, You shall not, directly or indirectly, in whole or in part: (i) use the Materials in any way that results in a profit or supports a profitable enterprise within or outside of Your school, district, community college, university, or educational entity; (ii) copy or reproduce the Materials, except as part of Your permitted use pursuant to Section 1; (iii) electronically share or transfer the Materials, store the Materials in a database or retrieval system, or duplicate the CD, without WestEd's prior written consent; (iv) modify or create derivative works based upon the Materials; (v) alter, remove, or obliterate any copyright notice, trademark notice, or other proprietary rights notice on the Materials; or (vi) do anything which adversely affects WestEd's right, title, or interest in or to the Materials.

3. *Ownership.* Title and ownership of all proprietary rights, including any copyright, patent, trade secret, trademark, or other intellectual property rights, in and to the Materials, and any copies thereof, are and will at all times remain the property of WestEd. WestEd retains all right, title, and interest in and to the Materials that are not specifically granted to You hereunder.

4. *Term and Termination.* This Agreement and the license granted herein shall remain effective until terminated. You may terminate this Agreement and the license at any time by destroying the CD and all copies of the Materials in Your possession or control. Your rights under this Agreement will terminate immediately without notice from WestEd if You fail to comply with any provision of this Agreement. Upon termination, You shall immediately cease use of the CD and the Materials, and destroy the CD and all copies of the Materials in Your possession or control.

5. *Disclaimer.* To the fullest extent permitted by applicable law, WestEd disclaims any and all warranties, express or implied, including, without limitation, the implied warranties of merchantability, fitness for a particular purpose, and non-infringement. The CD and Materials are provided "as is." WestEd does not warrant that the CD or the Materials will meet Your requirements, operate without interruption, or be error free.

6. *Limitations of Liability.* In no event will WestEd be liable for special, indirect, incidental, punitive, or consequential damages, regardless of the form of action, even if the claim was reasonably foreseeable or if WestEd was advised of the possibility of such damages. In no event will WestEd's aggregate liability under any and all claims arising out of this agreement exceed the total amount paid by You for the Materials. Some jurisdictions do not allow the exclusion or limitation of incidental or consequential damages, so these limitations may not apply to You.

7. *Miscellaneous.* If any provision of this Agreement is held to be unenforceable, such provision shall be reformed to the extent necessary to make it enforceable so as to affect the intent of the parties, and the remainder of this Agreement shall continue in full force and effect. A waiver of any default is not a waiver of any subsequent default. You may not assign or otherwise transfer any of Your rights hereunder without WestEd's prior written consent, and any such attempt is void. This Agreement is binding upon and is for the benefit of the respective successors and assigns of the parties hereto. The parties acknowledge and agree that a material breach of this Agreement adversely affecting WestEd's proprietary rights would cause irreparable harm to WestEd for which a remedy at law would be inadequate and that WestEd shall be entitled to injunctive relief in addition to any remedies it may have hereunder or at law. This Agreement is the complete agreement between You and WestEd concerning the subject matter hereof, and supersedes any and all prior agreements and representations between WestEd and You related to the same subject matter.

8. *Contact.* If You have any questions regarding this Agreement or would like to contact WestEd for any reason, please send an inquiry to WestEd, 730 Harrison Street, San Francisco CA 94107-1242; permissions@WestEd.org.